Our Singing Country

Folk Songs and Ballads

Collected and Compiled by
JOHN A. LOMAX
and
ALAN LOMAX

Music Editor
Ruth Crawford Seeger

Introduction to the Dover Edition by
Judith Tick

DOVER PUBLICATIONS, INC.
Mineola, New York

TO WILL C. HOGG

Classmate and Friend

Whose life was a ballad

Bibliographical Note

This Dover edition, first published in 2000, is an unabridged republication of
the work originally published by The Macmillan Company, New York;
copyright © 1941 by John A. Lomax. Judith Tick's introduction was written
specially for this edition, and the frontmatter has been slightly reordered and
repaginated to accommodate her insightful addition.

International Standard Book Number

ISBN-13: 978-0-486-41089-0
ISBN-10: 0-486-41089-7

Manufactured in the United States by LSC Communications
41089705   2016
www.doverpublications.com

CONTENTS

I. RELIGIOUS SONGS

Contents

II. SOCIAL SONGS

Contents

Contents

III. MEN AT WORK

Contents

IV. OUTLAWS

Contents

Contents

Introduction to the Dover Edition
REDISCOVERING *OUR SINGING COUNTRY*

John and Alan Lomax are the most important documentors of American folk music in this century—legends in a field crowded with legends. John Lomax (1867–1948) started his *Adventures of a Ballad Hunter* (the title of his 1947 autobiography) in 1910 with a volume of *Cowboy Songs* (from which came the fabled "Home on the Range"). In the 1930s John enlisted his son, Alan (b. 1915), as a collaborator and heir apparent, and the two nomads logged thousands of miles, crisscrossing the country in a make-shift pickup truck loaded down with unwieldy primitive recording equipment. By 1939 they had greatly enlarged the holdings of the Archive of American Folk Song at the Library of Congress by depositing over 700 aluminum and acetate disks, which totaled about 2800 items. Eventually their gifts to the Archive numbered more than 10,000 recordings. Using these field recordings as their main source, the Lomaxes published a series of popular anthologies, beginning with *American Ballads and Folk Songs* (1934): *Leadbelly* (1936), *Our Singing Country* (1941), and *Folk Song USA* (1947), their last joint project. All of these books are monuments to the collective cultural discovery we call the "folk revival."

In some ways *Our Singing Country* is an anomaly because it is the best of the three omnibus anthologies, even though it has been the least known. When it was published, it appealed to critics and professional folklorists more than the general public. Yet time has settled its stature in the field. John's daughter, Bess Lomax Hawes, herself a noted professional folklorist, believes it to be the finest of the family books. In his study *Anglo American Folksong Scholarship Since 1898*, D.K. Wilgus pronounced it a "superior volume" to the first Lomax anthology. The writer Gene Bluestein called it a "catalogue worthy of Walt Whitman's *Leaves of Grass*." Out of print for over 50 years, the book can now once again live up to its reputation.[1] For simplicity's sake, we've dubbed it "OSC" in this introduction.

A "FUNCTIONAL SONGBOOK"

Today we share the appreciation of critics in the 1940s, who praised OSC's diversity of songs, the high level of literary and musical beauty of the selections, and the documentary framework in which these songs were placed.

[xiii]

The music came from one side of the American continent to the other, and even occasionally beyond it. Thus a small selection of the place names conveys the breadth of the whole: from such legendary music sites as Livingston, Alabama; the Georgia Sea Islands; Murrells Inlet, South Carolina; and Galax, Virginia. From cities that surprise us, like New York, and from cities that don't, like New Orleans. From Arkansas, Ohio, Texas, Kentucky, California, and even the Bahamas. If today we understand the cultural contradictions embedded in the term "American tradition," it is partly because of the variety documented across 16,000 miles of collecting: spirituals, hollers, game songs, lullabies, whopper ballads, courting songs, chain-gang work songs, Cajun tunes, breakdowns, and play-party songs from a staggering inventory of song types and traditions.

OSC offers a mixture of the familiar and the rare. Many of its 200 or so tunes became standards in the next decades: "Cotton Eye Joe," "East Virginia," "The Dodger," "Darling Corey," "Take this Hammer," "Pauline," "Look Down that Lonesome Road," "Hush, Li'l Baby," "The Rising Sun Blues," "Little Bird, Go Through My Window." Unusual versions of famous Child ballads—such as "Sweet William" for "Barbara Allen" and "Black Jack Davy" for "The Gypsie Laddie"—share space with "A Wasp Bite Nobi On Her Conch Eye" from Bimini.

In making choices for OSC, the Lomaxes treated performance style as important a factor as the tunes themselves. The way a tune was sung could transport it from the commonplace into the realm of distinction. Most academic folklorists usually sidestepped aesthetic issues. But like all great documentors, the Lomaxes were connoisseurs as much as collectors. They did not shy away from critical judgments about the quality of a particular version of a tune as sung by a particular individual.

Taste mattered and for OSC they sought out the best. Sometimes a few details could make all the difference. In OSC, "Down in the Valley" reappears as "Little Willie's My Darlin." The Lomaxes write how this version, with its unexpected blue notes here and there, as "sung by a Negro convict in North Carolina, has more charm than any other version we have heard." The close-harmony improvisation of a group of men from Nassau, 1935, turns "Dig My Grave" into "one of the finest of Negro spirituals."

Because performance style counted for so much, OSC expanded the definition of folk music to include songs available on commercial recordings. At a time when most folklorists still considered words more important than music and disdained all commercial venues, the Lomaxes pushed the frontier of what was American folk music across borders that were then drawn between commercial and folk and later drawn between folk, country, and old-time. Alongside field recordings came songs like "Hard Times in the Country" from the "hillbilly" list of Columbia Records. "Jack O Diamonds" as sung by Pete Harris, Richmond, Texas, 1934, was probably derived from Blind Lemon Jefferson's record on Paramount. "Sweet Thing" is linked to a version of a tune popular on the radio and the phonograph known as "The Crawdad Song." Alan Lomax gave Burl Ives OSC's unusual version of "Darlin Corey," as sung by Aunt Molly Jackson, and Ives recorded it even before the book was published.

Sometimes the Lomaxes took pride in the way their versions differed from standard fare or from popular adaptations. Other times they accepted the influence of one on the other. Perhaps Ella Fitzgerald's swing version of "Atisket, Atasket," which reached the pop charts in 1938, affected country as well as city singers. No matter. Their version of Alabama school girls singing "Kitty Kitty Casket" in 1934 carried "its own evidences of originality." Similarly, the voice of Ozella Jones, in the haunting early blues lyric "I Been a Bad Bad Girl," had more to offer, they wrote, than "the brass-bound music-hall throat" of Bessie Smith. Even if today such competitive comparisons seem forced, back then this partisanship was an inevitable tactic to gain recognition for the underdog rural music maker.

OSC also stands out among Lomax books for its thorough, orderly approach to documentation. Because the Lomaxes had been criticized previously for their rather casual approach, for this book they reformed their ways. They provided each tune with archival reference numbers, information about parallel versions (or scholarly "concordances") in other sources, and added extensive bibliographical references. They avoided the practice of making a "composite" version of a folk song from its many variants, instead picking one version to represent the whole, and presenting it as faithfully as possible.

All of this scholarly apparatus—the lengthy headnotes, the references, the descriptions of context for songs—flows out of the documentary approach to culture pioneered in the 1930s. Instead of treating folk music as some kind of antiquarian relic, the Lomaxes touted the modernity of the material. No more quaintness, no more stereotypes of folk song as an example of primitive simplicity. Over and over, the literary commentary embedded music in lived experience. "This song was a song we used in hoisting the sails," says J.M. Hunt of "Haul Away, My Rosy." Reminiscing about the famous English collector Cecil J. Sharp, Liza Pace calls the Child Ballad "The Mermaid" a "love song": "Years ago when that funny old Englishman come over the mountains and wrote down these old love songs I know, I could sing like a mockingbird and wasn't no step I couldn't put my foot to in a dance."

This approach to folk music made OSC a "functional songbook" in Alan Lomax's eyes. The term is barely used now, but back then it stood for a new approach to the field, which Alan Lomax, along with other New Deal culture advocates like B.H. Botkin and Charles Seeger, actively promoted. They stressed the meaning of the material to the community and its relationship to "acculturation"—the way singers and songs adapted to change. As Bess Lomax Hawes recalls, "They deliberately set out to talk about the United States as a place with enormous musical creativity."

THE ALIVE MUSICAL MOMENT

How to communicate this creativity challenged the Lomaxes throughout their lives. In order to succeed, sound had to be translated into score through a process known as "transcription": taking field recordings and turning them into Western notation, sophisticated enough to convey the full richness of folk music, and yet simple enough to be used by readers with moderate musical literacy. Meeting that challenge fell to the composer Ruth Crawford Seeger (1901–1953), whom the Lomaxes hired as their music editor in the summer of 1937. At the time no one imagined that the process of working on OSC would thrust her into the front ranks of composer-transcribers in the twentieth century, or that it would initiate a collaboration between two families eventually involving three generations of urban folk-revival musicians.

Alan Lomax remembered what happened to them and to her. Ruth Seeger struggled "to really represent the tunes, to paint them somehow with notes . . . I was witness to that struggle," Lomax told Ruth's son and folk-revival musician Mike Seeger several decades later. It was the "struggle of the conservatory-trained musician . . . a musico-intellectual lambkin gambolling in the lion's jaws of oral tradition. We had given her the chance, and she, in total youthful wonderful confidence, set out to take the terrible European notational system and to do it, to make it communicate the ultimate originality of a living tradition." A process that was supposed to take one year took four. Crawford's step-son, the famous Pete Seeger, recalls how "once she was transcribing some Afro-American work songs. Is that a B or a B-flat? What to do? What would be the best thing? What an extraordinary intense concentration on things." In the end, Crawford Seeger's much-praised Music Preface for OSC was distilled from her eighty-page academic analysis of transcription method. (Her complete text, titled *The Music of American Folk Songs*, is scheduled for publication for the first time in 2001).[2]

It took so long because Crawford Seeger heard so much. The great triumph of OSC is the way her transcriptions communicate the coherence, elegance, and complexity of American folk music. "Precision and love" were her guides. So wrote Marc Blitzstein (famous for the opera *The Cradle Will Rock*) in a review for the magazine *Modern Music*, where he captured his experience of hearing the music of OSC through her ears:

> In particular, she hears a pause as a pause, not as a tied-over note or as an aimless wait until the next line: some of the rests, as in "God Don't Like It," are really thrilling in the way they evoke the singer's breathing apparatus and niceness of phrasing. Five-fours, six-eight-plus-three-fours, etc., hold no terrors for her; if it was sung like that, and that's the way it gets notated, and no nonsense . . . The Lomaxes and Mrs. Seeger have let us in on an alive musical moment, from which we . . . can reconstruct the variations and the possibilities. These tunes spring from the page in the same way they leapt from the throat.

To see precision and love in action, look at the transcription of the fiddle tune "Bonyparte." All its double-stops and switches in register are carefully notated in music that was swallowed whole by Aaron Copland and made famous as "Hoedown" in his ballet *Rodeo*. The African American holler "Trouble, Trouble" as sung in 1937 by James Hale in Atmore, Alabama, documents a musical moment in the life of a mule-driver with the controlled detail of a Dorothea Lange photograph. Tracking the singer by changing meters, Crawford Seeger brings home the spontaneity. Wavy lines and invented syllables convey the middle ground between speech and song, with notated "Giddaps" and "Whoa deres." Words, whoops, half-sung, half-talked pitches, bluesy slides: all of the crazy-quilt vocal artistry gets frozen into print.

OSC was finally published in November, 1941, less than a month before America officially entered World War II. In a way the timing was just right. "Never did we need so much at present to cultivate this democratic art of singing together the songs made and loved by the Folk," one reviewer wrote in the *New England Quarterly*. Yet to the great surprise and disappointment of the Lomaxes and the Seegers, their dedication and idealism turned to nought. OSC was not a commercial success, in spite of many good reviews and much attention paid. Its fate hit Alan Lomax particularly hard—a "terrible blow," he said many years later.

Although Alan would later blame OSC's failure on the complexity of the transcriptions, the real problem was the new competition in the folk-music book market. Shortly before OSC was published, the composer Elie Siegmeister and the critic Olin Downes put out *The Treasury of American Folksong*, supplying each folksong with a piano accompaniment, and thereby making it much easier for amateurs to use. Both the Lomaxes and Ruth Crawford Seeger adopted this approach in later books. For many years Alan Lomax considered redoing OSC in this format as well.

That need has gone by in these post-folk-revival times. Commercial music as a corporate product dominates the public, who generally listens rather than sings. Questions rather than answers shape the discourse over authenticity and the very meaning of folk music itself. How remarkable, then, that the clarity of vision in OSC sustains itself even today. Through OSC we can still "gambol in the lion's jaws of oral tradition." Singers and songs retain their power to astonish us, and even in this music culture, as noisy as a fleet of jets, the sounds of an epic cultural revolution still make themselves heard.

Judith Tick

Judith Tick is the author of *Ruth Crawford Seeger: A Composer's Search for American Music* (Oxford University Press, 1997), which won an ASCAP Deems Taylor Award for excellence in writing about music. On the faculty of Northeastern University, she has also published articles about women's history and other American composers.

---

[1] All quotations come from Judith Tick, *Ruth Crawford Seeger: A Composer's Search for American Music* (1997). Also, see Nolan Porterfield, *Last Cavalier: The Life and Times of John A. Lomax* (1996).

[2] Larry Polansky is editing *The Music of American Folk Songs* for Frogpeak Press.

INTRODUCTION TO THE 1941 EDITION

In any country it is the people who make the differences. The landscapes with the thumb-mark and the heel-mark of the people on them are the landscapes you remember. In Chile it is not the mountains which make the unbelievable loveliness of that country but the rows of poplars standing under the stone of the Andes, leaf against granite. It is the same way in other countries. France with the fields so and the roads so and the villages square to them. England with the roofs set this way—not in any other way. Persia with the water courses in the wild gardens and the peach boughs over the mud walls. Japan where the pines on the ridge-poles of the mountains are warped by the wind but not by the wind only. It is the mark of the people on any country which gives it the feel it leaves in a man's mind. Even the sense of time in a country is the sense of the people in it now and before now.

But it is not only the heel-marks on the hill-sides and the way the roads run that show the traces of the people. There are other marks in other materials and not least in the substance of words and the substance of music. Music and words will wear under the use of a people as easily as the earth will wear—and the marks will last longer. Devoted writers write as though the body of the people of a country made songs for themselves and poems for themselves—the "folk songs" and the "folk music." But to speak prosaically *the people* do not make songs and poems for themselves. The folk songs and the folk poems come from far back and like any song or any poem they have had beginnings in a single mind. What the people of a country do with the music they take over for themselves and the poems they take over for themselves is to pass them along from hand to hand, from mouth to mouth, from one generation to the next, until they wear smooth in the shape the people—this particular people—is obliged to give them.

The people "make" their songs and poems the way the people make a stone stair in an old building of this republic where the treads are worn down and shaped up the way their users have to have them. The folk songs and the folk poems show the mark of a people on them the way the old silver dollars show the mark of shoving thumbs—but with far more meaning. They show the people's mark more even than the line of the roads in a country or the shape of the houses—hopeful or not so hopeful—and they last longer. The people (or the poets either) who can leave their mark on the words or on the music of a country, leave it for a long time and in an honorable place.

This second volume of American ballads and folk songs collected by

Introduction

John Lomax of Texas and his son Alan, the two men who created, under the brilliant direction of Herbert Putnam, the Archive of American Folk Song in the Library of Congress, is a body of words and of music which tells more about the American people than all the miles of their quadruple-lane express highways and all the acres of their bill-board-plastered cities—a body of words and of music which tells almost as much about the American people as the marks they have made upon the earth itself. It is a book which many Americans will delight to open, and not once but many times.

But behind this book is another body of material (also a product of the work of Mr. Putnam and the Lomaxes) which reveals with even greater precision the character and the distinction of the mark left upon their music and their words by the people of this country. Behind it are the actual field recordings of the songs as their own singers sang them in the unreproduceable rhythm and inflection and beat of the songs themselves.

Down to last year these recordings were available only to specialists who visited the Library—and not always to them. Many of the disks were too fragile to play more than a few times and none of them could be made publicly available. The Archive was an archive indeed, a rich store of priceless materials—but few men had ever used it or ever could.

As part of our present effort in the Library of Congress to make the American record, as it is stored here, truly and broadly available to the American people themselves, we approached the Carnegie Corporation of New York in the fall of 1939 with the request that funds be granted to enable the Library to establish a Sound Studio which could manufacture pressings of the recordings of the Archive, and of other comparable materials, for sale at cost to schools, colleges, students of folk song, and the public generally.

Thanks to the imagination and understanding of Dr. Frederick P. Keppel, President of the Carnegie Corporation of New York, the grant was made in March 1940 and the Studio began work in June 1940. An order list of the recordings available is now in process of publication and will shortly be ready for public distribution. It is our hope that the Sound Studio, which works closely with the Archive of American Folk Song though under the direction of Mr. Jerome B. Weisner as Chief Engineer, will be of increasing service to lovers of folk music and particularly to those, in American schools and colleges, whose labor it is to teach the next generation of Americans what their country is and to what people they belong.

ARCHIBALD MacLEISH.

Washington,
August, 1941.

PREFACE

If, then, to meanest mariners, and renegades and castaways, I shall here-
after ascribe high qualities, though dark; weave round them tragic graces;
if even the most mournful, perchance the most abased, among them all,
shall at times lift himself to the exalted mounts; if I shall touch that work-
man's arm with some ethereal light; if I shall spread a rainbow over his
disastrous set of sun; then against all mortal critics bear me out in it, . . .
thou great democratic God! who didst not refuse to the swart convict,
Bunyan, the pale, poetic pearl; Thou who didst clothe with doubly ham-
mered leaves of finest gold, the stumped and paupered arm of old Cer-
vantes; Thou who didst pick up Andrew Jackson from the pebbles; who
didst hurl him upon a war-horse; who didst thunder him higher than a
throne! Thou who, in all thy mighty, earthly marchings, ever cullest Thy
selectest champions from the kingly commons; bear me out in it, O God!"
                                                    —*from* Moby Dick

At the crossings of many of the rivers on the cattle trails from Texas to
Montana, there are little wind-blown graveyards—the resting place of
cowboys drowned while swimming longhorn cattle across swollen streams.
Scratched on one leaning headstone is: "He done his damdest."

The function of this book is to let American folk singers have their say
with the readers. Most of these singers are poor people, farmers, laborers,
convicts, old-age pensioners, relief workers, housewives, wandering guitar
pickers. These are the people who still sing the work songs, the cowboy
songs, the sea songs, the lumberjack songs, the bad-man ballads, and other
songs that have no occupation or special group to keep them alive. These
are the people who are making new songs today. These are the people
who go courting with their guitars, who make the music for their own
dances, who make their own songs for their own religion. These are the
story-tellers, because they are the people who are watching when things
happen. These are the great laughers and the great liars, because they

[xxi]

know that life is so much more ridiculous than anyone can ever hope to tell. These are the people who understand death, because it has been close to them all their lives. They have looked at the faces of young men whose lives have been torn from them in industrial accidents. They have been acquainted personally with young girls who killed themselves when they were deserted by false-hearted lovers. They have sheltered the families of men who were sent to prison for murder. These people make deep, slow jokes while they are waiting for things to happen, and they know that what a man isn't willing to fight for must not be true for him. These people have a lot to say and a lot to remember, and that is why this book is mostly in quotation marks.

These people have been wanderers, walking and riding alone into the wilderness, past the mountains and the broad rivers, down the railroad lines, down the highways. Like all wanderers, they have been lonely and unencumbered by respect for the conventions of life behind them. Remembering the old songs in their loneliness, throwing up their voices against prairie and forest track, along new rivers, they followed the instincts of their new experience and the old songs were changed so as to belong to their life in the new country. New songs grew up inconspicuously out of the humus of the old, thrusting out in new directions in small, but permanent, fashion. There grew up a whole continent of people with their songs as much a part of their lives as their familiar ax, gun, or silver dollar. It took them long to recognize that new lives and new songs had been made here.

Yet, in mass, the songs are perhaps more unconventional than the new lives. The songs are the product of the mixing or extension of several peasant musical stocks—British, African, Spanish, French, and German. They are sung in styles which offend the cultivated ear; they are accompanied, if at all, in various unpredictable ways on a number of "limited," inexpensive, and portable instruments. They are often repetitious; they are frequently trite and sententious; but, taken all together, they reflect the life with more honest observation, with more penetrating wit and humor, with more genuine sentiment, with more true, energetic passion than other forms of American art, cultivated or subsidized.

We have known country fiddlers who couldn't read or write, but could play two, three, or four hundred tunes. We have known white ballad singers who remembered one, two, three hundred ballads. We have known Negroes who could sing several hundred spirituals. We have shaken hands with a Mexican share-cropper who carried in his head the text, tunes, and stage directions for a Miracle play requiring four hours and twenty actors to perform. We have been in constant touch with people who felt that inability to improvise by ear unfamiliar tunes in three- or four-part harmony marked one as unmusical. Such artists with their audiences have created and preserved for America a heritage of folk song and folk music equal to any in the world. Such folk have made America a singing country.

We name the names of some of the best singers that we have met:

Mrs. Griffin, a "Georgy cracker" who "has done everything that an honest woman could do except lie and steal"—picked cotton, cleared land, danced in a minstrel show, raised twelve children, run her own sawmill; who came to northern Florida overland and on foot from southern Georgia; from whom seventy-five or more ballads and songs have been recovered, including one called "Lord Derwentwater."

Old Lize Pace of Hyden, Kentucky, from whom Cecil Sharp collected some of his best songs, and whose story is found on page 151 of this book.

Blind old Mrs. Dusenberry of the Ozarks, living in a little old log cabin in the hills, holding in her memory nearly two hundred songs and ballads.

Maggie Gant and her children, dispossessed east Texas share-croppers, whose story is found on page 156.

Mrs. Ward of the Wards of Galax, Virginia, a gentle-voiced and calm farmer's wife who has passed on a store of ballads and songs to a whole generation of her descendants.

Elida Hofpauir, fifteen, who knew a bookful of French and Cajun ballads, who worked in a tomato canning factory and wanted a dollar "store-bought" dress for a present.

Aunt Molly Jackson, who has filled seventy-five twelve-inch records for the Library of Congress with her songs and reminiscences about them, who was midwife to Clay County, the daughter of a coal miner and preacher, the wife of a miner, and a union organizer in her own right.

Johnny Green, rantankerous old Irish fisherman and lumberjack and lake sailor of Beaver Island, Michigan, who has "dug up" out of his own memory nearly three hundred come-all-ye ballads, the saga of his people in Ireland, in English wars, in American forests, and on the American lakes.

Elmer George, one-time lumberjack, now automobile salesman of North Montpelier, Vermont.

Dick Maitland, seaman of Sailors' Snug Harbor, eighty-odd, still as sturdy and foursquare as an oak ship, called by Joanna Colcord the best sea shanty singer she knows.

J. C. Kennison, scissors grinder, shacked up on the windy top of one of the Green Mountains in Vermont, holding proudly in his mind the memories of Young Beichan and his Turkish Lady and of Jim Fiske, "the kind of man would pat a dog on the head."

Preface

Captain Pearl R. Nye, rotund and apple-cheeked, who claims to know the name of "every canalboat and every skipper that sailed the 'silver ribbon' of the Ohio ship canal," who sent to us in the Library of Congress the texts of seven hundred songs and ballads once current on the canal, copied out on scrolls of cheap yellow paper —songs he said had "bobbed up" recently out of his memory. (Captain Nye remarked once, "My mind is canal.")

Alec Moore, retired cowpuncher, who sings everything from "Bold Andrew Barton" to "The Bloody Sioux Indians," whose present occupation is riding herd on an ice-cream wagon on the streets of Austin, Texas.

The Sheriff of Hazard County, Kentucky, who gets re-elected each year partly by the speed, ferocity, and style of his banjo-picking at county meetings.

Woody Guthrie, dust-bowl ballad-maker, proud of being an Okie, familiar with microphones and typewriters, familiar, too, with jails and freight trains, "with relatives under every railroad bridge in California," who knows scores of the old songs and makes up a new one whenever he feels that one is needed about the Vigilante Men or Pretty Boy Floyd or Tom Joad.

And now the names of some of the singers who have moved us beyond all others that we have heard between Maine and New Mexico, Florida and Michigan—the Negroes, who in our opinion have made the most important and original contributions to American folk song:

Aunt Harriett McClintock of Alabama, seventy-eight years old, who sat by the roadside and sang:

> Poor little Johnny, poor little feller,
> He can't make a hunderd today;
> Down in the bottom
> Where the cotton is rotten,
> He can't make a hunderd today.

Aunt Molly McDonald, who sat on the sunny porch of her shanty and swapped sixty little songs out of the slavery days with Uncle Joe, her husband, and laughed heartily between the stanzas.

Iron Head, grim-faced prison habitué, who always claimed that his choice, aristocratic repertoire of songs all came from one fellow prisoner.

Big John Davis, who was the best man, the biggest drinker, the most powerful argufier, and the best singer in Frederica, Georgia.

Allen Prothero, whose singing of "Jumping Judy" and "Pauline" is giving him posthumous fame, who "just nachully didn't like the place" where we found him, and died there in the Nashville Penitentiary of T.B.

Henry Truvillion, still leader of a railroad gang in the piney woods of No Man's Land between Texas and Louisiana, who each day sings and shouts his men

Preface

into concerted activity by original and beautifully phrased songs, who owns a farm and a white cottage by the side of the road and yet has time to be the pastor of two country churches: "I collected $7.45 last Sunday, all mine; the Lord owns the whole world, He don't need no money."

Lightning, a dynamic black Apollo song-leader, called "Lightnin'" by his comrades because "he thinks so fast he can git around any of them white bosses," who sings "Ring, Old Hammer" so realistically that one can see the old blacksmith shop with swinging bellows and hear again the cheerful ring of the forgotten anvil.

Willie Williams, who could sing holler at his mules ("Don't 'low me to beat 'em, got to beg 'em along") or lead spirituals with equal power and fervor.

Dobie Red, Track Horse, Jim Cason, Big Nig, and many another Negro prisoner, from whom we have obtained our noblest songs.

Vera Hall and Dock Reed, cousins, who can sing all the unique spirituals that seem to have emerged from the countryside about Livingston, Alabama, the beauty of whose singing has been made known to the world through the interest and devotion of Mrs. Ruby Pickens Tartt.

Clear Rock (Texas), Kelly Page (Arkansas), and Roscoe McLean (Arkansas) are other unsurpassed song leaders.

Seldom does one discern in these folk a delicate concern "with the creation of an imaginary world peopled with characters quite as wonderful, in their way, as the elfin creations of Spenser." * Nor does one find in them an overwhelming desire to forget themselves and everything that reminds them of their everyday life. The American singer has been concerned with themes close to his everyday experience, with the emotions of ordinary men and women who were fighting for freedom and for a living in a violent new world. His songs have been strongly rooted in his life and have functioned there as enzymes to assist in the digestion of hardship, solitude, violence, hunger, and the honest comradeship of democracy.

The songs in this book, therefore, have been given a roughly "functional" arrangement—that is, according to the way they grew up and lived in the American community. The first half of the book contains those songs that have been sung in a normal community by or for or before men, women, and children—*i.e.*, religious songs, dance songs, lullabies, love songs, and ballads. The last half contains those songs which grew up in circles mostly male, and were male in content and audience—the occupational songs and ballads, the work songs; and those songs which grew up in groups where the exceeding hardness and bitterness of existence tended to obliterate distinctions—the blues and songs of drink, gambling, and crime.

* *English Folk Songs of the Southern Appalachians*, by Cecil Sharp and Maude Karpeles, p. xxxvii.

Preface

Only recently have artists and scientists seemed to care to know what the people thought and felt and believed, what and how they sang. With the development of the portable recording machine, however, one can do more than transcribe in written outline what they say. The needle writes on the disc with tireless accuracy the subtle inflections, the melodies, the pauses that comprise the emotional meaning of speech, spoken and sung. In this way folklore can truly be recorded. A piece of folklore is a living, growing, and changing thing, and a folk song printed, words and tune, only symbolizes in a very static fashion a myriad-voiced reality of individual songs. The collector with pen and notebook can capture only the outline of one song, while the recorder, having created an atmosphere of easy sociability, confines the living song, without distortion and in its fluid entirety, on a disc. Between songs, sometimes between stanzas, the singers annotate their own song. The whole process is brief and pleasurable. They are not confused by having to stop and wait for the pedestrian pen of the folklorist: they are able to forget themselves in their songs and to underline what they wish to underline. Singing in their homes, in their churches, at their dances, they leave on these records imperishable spirals of their personalities, their singing styles, and their cultural heritage. The field recording, as contrasted with the field notebook, shows the folk song in its three-dimensional entirety, that is, with whatever rhythmic accompaniment there may be (hand-clapping, foot-patting, and so on), with its instrumental background, and with its folk harmonization. A funeral service in the South, a voodoo ceremony in Haiti, a wedding in French southwestern Louisiana, or a square dance in the country may be recorded for future study; a "movie" would complete the picture.

It is always a dramatic moment for any one when his own voice comes back to him undistorted from the black mouth of a loud-speaker. He seems to feel the intense and absorbing pleasure that a child experiences when he first recognizes himself in a mirror. One old hard-bitten Mexican vaquero in the mesquite country of southwest Texas, when his song was played to him unexpectedly, said with soft amazement, "Madre de Dios!" then after a time, "Muy hombre!" A Negro prisoner, wishing to communicate his extravagant and uncontrollable surprise, fell flat on his back and lay there till his buddies picked him up. A mountaineer, when asked if he would like to hear his record played back, said: "I reckon so. Anything I'll do oncet, I'll do hit twicet." "Ain't men sharp?" he added, when the record was finished. "A man can't stutter none talking into one of them things; got to stick to plain English. If he don't, it'll tell on him." On hearing

Preface

his voice come back, an Alabama Negro exclaimed, "Dat's pure hit! Dat's hit directly!" Another decided: "That machine can sho beat me singin'." Aunt Harriett heard the sputter of the batteries, saw the spinning turntable. She didn't understand what was happening, but she pointed at the machine and said, "Stop dat ghost!"

Occasionally the singer's belief in the power of the recording he has made is pathetic beyond tears. In the Tennessee State Prison a young Negro convict came up to us shyly and asked to be allowed to make a record. When we asked what he wanted to record, he said, "Boss, I can beat on a bucket just as sweet as you please." All the prisoners present agreed that this was true. When the record was completed, he murmured, half to himself, "Well, I guess when they hear that up there in the White House, them big men sho goin' do something for this po' nigger."

There are now over four thousand aluminum and acetate discs by such singers in the Archive of American Folk Song, about two-thirds of them recorded in the field by ourselves. An order list of these records will be published shortly, containing over twelve thousand English titles, and foreign language supplements later on. A recent grant from the Carnegie Foundation for the installation of duplicating equipment will make these records available at cost to the public. We hope that the American people will learn from these records to know itself better, learn to sing its own folk songs in the rich and varied styles of our folk singers. It is possible to use some commercial records out of the groups called "hillbilly" and "race" to the same ends.*

This might seem to be the last book in the world which should owe its existence to the man who invented the L.C. card, Dr. Herbert Putnam. And yet, when one reflects that this same reserved and iron-willed Bostonian liberal also made the Library of Congress the only great democratic library in the world, it is not strange that he understood and wished to preserve—although he could seldom bear to listen to—the songs of the American people. Ruby Pickens Tartt and Genevieve Chandler, two intelligent and creative Southern women, explored the singing resources of their communities and welcomed us with our recording machine. Dr. W. P. Davis and his Bogtrotters of Galax, Virginia, introduced us to an unexplored and tune-packed section of the Virginia mountains, and it is with his kind permission that Galax songs are reproduced in this book. Dr. Harold Spivacke has been personally helpful and administratively generous throughout the

* A large mimeographed list of such records is available on application to the Archive of American Folk Song, Library of Congress.

making of this volume. Acknowledgment is hereby made to the Federal Writers Project and the Historical Records Project of the Works Progress Administration, under whose auspices a number of these songs were collected. Aunt Molly Jackson spoke the lines that make up much of the continuity of *Our Singing Country*.

Our Singing Country: A Second Volume of American Ballads and Folk Songs, with many regrets for all the songs we have to omit, stands only for work (as noted in the headnotes) we ourselves have done and for our tastes and interests. It neither does justice to our collection, perhaps, nor, except in minor instances, draws upon work done, upon records made, or upon texts collected by any one else. We hope that the book is merely a foretaste of what may grow into a fairly complete collection of American folk tunes, and of the books, symphonies, plays, operas for which it should eventually provide material. Since the songs cannot be heard in all of their living quality, we have not hesitated to adopt certain means for conveying as much of their content as possible to the readers. We have in certain cases created composite versions of the texts of ballads or songs (as noted in the headnotes), so that the non-ballad-student among readers may quickly survey all the choicest lines that any group of song variants contains. We have not quibbled about the definition of folk song, but we have included whatever songs and ballads prove to have been current among the people and to have undergone change through oral transmission. To introduce the songs, we have generally used quotations from the records themselves. We have let the song-makers and the song-rememberers speak for themselves.

A. L. AND J. A. L.

WASHINGTON, D.C.
March, 1941

MUSIC PREFACE

With the exception of thirteen songs,* the tunes included in this volume were transcribed by the Music Editor direct from duplicate discs of phonograph recordings made by John A. and Alan Lomax with portable electrical sound-recording apparatus. Copies of these, as of many other recordings in the Archive of American Folk Song, in the Division of Music of the Library of Congress, are now available to the public.

I

Up in the Archive of American Folk Song, in one of the attics of the Library of Congress, John Lomax and Alan and Bess Brown and I, with Elizabeth and "Deanie" often sitting along the sidelines, gathered around the phonograph about three years ago. The occasion for these conclaves was the selection of songs to be included in this volume. We played spirituals ad lib., work songs, hollers, white ballads, Negro game songs, Cajun tunes, breakdowns, fiddle tunes, come-all-ye's, and so on.

On each song I was asked to cast my vote. And I found myself very often hesitant to give it. What standards had I—a mere composer—for judgment? My basis for evaluation was that of written rather than unwritten music—of fine art, not folk art. As a professional musician, my inclination was to ask: How "different" is this song? Is it quaint, archaic? Does it contain irregularities of meter, rhythm, counterpoint, harmony, intonation, scale, mode, which set it apart as something unusual, unique?

These questions I could answer without difficulty. But to one who had yet to learn the idioms, their opposites were not so easy: How *typical* is this song? To what extent does it *conform*? How "nice and common" (in one singer's words) is it? Of that sort of commonness which keeps a thing alive and growing? And where lies the dividing line between the common and

---

* Included from other publications: "The Romish Lady," "Over Jordan," "The High Barbaree," "Down, Down, Down." Dictated to the Music Editor by the singer: "Cotton Eye Joe," "Old Bangham," "Old King Cole," "Po' Farmer," "Bugger Burns," "I Got to Roll," "Godamighty Drag." Transcribed from commercial recordings: "The Sporting Cowboy," "Hard Times in the Country."

the commonplace? Is "The Lexington Murder" cheap, and "Little Willie's My Darlin'" sentimental? Is "Careless Love," or "Adieu to the Stone Walls," banal?

In many cases I could, of course, vote an immediate No or Yes—No to a holler whose fluid tonal and rhythmic subtleties could on no stretch of the imagination be put into notation suitable for sight-reading; Yes to a ballad or spiritual or work song whose authenticity was unmistakable, and whose balance between the usual and the unusual made choice easy. But for the most part I gained a reputation for "thinking it over"—for wishing to postpone decision until I felt I had heard a large enough body of these songs and had myself sung enough of them to gain some sort of feeling for the various idioms as wholes before attempting to pass judgment on individual adherence to or departure from them.

Since we all felt that at least a majority of the songs should be of the sort which could be more or less easily sung, there was a great deal of singing in those sessions. And throughout the succeeding years, during which I sporadically transcribed the three hundred tunes from which the final hundred and ninety were selected, I continued to sing these songs and others like them. And found my tastes expanding. Interest in the unusual did not diminish—in a work song in $\frac{5}{2}$ meter, a Cajun tune consistently in $\frac{10}{8}$ throughout, a Ravel-like banjo accompaniment, a ballad of archaic tonal texture, a Bahaman part-song of contrapuntal bareness. But appreciation of the "nice and common" took root and grew strong, with promise of growing stronger as time goes on. And along with this growth have come surer answers to some of those questions of three years ago. "Careless Love" and "Adieu to the Stone Walls" are not sentimental, banal —that is, not if they are sung more or less in the manner in which the folk musician sings them.

No one who has studied these or similar recordings can deny that the song and its singing are indissolubly connected—that the character of a song depends to a great extent on the *manner of its singing*. It is often to be noticed that the city person, unacquainted with folk idioms, will endow a folk song with manners of fine-art or popular performance which are foreign to it, and will tend to sentimentalize or to dramatize that which the folk performer presents in a simple straightforward way. I have heard "Careless Love" sung by a considerable number of folk musicians, but not once "dreamily," "with expression," "patético," "con amore." Some sing it moderately fast, some fast. The tempo of one recording was very fast from beginning to end.

Music Preface

It has been my wish, in transcribing these songs, *to include as many characteristics of singing-style as is possible, yet to keep most of the notations simple enough to be sight-read by the average amateur.* If I have been successful in this, those familiar with the idioms can expect to make from these notations fairly adequate reconstruction of the music. To those not familiar with the idioms (and as a reminder to those who are!) the following suggestions are offered, based on observations made during transcription of the songs from the recordings.

II

SUGGESTIONS FOR SINGING THE SONGS IN THIS BOOK

It should be remembered that these are neither rules nor directions. They are suggestions, based on acquaintance with these songs and others like them, as heard from the singers themselves and from direct sound-recordings.

1. *Do not hesitate to sing because you think your voice is "not good"— i.e., has not been "trained."* These songs are better sung in the manner of the natural than the trained (bel canto] voice.* Do not try to "smooth out" your voice. If it is reedy or nasal, so much the better.

2. *First try the tune through several times without attention to signs indicating extended tones and extended or inserted rests* ($\overset{2}{\curlywedge}$, $\overset{4}{\curlywedge}$, etc., and , and ,, , explained on pages xxii and xxiii). When you are more or less at home with the tune, you can then decide whether to add these irregularities to the simple structure you have just learned. You may find, in time, that they "come natural."

3. *Do not sing "with expression," or make an effort to dramatize.* Maintain a level of more or less the same degree of loudness or softness from beginning to end of the song.

4. *Do not slow down at ends of phrases, stanzas, or songs.* Frequent, stereotyped ritardandos are rarely heard in the singing of these songs.

5. *Do not hesitate to keep time with your foot. Unless otherwise indicated, sing with a fairly strong accent.*

6. *Do not "punch" or "typewrite out" each tone.* When two or more tones are to be sung to one syllable of text, bind them together rather

* J. W. Work, in his Introduction to Frederick J. Work's *Folk Song of the American Negro* (Work Brothers, Nashville, Tenn., 1907), wrote: "To sing this music effectively the singer . . . must not try to sing: that is, he must not try to impress people with his voice or voice culture."

than articulate each separately. Bear this in mind when singing grace notes and such figures as 𝄢. (see "Marthy Had a Baby"), which have been used to indicate rapid slides in the voice.

7. *Do not make too much difference between major and minor degrees, in songs containing both* (see "Pass Around Your Bottle"). Many such tones are merely "closer to major than to minor," or vice versa.*

8. *Do not let the presence of extra syllables in succeeding stanzas deter you from singing the song through.* Most singers crowd them, but not too hurriedly, into the established measure-length. Others insert extra beats to care for them in more leisurely fashion.

9. *Do not feel that, in group singing, these songs require "harmonizing."* Those which lend themselves to group singing are, with a few exceptions, most appropriately sung in unison or octave.†

10. *Do not hesitate to sing without accompaniment.*

11. *When singing without accompaniment, do not make noticeable pause between stanzas.* Most singers, when unaccompanied, continue with little or no break from stanza to stanza throughout the song. (The amount of breathing-time allowed at the end of the stanza by the original singer has, with a few exceptions, been included in each notation. It is more or less typical of that allowed between other stanzas throughout the song.)

12. *When accompaniment is desired, a guitar or banjo is to be preferred.* The harmonica, fiddle, dulcimer, auto-harp, and accordion are also appropriate. The piano, if it must be used, should not obtrude; it can easily submerge the voice in conventions foreign to the spirit of the songs. Use simple chords—for most songs, primary triads (I, IV, V) with an occasional V⁷. Do not feel that you must change chords too often. Accompaniment of an entire song with the tonic (I) is fairly common, either with or without an added melodic line in the bass.

13. *When singing with accompaniment, the voice should rest occasionally between stanzas to allow for instrumental interludes*—which, often as not, will repeat the tune. The banjo, on these recordings, gives more frequent interludes than the guitar. Accompaniments usually

---

* Indication of "blue notes" and neutral intervals has been felt to be out of place in the notations in this volume. See Winthrop Sargeant on "The Scalar Structure of Jazz," in *Jazz: Hot and Hybrid*, Arrow Editions, New York, 1938.

† Twenty-one of the songs in this volume were sung in parts. They are, in the main, spirituals, Bahaman songs, and Negro work songs. In twelve of these, the parts have been transcribed (see "Dig My Grave").

As used here, the term "in parts" signifies continuous or consistent deviation from unison or octave singing, and possesses no harmony-book implications.

continue without break throughout an entire song, regardless of extended or contracted tones or rests in the voice. (The duration of the short interlude has, as often as possible, been included in the notation—either in the form of rests (as in "Pretty Polly") or of long held tones (as in "The White House Blues"). It is more or less typical of that found between other stanzas throughout the song. For obvious reasons, durations of the longer interludes have not been indicated.)

14. *Remember that most songs which begin with the chorus end with the chorus.* In these as in all others, the end of the song is indicated by the heavy double bar.

15. *Do not "sing down" to the songs.* Theirs are old traditions, dignified by hundreds of thousands of singers over long periods of time.

16. *Listen to phonograph recordings of these songs and others like them.*

III

EXPLANATION OF TERMS AND SIGNS

The tunes have been transposed to a range suitable for medium voice. The original pitch of the last tone of each tune, as given by the duplicate disc used for transcribing, has been indicated at the beginning of the headnote to each song, by means of a letter in italics (see Explanation of Headnotes, page xxv). Keys of more than three sharps or flats have been avoided. Excepting the part-songs, all tunes are represented in the G or treble clef, with which the general reader is most likely to be familiar. For simplicity in reading, instrumental notation has been used in place of vocal (as, for instance, ♩♩♩ *instead of ♩ ♩ ♩ ♩); when more than one tone is sung to a single syllable of text, this is indicated by a slur (as* 🎵 *). As often as space permits, the linage of the music follows the linage of the words (see "Lolly Too-Dum").*

Key signature

Most of the readers of this book will have been taught to sight-read in the conventional major and minor modes, and to judge the key (and hence, the tonic or key-tone) from the key signature at the beginning of the notation. In these notations, therefore, that key signature has been chosen for each song which will enable the reader most easily to locate its tonic or key-tone. In tunes of 4, 5, 6, or 7 scale degrees, which do not employ, or which cancel, an accidental (sharp or flat) contained in the key signature, this accidental has been enclosed in parentheses (as ♯ or ♭). Exceptions will be found in "King William Was King George's Son," "Oh, Lovely Appearance of Death," and "Trouble, Trouble."

Metrical signature and tempo

Tempo refers to the speed at which a song is sung.

Precise indications of speed have been given in terms of the metronome, at the heading of each song. Thus, ♩=66 indicates that there are 66 half-notes to the minute. The note-value used in the metronome mark is, in most cases, that of the denominator of the metrical signature. It represents the pulse—or foot-beat, either present or implied. The numerator of the metrical signature indicates the number of pulses per measure. Further indication of pulse is given in the length of beams connecting eighth and sixteenth notes (as ♫ in "Billy Barlow" or ♬ in "Hop Up, My Ladies"). The eleven songs not transcribed from recordings have been given no metronome indications.

General indications of speed are expressed by the terms "Fast," "Moderately fast," "Moderate," "Moderately slow," and "Slow," placed before the metronome mark at the heading of each song. Unless otherwise indicated, the song should be understood to have been sung more or less in strict time (Tempo giusto), with regularly recurring, strongly defined pulse, and well accented. The indications "Free" and "Somewhat free" have been used to designate the tempo of songs in which a regular pulse is either (a) vague or indeterminate, or (b) established, departed from and returned to periodically throughout the stanza (rubato).

Ritenuto	Abrupt change to a slower tempo
Ritardando	Gradual decrease of speed
Accelerando	Gradual increase of speed
⌢	A hold of indefinite length (fermata)
⌢̇	A hold of definite length, indicating that a second beat, of the value of the denominator of the metrical signature, should be added to the tone over which this sign appears. Thus (as in "The Wild Colonial Boy"): 𝄽 ♪ ♪ ♪̂ - 𝄽 ♪ ♪ ♪♪ (or ♪ ♪ ♪)

$\overset{3}{\curvearrowright}$	A hold of definite length, indicating that a second and a third beat, each of the value of the denominator of the metrical signature, should be added to the tone over which this sign appears. Thus (as in "The Little Brown Bulls"):

(musical notation example)

or (as in "Texas Rangers"):

(musical notation example)

$\overset{4}{\curvearrowright}$, $\overset{5}{\curvearrowright}$, etc.	Holds of definite length, to be interpreted as above
,	An extended or an inserted rest, indicating that one beat, of the value of the denominator of the metrical signature, should be added or interpolated. Thus (as in "My Father Gave Me a Lump of Gold"):

(musical notation example)

or (as in "The Irish Lady"):

(musical notation example)

,,	An extended or inserted rest of two beats, to be interpreted as above
DC (Da Capo)	Go back to the beginning
DS 𝄋 *(Dal Segno)*	Go back to the sign 𝄋
Fine	The end of the song
DC al Fine	Go back to the beginning, then continue to *Fine*
↓	A tone half sung, half spoken
♫	Small notes have been employed to indicate (a) occasional variations in succeeding stanzas, and (b) additional parts sung simultaneously with the principal tune. There need be no confusion between these two usages, since the latter is always accompanied by some such indication as "Second part," "Second singer," "Tenor," or "Bass."

* * *

Music Preface

Appreciation is due to Bess Brown Lomax, with whom most of the transcriptions were discussed and sung. I am also indebted to Sidney Robertson for her detailed reading of the entire music proof. Dr. George Herzog has kindly checked the transcriptions of "Callahan" and "Pauline," and made suggestions which were incorporated in the notation of the latter. Carolyn LeFevre Spivacke has played through the two fiddle tunes, and checked their transcriptions with the recordings. Above all, acknowledgment is due to Charles Seeger, for day-to-day encouragement, consultation and collaboration.

R. C. S.

WASHINGTON, D.C.
March, 1941

EXPLANATION OF HEADNOTES

A headnote in small type appears above the notation of each song, and contains the following information:

(1) the pitch of the final tone of each tune, as shown on the duplicate phonograph disc (played at 78 RPM) from which the tune was transcribed;

(2) the number of the original disc in the Archive of American Folk Song in the Music Division of the Library of Congress;

(3) the name(s) of the singer(s), and of the accompanying instrument(s) and player(s), if any;

(4) the place where the recording was made;

(5) the date at which the recording was made;

(6) one or several references to sources where similar songs can be found in print.

The pitch of the final tone of each tune is shown by means of a letter in italics, as follows:

C to B   c to b   c' to b'

When the pitch rises or falls during the course of a song, this change is indicated (as "*e* to *f*"). When several voice-parts have been shown in the notation, the final tone of each is indicated here, from lowest to highest (as "*G, g, d'* ").

It should be noted that the original discs, as well as the duplicate discs from which the tunes were transcribed, were made on several different assemblies of equipment under varying conditions. It is a question, therefore, whether the pitch of the duplicates as given on the following pages is in all cases the same as that of the original singing, or of the original recording. The pitches given here are offered as having value for at least an approximate pitch placement, and as an indication of the amount of *variation* in pitch within the limits of any one song.

There follows a list of books to which reference has been made in the headnotes. Most of the books may be found in any large library. The references here noted are not intended to be complete, but rather to lead the student or the interested reader to sources where versions of the song may be found, where the song may be located in a context of similar songs with discussion of these songs, or from which the song may

[xxxvii]

Explanation of Headnotes

be traced to European or American sources. Each reference book appears in the headnote in a short form which may be identified by reference to the following list of books. In most cases, the references pertain to the text rather than the music.

Ba. . . . . BARBEAU, MARIUS, *Romancero du Canada.* Toronto: Macmillan Co. of Canada, 1937.

BaS. . . . BARBEAU, MARIUS, AND SAPIR, E., Folk Songs of French Canada. New Haven: Yale University Press, 1925.

Be. . . . BELDEN, H. M., *Ballads and Songs Collected by the Missouri Folk Song Society.* Columbia, Mo.: University of Missouri Press, 1940.

Boa. . . . BOATNER, E., *Spirituals Triumphant, Old and New.* Nashville, Tenn.: National Baptist Convention Publishing Board, 1927.

BB. . . . BOLTON, D. G., AND BURLEIGH, H. T., *Old Songs Hymnal.* New York: Century Co., 1929.

Bo. . . . BONE, DAVID W., *Capstan Bars.* New York: Harcourt, Brace & Co., 1932.

Bot. . . . BOTKIN, B. A., *The American Play Party Song.* Lincoln: University of Nebraska, 1937.

Ca. . . . CAMBIAIRE, C. P., *East Tennessee and Western Virginia Mountain Ballads.* London: Mitre Press, 1934.

Co. . . . COOMBS, J. H., *Folk Songs du Midi des Etats Unis.* Paris: Presses Univ. de Paris, 1925.

Col. . . . COLCORD, JOANNA, *Songs of American Sailormen.* Indianapolis: Bobbs-Merrill Co., 1924.

Cox. . . . COX, J. H., *Folk Songs of the South.* Cambridge: Harvard University Press, 1925.

Cr. . . . CREIGHTON, HELEN, *Songs and Ballads from Nova Scotia.* Toronto and Vancouver: J. M. Dent & Sons, 1932.

Da. . . . DAVIS, A. K., *Traditional Ballads in Virginia.* Cambridge: Harvard University Press, 1929.

Ed. . . . EDDY, MARY O., *Ballads and Songs from Ohio.* New York: J. J. Augustin, 1939.

Fe. . . . FENNER, T. P., *Cabin and Plantation Songs by Hampton Students.* New York: G. P. Putnam, 1877.

Fl.1. . . FLANDERS, H. H., AND BROWN, GEORGE, *Vermont Folk Songs and Ballads.* Brattleboro: Stephen Daye Press, 1932.

Fl.2. . . FLANDERS, H. H., AND OTHERS, *The New Green Mountain Songster.* New Haven: Yale University Press, 1939.

Ga.1. . . GARDNER, E. E., *Folklore from the Schoharie Hills.* Ann Arbor: University of Michigan Press, 1937.

Ga.2. . . GARDNER, E. E., AND CHICKERING, G. J., *Ballads and Songs of Southern Michigan.* Ann Arbor: University of Michigan Press, 1939.

Explanation of Headnotes

Go. . . . GORDON, ROBERT, "Folk Songs of America"—series of articles in *New York Times Magazine*, beginning Jan. 2, 1927.

Gra. . . . GRAY, R. P., *Songs and Ballads of the Maine Lumberjack.* Cambridge: Harvard University Press, 1924.

Gr. . . . GREENLEAF, E., AND MANSFIELD, G. L., *Ballads and Sea Songs of Newfoundland.* Cambridge: Harvard University Press, 1933.

Hu. . . . HUDSON, A. P., *Folk Songs of Mississippi.* Chapel Hill: University of North Carolina Press, 1936.

Ja.1. . . JACKSON, G. P., *Spiritual Folk-Songs of Early America.* New York: J. J. Augustin, 1937.

Ja.2. . . JACKSON, G. P., *White Spirituals from the Southern Uplands.* Chapel Hill: University of North Carolina Press, 1933.

Jo.1. . . JOHNSON, J. W. AND J. R., *The Book of American Negro Spirituals.* New York: Viking Press, 1925.

Jo.2. . . JOHNSON, J. W. AND J. R., *The Second Book of American Negro Spirituals.* New York: Viking Press, 1926.

Jo.3. . . JOHNSON, J. R., *Rolling Along in Song.* New York: Viking Press, 1937.

JAFL. . *Journal of American Folk-Lore.* New York: American Folk-Lore Society.

Lo.1. . . LOMAX, J. A. AND A., *Cowboy Songs,* rev. ed. New York: Macmillan Co., 1938.

Lo.2. . . LOMAX, J. A. AND A., *American Ballads and Folk Songs.* New York: Macmillan Co., 1934.

Lo.3. . . LOMAX, J. A. AND A., *Negro Folk Songs As Sung by Lead Belly.* New York: Macmillan Co., 1936.

Ma. . . . MACKENZIE, W. R., *Ballads and Sea Songs from Nova Scotia.* Cambridge: Harvard University Press, 1928.

Me. . . . MCILHENNY, E. A., *Befo' de War Spirituals.* Boston: Christopher Publishing House, 1933.

Mem. . . *Memoirs of the American Folk-Lore Society.* New York: American Folk-Lore Society.

Na. . . . *National Jubilee Melodies.* Nashville, Tenn.: National Baptist Publishing Board, no date.

Ne. . . . NEWELL WM. W., *Games and Songs of American Children.* New York: Harper and Brothers, 1903.

Ni. . . . . NILES, J. J., *Seven Negro Exaltations.* New York: G. Schirmer, 1929.

Od.1. . . ODUM, H., AND JOHNSON, G. B., *The Negro and His Songs.* Chapel Hill: University of North Carolina Press, 1925.

Od.2. . . ODUM, H., AND JOHNSON, G. B., *Negro Workaday Songs.* Chapel Hill: University of North Carolina Press, 1926.

Po. . . . POUND, LOUISE, *American Ballads and Songs.* New York: Charles Scribner's Sons, 1922.

Explanation of Headnotes

PTFLS.   *Publications of the Texas Folk-Lore Society,* ed. J. Frank Dobie. Austin, Texas, 1916– .

Ri. . . . . RICKABY, FRANZ, *Ballads and Songs of the Shanty-Boy.* Cambridge: Harvard University Press, 1926.

Sa. . . . SARGEANT, WINTHROP, *Jazz, Hot and Hybrid.* New York: Arrow Editions, 1938.

Sc.1. . . . SCARBOROUGH, DOROTHY, *On the Trail of Negro Folk-Songs.* Cambridge: Harvard University Press, 1925.

Sc.2. . . . SCARBOROUGH, DOROTHY, *A Song Catcher in the Southern Mountains.* New York: Columbia University Press, 1937.

Sh. . . . SHARP, CECIL J., AND CAMPBELL, O., *English Folk Songs from the Southern Appalachians.* 2 vols. New York: G. P. Putnam's Sons, 1917.

Tho.1. . THOMAS, JEAN, *Devil's Ditties.* Chicago: W. Wilbur Hatfield, 1931.

Tho.2. . THOMAS, JEAN, *Ballad Makin' in the Kentucky Mountains.* New York: Henry Holt & Co., 1939.

Wha. . . WHALL, W. B., *Sea Songs and Shanties.* Glasgow: J. Brown & Son, 1920.

Whi. . . WHITE, N. I., *American Negro Folk-Songs.* Cambridge: Harvard University Press, 1928.

I

RELIGIOUS SONGS

1. Negro Spirituals
2. White Religious Songs
3. The Holiness People

I. 1. NEGRO SPIRITUALS

PRAYER

No. 233. Negro, Raleigh, N.C., 1936.

This evening, our Father,
We begin before death in early judgment—
This evening, our Father,
I come, in the humblest manner I ever knowed
Or ever thought it,
To bow.

I'm thanking Thee, O Lord,
O Lord, thanking Thee this evening, my Father,
That my laying down last night wasn't my cooling board;
O Lord, thanking Thee this evening, my Father,
That my cover was not my winding sheet;
O Lord, thanking Thee this evening, my Father,
That my dressing room this morning was not my grave;
O Lord, thanking Thee this evening, my Father,
That my slumber last night was not for eternity.

O Lord,
Just bless the widows and orphans in this land,
I pray Thee in Jesus' name,
Take care of them, my Father,
And guide them;
And then, my Father,
When they all is standing in Glory
And Thou art satisfied at my staying here,
Oh, meet me at the river, I ask in Thy name.
Amen.

ADAM IN THE GARDEN PINNIN' LEAVES

e'. No. 105. Alberta Bradford, 72, and Becky Elsy, 86.
Avery Island, La., 1934. Text partly from Me, p. 37.

Moderately fast ♩ = 84

CHORUS
FIRST SINGER

SECOND SINGER
foot-tapping

"Oh, Eve,— where is Ad-am? Oh, Eve,— where is Ad-am?

Oh, Eve, where is Ad-am?" "Ad-am in the gar-den pin-nin' leaves."

STANZA

I know my God is a man— of war,— Oh,

Ad-am in the gar-den pin-nin' leaves, Yes, he fought that bat-tle at

Jer-i-cho walls,— Oh, Ad-am in the gar-den pin-nin' leaves.

Stanza 1 adds the following before returning to the chorus:

I know my— God— is a man— of war,—

Ad-am in the gar-den pin-nin' leaves.—

*Sung by two women. The above notation is a transcription of the two parts heard on the record.

[4]

Chorus:
"Oh, Eve, where is Adam?
Oh, Eve, where is Adam?
Oh, Eve, where is Adam?"
"Adam in the garden pinnin' leaves."

1 I know my God is a man of war,
Oh, Adam in the garden pinnin' leaves,
Yes, he fought that battle at Jericho walls,
Oh, Adam in the garden pinnin' leaves.

2 First time God called, Adam 'fused to answer,
Adam in the garden layin' low,
Second time God called, Adam 'fused to answer,
Adam in the garden layin' low.

3 Nex' time God called, God hollered louder,
Adam in the garden, pinnin' leaves,
Nex' time God called, God hollered louder,
Adam in the garden pinnin' leaves.

Alternate Chorus:
"You, Eve, can't see Adam,
You, Eve, can't see Adam,
You, Eve, can't see Adam."
"Adam 'hin' the fig-tree pinnin' leaves."

SAMSON

f. No. 2659. Sylvester Johnson, Knight, La., 1939. Additional stanzas: Jesse Allison and Dock Reed, Livingston, Ala., 1939; Willie Johnson, Golden Gate Quartet, New York City, 1940.

De - li - lie was a wo - man, fine an' fair,___
De - li - lie she gained old Sam - son's mind_
Oh, whether he went to Tim- o - thy, I can't tell,___
He 'plied to his fa - ther go an' see,___

A - ve - ry plea-sant-look-in' an' coal-black hair;
When he saw the wo-man an' she looked so fine.
But the daugh-ters of Tim-o -thy, they treated him well.
"Can't you get this beau-ti - ful wo-man for me?"

CHORUS

He said, "An' if I___ had -n my way,"___ He says, "An'

if I had -n my way,"___ He says, "An' if I___

had -n my way, __ I'd tear the build - in' down."

He cried, "O Lord,_____ O Lord,_____

D.S. al Fine

O Law Lord - y, Lord-y, O Lord." O Lord, yes!"

[6]

1 Delilie was a woman, fine an' fair,
  A-very pleasant-lookin' an' coal-black hair;
  Delilie she gained old Samson's mind
  When he saw the woman an' she looked so fine.
  Oh, whether he went to Timothy, I can't tell,
  But the daughters of Timothy, they treated him well.
  He 'plied to his father to go an' see,
  "Can't you get this beautiful woman for me?"

Chorus:
        He said, "An' if I had-n my way,"
        He says, "An' if I had-n my way,"
        He says, "An' if I had-n my way,
        I'd tear the buildin' down."
        He cried, "O Lord, O Lord,
        O Law Lordy, Lordy, O Lord."
        He cried, "O Lord, O Lord,
        O Law Lordy, Lordy, O Lord, yes!"
        He said, "An' if I had-n my way,"
        He says, "An' if I had-n my way,"
        He says, "An' if I had-n my way,
        I'd tear the buildin' down."

2 Samson's mother 'plied to him,
  "Can't you find a wife among our kin?"
  Samson's father said, " 'T grieve your mother's mind
  To see you marry a woman of the Philistines."
  Read about Samson from his birth,
  He was the strongest man that ever lived on earth.
  Read away down in ancient times
  He killed three thousand Philistines.

3 Stop an' let me tell you what Samson done,
  He looked at the lion, an' the lion run;
  It's written that the lion had killed men with his paw,
  But Samson had his hand in the lion's jaw.
  He kilt the lion, the lion is dead;
  Bees made honey in the lion's head.
  Samson was a man, large in size.
  Overpowered a man and plucked out his eyes.

[7]

4 Samson burnt up a field of corn,
  They looked for Samson but he was gone;
  A-so many thousand formed a plot,
  It wasn't many days 'fore he was caught.
  They bound him with rope and, while walkin' along,
  He looked on the ground and he saw an old jawbone;
  He moved his arms, the rope popped like threads,
  When he got through killin', three thousand was dead.

5 Samson, he went wanderin' about,
  Samson's strength was never found out,
  Till his wife sat on his knee,
  She said, "Tell me where your strength be, if you please."
  Samson's wife, she talked so fair,
  Samson told her, "Shave off my hair,
  Shave my head as clean as my hand
  And my strength will be like a natural man."

6 Shave his hair like the pa'm o' his hand,
  His strength become as a natural man.
  Took po' Samson to the judgment hall,
  Bind him and chained him to the wall;
  He called a little boy about three foot tall,
  Said, "Place my hands up against the wall."
  He placed his hands up against the wall
  And he tore that buildin' down.

Second Chorus:
      He said, "An' now I got my way,"
      He says, "An' now I got-n my way,"
      He says, "An' now I got-n my way,
      I'll tear the buildin' down."
      He cried, "O Lord, O Lord,
      O Law Lordy, Lordy, O Lord,"
      He cried, "O Lord, O Lord,
      O Law Lordy, Lordy, O Lord, yes!"
      He said, "An' now I got-n my way,"
      He says, "An' now I got-n my way,"
      He says, "An' now I got-n my way,
      I'll tear the buildin' down."

[8]

THE MAN OF CALVARY
No. 186. Sin Killer Griffin, Darrington, Texas, 1934.

Reverend Sin Killer Griffin is pastor of one of the largest congregations in the world—the Negro convicts of the penitentiary. This is a fragment of his Easter Sunday sermon, transcribed from a group of records made in 1934. His sermon is at once poetry and song and must be chanted and sung in a highly dramatic manner. (See record for the manner of rendition.)

Roman soldiers come ridin' at full speed on their horses and splunged
    Him in the side.
We seen the blood and water come out.
Oh-h, Godamighty placed it in the minds of the people,
Why, the water is for baptism
And the blood is for cleansin'.
I don't care how mean you've been,
Godamighty's blood 'll cleanse you from all sin.
I seen, my dear friends,
The time moved on. . . .
I seen while he was hangin',
The mounting begin to tremble on which Jesus was hangin',
The blood was dropping on the mounting,
Holy blood, dropping on the mounting,
My dear friends, corrupting the mounting.
I seen about that time while the blood was dropping down,
One drop after another,
I seen the sun Jesus made in creation;
The sun rose, my dear friends,
And it recognized Jesus hanging on the cross.
Just as soon as the sun recognized its Maker,
Why, it clothed itself in sack clothing and went down,
Went down in mourning!
"Look at my Maker hangin' on the cross."
And when the sun went down,
We seen the moon—that was his maker, too,
Oo-oo, he made the moo-oon,
My dear friends, yes, both time and the seasons.
We seen, my dear friends,
When the moon recognized Jesus hangin' on the cross,
I seen the moon, yes, took with a judgment hemorrhage and bleed away.

[9]

Good God, the dying thief on the cross
Saw the moon going down in blood,
Saw it go down and bleed away.
I seen the little stars, great God, that was there;
They remembered Jesus when he struck on the anvil of time;
And the little stars recognized their Maker dying on the cross;
Each little star leaped out of its silver orbit
To make the torches of a dark and unbenointed world.

It got so dark until the men who was puttin' Jesus to death,
They said they could feel the darkness with their fingers.
Great Godamighty! they was close to one another,
And it was so dark they could feel one another,
And feel one another talk, but they couldn't see one another.
I heard one of the centurions say,
"Sholy, sholy, this must be the son of God."
'Bout that time we seen, my dear friends—
The prophet Isaiah said the dead in the graves would hear His voice and
    come forward—
We seen the dead getting up out of their graves on the east side of
    Jerusalem,
Getting out of their graves,
Walking about,
Going down in town,
Oh-h-h, way over on Nebo's mounting!
I seen the great lawgiver
Get up out of his grave and begin to walk about, my dear friends,
Walk about, because Jesus said it was finished.

I shouldn't wonder, my dear friends,
That the church will save you when you get in trouble.
I heard the church so many times singing when you get in trouble,
The church would sing, *How can I die while Jesus lives?* *

I seen the horse come steppin' on Calvary's bloody brow,
Pawing, my dear friends, with thunder in his train,
And the lightnin' was playing on the bridle reins which Death had in his
    hands.
He come ridin'! He come ridin'!

* Here the pastor sings a hymn beginning with these seven words, and the men join in.

[10]

And the dyin' thief looked Death in the face,
Caught sight of the object side of the horse,
He saw a new name written there,
He read the name, and the name read like this—
"Death and Hell followeth him."
I heard the dying thief say,
"Lord, O Lord! Lord, O Lord!
When thou come to thy father's kingdom,
I pray remember me.
Oh, motherless child,
Hangin' on the cross,
An' I want you to remember me."

Jesus, my dear friends—
The dying thief had so much confidence in Him—
Jesus, hung just like He was,
Jesus, daggered in the side,
Blood dripping, great God!—
Jesus caught ahold of the bridle, my dear friends,
Caught it by the bridle,
And the old horse began to paw,
Oh-h-h, Elijah didn't catch ahold of him, when he was comin',
Oh-h-h, Job didn't catch ahold of him when he was comin',
Oh-h-h, Great Godamighty!
Moses, the great lawgiver, didn't catch ahold of him,
But over yonder, the incarnate Son of God
Caught the horse by the bridle and held him still.

Jesus begin to speak,
Yes! says to the dyin' thief,
"Pay no attention to death."
Says to the dyin' thief,
"This day your spirit will be with me in heaven."
Says, "Oh, yes, this day it will be with me. . . ."

*   *   *

God met the Devil when He seen him comin',
We began to wonder where he was goin'
(You needn't wonder, but just keep still,
He'll let you know what He's comin' for);

[11]

And then He fastened the great dragon,
Great God! bound him for so many thousand years,
Seen Him, my dear friends, when He got ahold of Death,
Twist the stinger away from Death—
Death haven't got no dominion over a child of God!

I seen Jesus whisper from hell to His Father,
Told Him to send down angels of grace—
"Let them roll back the stone,
Then stay there and let my mother know I am gone as I said."
Great Godamighty!
We seen when Godamighty with His omnipotent power,
Good God!
Called Michael and Gabriel,
Both peaceful angels,
"Both angels that obey me."
Praise God! Seen when Jesus told the boys,
"Don't, don't harm those peoples that is settin' at the grave,
Don't say nothin' to 'em,
I'll give power,
I'll cause the earth to quake ahead of yuh!"

Those angels left Godamighty's throne,
Leaped over the battlements of glory.
I seen forty and four thousand angels in heaven,
Just in a moment, the twinklin' of an eye,
Great God! bowed on their knees,
Hung up their harps on the willow,
Great God! Three and twenty elders
Left their seats, each one cryin',
"Ho-ly, ho-ly, holy!"
And when the angels got near the earth,
The earth began to quake and tremble,
The peoples began to say, "What's the matter here?"
Good Godamighty!
First and second day, no harm, nothing happened;
But here on the third mornin',
Looky here! the earth quakin'!
Good God! the earth began to quake!

[12]

'Bout that time while they were a-watchin' the earth,
The angels darted down and took a seat right by the side of 'em,
Rolled back the stone,
Took a seat by the side of 'em,
Never said a word to 'em, but just set there.
And when the angels took their seats,
Good God! Jesus got up!
Yes, got up out of His grave,
Began pulling off His graveclothes,
Great God! taken the napkin from 'round His jaws,
Laid 'em down in the grave.
We seen the angels watch old Mary and Marthy;
Shook the girls and told 'em just about when the morning star would
    appear,
Told the girls to go on down into the grave,
Told the girls not to grieve and cry,
Because He would come again.
Every child of God has something to carry to Jesus!
Oh-h-h, how you abused me in this world,
And how you caused me to shed briny tears,
How you caused me to stand with folded arms!
But some day, some day,
Some long, lonesome day, when the final roll is called,
I will fly to the arms of Jesus and be at rest.

JOB

g. No. 1321. Vera Hall and Dock Reed, Livingston, Ala., 1937.

"Job" is an early type of spiritual in which the leader sings a story in short phrases and the congregation responds by singing "uh-huh" after each phrase and by joining in on the chorus at the conclusion of each stanza.

* In group singing, the part sung here by the woman would be sung by the group. The "uh-huh's" are nasalized throughout.

Religious Songs

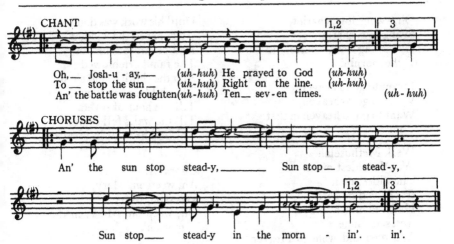

CHANT

Oh,— Josh-u - ay,— (*uh-huh*) He prayed to God (*uh-huh*)
To — stop the sun — (*uh-huh*) Right on the line. (*uh-huh*)
An' the battle was foughten (*uh-huh*) Ten— sev-en times. (*uh-huh*)

CHORUSES

An' the sun stop stead-y,——— Sun stop— stead-y,

Sun stop— stead-y in the morn - in'. in'.

1 O Job, Job, (*uh-huh*)
Oh, what you reckin? (*uh-huh*)
Your children's dead. (*uh-huh*)
O Job, Job, (*uh-huh*)
Oh, what you reckin? (*uh-huh*)
Your servant's dead. (*uh-huh*)
O Job, Job, (*uh-huh*)
Oh, what you reckin? (*uh-huh*)
Your daughter's dead. (*uh-huh*)
Just listen at Job, (*uh-huh*)
What Job said, (*uh-huh*)
"Oh, blessèd be (*uh-huh*)
The name of the Lord. (*uh-huh*)
The Lord he giveth, (*uh-huh*)
And the Lord take away, (*uh-huh*)
An' blessèd be (*uh-huh*)
The name of the Lord." (*uh-huh*)

Chorus:
Oh, run Mount Zion,
Run Mount Zion,
Oh, run Mount Zion in the
    mornin'.

2 Oh, Joshu-ay, (*uh-huh*)
He prayed to God (*uh-huh*)
To stop the sun (*uh-huh*)
Right on the line. (*uh-huh*)
An' the battle was foughten (*uh-huh*)
Ten seven times. (*uh-huh*)

Choruses:
An' the sun stop steady,
Sun stop steady,
Sun stop steady in the mornin'.

Oh, swing low, chariot,
Swing low, chariot,
Oh, swing low, chariot, in
the mornin'.

I want to go to heaven,
Want to go to heaven,
Want to go to heaven in that
mornin'.

3 Well, Methuselah
Was the oldest man,
The oldest man
Ever lived on earth,
He lived nine hundred
And sixty-nine,
And died and went to Heaven,
Well, in due time.

4 Joshu-ay
Was the son of Nun,
And God was with him

Until his work was done.
God opened the window
And began to look out,
The ram horn blowed
And the children did shout,
The children did shout
Till the hour of seven,
Till the walls fell down
An' God heard it in Heaven.

Choruses:

Ah, weep on, Mary,
Weep on, Mary,
Oh, weep on, Mary, in the
mornin'.

Oh, mourn on, Marthy,
Mourn on, Marthy,
Oh, mourn on, Marthy, in
the mornin'.

JOHN DONE SAW THAT NUMBER

No. 1335. Vera Hall, Livingston, Ala., 1937. See Sa, p. 155.

Moderate ♩ = 84

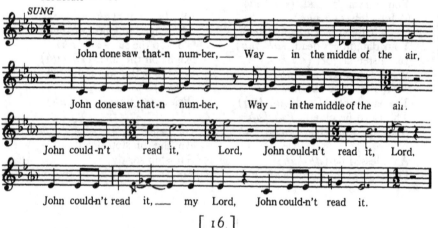

SUNG

John done saw that-n num-ber,___ Way___ in the middle of the air,

John done saw that-n num-ber, Way___ in the middle of the air.

John could-n't read it, Lord, John could-n't read it, Lord.

John could-n't read it,___ my Lord, John could-n't read it.

Religious Songs

CHANTED

See, see, ___ see, man, read, Read the Rev - e - la -tion, Third

chap-ter, third verse, And there you'll find it

there; There was a man of the Phar - i - sees, Named Nic-o-

de-mus, rul - er the Jews, Same ___ came to him by night,

Says, "No man ___ can do these mi'a - cles Ex - cept

SUNG

God be ___ with him there." ___ Cry'n', "Ho - ly, Lord," ___ Cry'n',

"Ho - ly, Lord," ___ Cry'n', "Ho - ly, ___ my Lord," Cry'n', "Ho - ly."

John could-n't read it, Lord, ___ John could-n't read it, Lord,

John could-n't read it, ___ my Lord, John could-n't read it.

CHANTED

God told the an-gel, "Go down, see 'bout old John."

An - gel flew __ from the bot-tom of the pit, Gathered the

sun all in her fist; Gath-ered the moon all

'round her wrist; Gath-ered the stars all un-der her

feet; __ Gath-ered the wind all 'round her waist.

SUNG

Cry'n', "Ho-ly, Lord," __ Cry'n', "Ho-ly, Lord," __

Cry'n', "Ho-ly, __ my Lord," Cry'n', __ "Ho-ly."

John could-n't read it, Lord, __ John could-n't read it, Lord, __

John could-n't read it, __ my Lord, John could-n't read it.

Sung:

1 John done saw that number,
   Way in the middle of the air,
   John done saw that number,
   Way in the middle of the air.

2 John couldn't read it, Lord,
   John couldn't read it, Lord,
   John couldn't read it, my Lord,
   John couldn't read it.

Chanted:

3 See, see, see, man, read,
   Read the Revelation,
   Third chapter, third verse,
   And there you'll find it there;
   There was a man of the Pharisees,
   Named Nicodemus, ruler the Jews,
   Same came to him by night,
   Says, "No man can do these mi'acles
   Except God be with him there."

Sung:

4 Cry'n', "Holy, Lord,"
   Cry'n', "Holy, Lord,"
   Cry'n', "Holy, my Lord,"
   Cry'n', "Holy."

5 John couldn't read it, Lord,
   John couldn't read it, Lord,
   John couldn't read it, my Lord,
   John couldn't read it.

Chanted:

6 There was a beast came out of the sea
   Havin' ten horns and ten crowns,
   On his horns was a-written blaspheme—

Sung:

7 Weep like a willow, mourn like a dove,
You can't get to heaven 'thout you go by love.

8 John saw that number,
Way in the middle of the air,
John saw that number,
Way in the middle of the air.

9 John couldn't read it, Lord,
John couldn't read it, Lord,
John couldn't read it, my Lord,
John couldn't read it.

10 Cry'n', "Holy, Lord,"
Cry'n', "Holy, Lord,"
Cry'n', "Holy, my Lord,"
Cry'n', "Holy."

Chanted:

11 God told the angel,
"Go down, see 'bout old John."
Angel flew from the bottom of the pit,
Gathered the sun all in her fist;
Gathered the moon all 'round her wrist;
Gathered the stars all under her feet;
Gathered the wind all 'round her waist.

Sung:

12 Cry'n', "Holy, Lord,"
Cry'n', "Holy, Lord,"
Cry'n', "Holy, my Lord,"
Cry'n', "Holy."

13 John couldn't read it, Lord,
John couldn't read it, Lord,
John couldn't read it, my Lord,
John couldn't read it.

JOHN WAS A-WRITIN'

F, f. No. 257. Group of Negro men in State Penitentiary, Milledgeville, Ga., 1934.

* The group sings in parts.

1 God, He called John while he was a-writin', (3)

> *Chorus:*
> "Oh, John, John, seal up your book, John,
> John, don't you write no more."
> Lord told John, "Don't you write no more."

2 Yes, he wrote the Revelation while-a he was a-writin', (3)

[22]

3 Yes, he wrote my mother's name while he was a-writin', (3)

4 Yes, he wrote my father's name while he was a-writin', (3)

DEM BONES

b. No. 177. Group of Negroes, Nashville, Tenn., 1933.

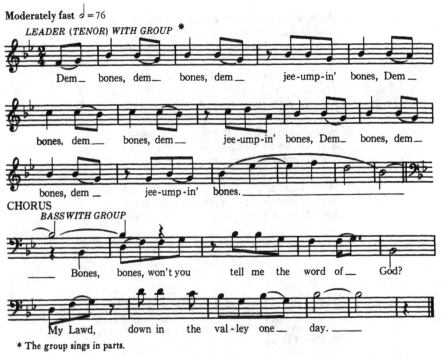

* The group sings in parts.

1 Dem bones, dem bones, dem jee-umpin' bones,
Dem bones, dem bones, dem jee-umpin' bones,
Dem bones, dem bones, dem jee-umpin' bo-o-ones.

Chorus:

Bones, bones, won't you tell me the word of God?
My Lawd, down in the valley one day.

[23]

2 Well, de toe bone jump to de foot bone,
   And de foot bone jump to de ankle bone,
   And de ankle bone jump to de leg bone.

3 Well, de leg bone jump to de knee bone,
   And de knee bone jump to de thigh bone,
   And de thigh bone jump to de hip bone.

4 Well, de hip bone jump to de back bone,
   And de back bone jump to de neck bone,
   And de neck bone jump to de head bone.

5 Well, de finger bone jump to de hand bone,
   And de hand bone jump to de wrist bone,
   And de wrist bone jump to de arm bone.

6 Well, de arm bone jump to de elbone,
   And de elbone jump to de muscle bone,
   And de muscle bone jump to de shoulder bone.

7 Well, de shoulder bone jump to de back bone,
   And de back bone jump to de neck bone,
   And de neck bone jump to de head bone.

8 Dem bones, dem bones, dem jee-umpin' bones, (3)

THE BLOOD-STRAINED BANDERS *

$f^\sharp$. No. 744. Acc. on guitar and sung by Jimmie
Strothers. Virginia State Prison Farms, 1936. Recorded by
Dr. Harold Spivacke. See Fe, p. 38.

The itinerant street singer has been an important factor in the life of the
Negro spiritual. Usually blind, piloted by his wife or by some little boy,
he inches along through the streets and down the alleys of Negro working-
class neighborhoods, shouting and groaning out a spiritual in his hoarse,
twelve-hour-a-day voice, reminding saints and sinners that the blind must
eat. The comrade of his dark, slow journeys is the battered guitar he plays.

* Blood-stained bandits—probably.

It provides his drum and tambourine accompaniment, it hums his background harmony, it comes in strong on the chorus, it stomps his two-four rhythm and claps a counter-rhythm against itself. And when his breath is gone, "Talk it for me, now," says the blind singer, and his old box sings the words of the chorus, plaintively and high on little E.

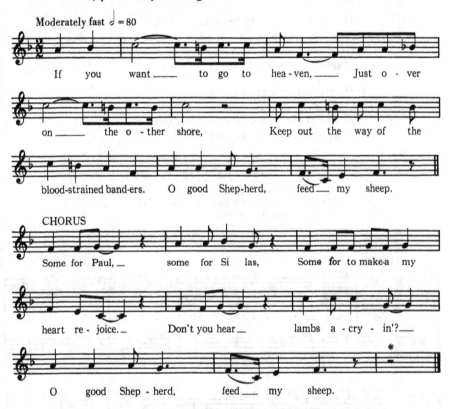

Moderately fast ♩ = 80

If you want___ to go to hea-ven,___ Just o - ver

on___ the o - ther shore, Keep out the way of the

blood-strained band-ers. O good Shep-herd, feed___ my sheep.

CHORUS

Some for Paul,___ some for Si las, Some for to make-a my

heart re - joice.___ Don't you hear___ lambs a-cry - in'?___

O good Shep - herd, feed___ my sheep.

* This rest is always omitted by the singer, who proceeds without pause.

1 If you want to go to heaven,
  Just over on the other shore,
  Keep out the way of the blood-strained banders.
  O good Shepherd, feed my sheep.

Chorus:

> Some for Paul, some for Silas,
> Some for to make-a my heart rejoice.
> Don't you hear lambs a-cryin'?
> O good Shepherd, feed my sheep.

2 If you want to go to heaven,
   Just over on the other shore,
   Keep out the way of the gunshot devils.
   O good Shepherd, feed my sheep.

3 If you want to go to heaven,
   Over on the other shore,
   Keep out the way of the long-tongued liars.
   O good Shepherd, feed my sheep.

GOD MOVES ON THE WATER

d, g, d'. No. 188. Lightnin' (Washington) with group
of Negro convicts, Darrington State Farm, Texas, 1933.
See Whi, p. 347; Ga.2, p. 295.

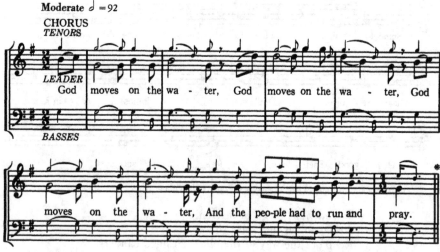

* The above notation is a transcription of the principal (continuous) voice parts heard on the record.

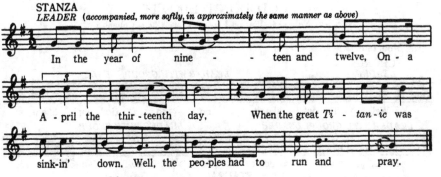

STANZA
LEADER (*accompanied, more softly, in approximately the same manner as above*)

In the year of nine - - teen and twelve, On - a A - pril the thir - teenth day, When the great *Ti - tan - ic* was sink-in' down. Well, the peo-ples had to run and pray.

Chorus:
God moves on the water, (3)
And the people had to run and pray.

1 In the year of nineteen and twelve,
On-a April the thirteenth day,
When the great *Titanic* was sinkin' down,
Well, the peoples had to run and pray.

2 When the great *Titanic* was sinkin' down,
Well, they throwed lifeboats around,
Cryin', "Save the womens and childrens
And let the mens go down."

3 When the lifeboats got to the landin'
The womens turned around,
Cryin', "Look 'way across that ocean, Lawdy,
At my husband drown."

4 Cap'n Smith was a-lyin' down,
Was asleep for he was tired;
Well, he woke up in a great fright
As many gunshots were fired.

5 Well, that Jacob Nash was a millionaire,
Lawd, he had plenty of money to spare;
When the great *Titanic* was sinkin' down,
Well, he could not pay his fare.

[27]

GOD DON'T LIKE IT

e^b. No. 1026. Pearson Funeral Home Choir, Columbia, S.C., 1937. See Ni, p. 2; Jo.3, p. 85.

Moderate ♩ = 76

CHORUS
LEADER
Well, God don't like it, no, no,— God don't like it,

LEADER WITH GROUP LEADER
no,— no,— God don't like it, no, no,— It's a scan-da-lous

STANZA
LEADER
and a shame.— Some peo-ple stay in the chur-ches, They

set-tin' in a dea-con's— chair,— They drink-in'

beer and whis-ky, And they say that they don't care.

* The group sings in parts.

Chorus:

Well, God don't like it, no, no,
God don't like it, no, no,
God don't like it, no, no,
It's a scandalous and a shame.

1 Some people stay in the churches,
They settin' in a deacon's chair,
They drinkin' beer and whisky,
And they say that they don't care.

2 Some people say that yaller corn
Can make you the very best kind;
They better turn dey yaller corn into bread
And stop that makin' 'shine.

[28]

3 Some member in the churches,
　They dressed and they dressed so fine;
　But when you come to find out,
　They been somewhere drinkin' 'shine.

4 You say you've been converted,
　You ought to quit telling lies;
　Quit drinking so much whisky,
　Live more civilized.

5 Preacher in the pulpit,
　Preaches so loud and bold;
　He's preachin' all about money,
　Nothin' about savin' your soul.

6 Your brother borrow your money,
　He promise shore to pay;
　When he see you comin'
　He turn some other way.

7 When the preacher was a-preachin' while ago
　Sister was about to shout;
　Now deacon wants a little collection,
　You got your lips poked out.

8 Fuss comes up in the church house,
　Comes from the deacons' side;
　If you ask them anything about it,
　They will ask you out to fight.

9 Some preachers are out preachin'
　Just for the preacher's name;
　Their doctrine and preachin'
　Are a scandal and a shame.

10 Some deacons in the churches
　Are livin' with two wives;
　You tell them of true glory
　And you'll see their tempers rise.

11 Some preacher come to your house;
You ask him to rest his hat;
He sits right down and begins to grin,
Saying, "Sister, where's your husband at?"

SOON ONE MORNIN' DEATH COME CREEPIN'

g'. No. 1319. Vera Hall and Dock Reed, Livingston,
Ala., 1937. See Whi, p. 78; Boa, No. 19; Jo.2, p. 174.

* In stanza 2, this incomplete measure and the upbeat to stanza 3 are omitted entirely. In all stanzas, the 2nd and 3rd beats are omitted.

1 Soon one mornin' death come creepin' in my room, (3)
    O my Lord, O my Lord, what shall I do to be saved?

2 Death done been here, tuck my mother an' gone,

3 Death done been here, left me a motherless child,

4 Don't move my pillow until my Jesus comes,

5 When Jesus comes, you can turn my bed around,

6 I'm so glad I got my religion in time,

I FEEL LIKE MY TIME AIN'T LONG

d'. No. 1310. Vera Hall, Livingston, Ala., 1937. See
Na, p. 144.

We're going home, where they ain't no shedding tears,
Where you can't hear the hum of sewing machines
Making the winding sheets for the dead,
It's home, home,
Don't have no backbiters,
Where liars can't go,
Where every day is Sunday and the congregation ain't never dismissed;
It's home,
Got no high sheriff to ride in it,
No deputy to serve warrants.—
Many of you got a mother,
And ev'y morning she walks out on the battlements of glory.
A few more rising suns
And the silver tune'll be heard in my heart.

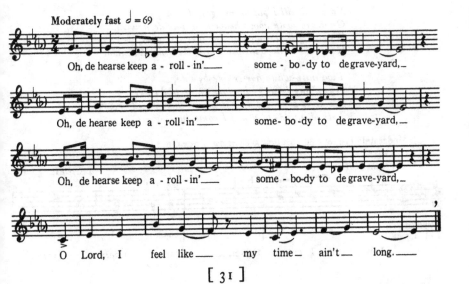

1 Oh, de hearse keep a-rollin' somebody to de graveyard,
  Oh, de hearse keep a-rollin' somebody to de graveyard,
  Oh, de hearse keep a-rollin' somebody to de graveyard.
  O Lord, I feel like my time ain't long.

2 Oh, my mother outrun me, an' she gone on to glory,

3 Oh, hush cryin', Mary, you'll see your brother,

4 Lord, I know I'll see him resurrection mornin',

5 Oh, look a-here, Mary, I am the resurrection mornin',

6 Oh, the bell keep a-tonin', somebody is dyin',

7 Oh, my father outrun me, an' he gone on to glory,

8 Oh, my brother outrun me, an' he gone on to glory,

IF I GOT MY TICKET, CAN I RIDE?

g'. No. 209. Jim Boyd and Percy Ridge, Huntsville,
Texas, 1934. See Boa, No. 76.

Now wait till I put on my gospel shoes,
Gwine to walk about heaven an' tote de news.
When I gits to heaven gwine take my stand,
Gwine to rassle with my Lord like a natchal man.

Two milk-white horses side by side,
Me an' my Jesus gwine take an evenin' ride;
Gwine to argy wid de Father an' chatter wid de Son,
Talk about de old world I come fum.

Moderately fast ♩ = 80 *increasing to 88 at end of recording*

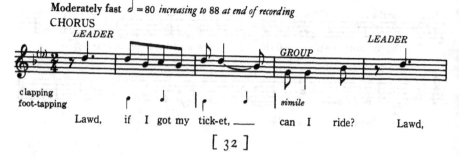

[32]

if I got my tick-et, ___ can I ride? Lawd, if I got my

tick-et, ___ can I ride? Ride a - way ___ to the heav-en that morn - in'. ___

Tell you one thing, ___ it cer-tain-ly is sho', ___ The Judg-ment's

com - in' an' ___ I don't know; Want to be read-y when I'm ___ called to

go, If an - y - thing ___ lack - in', Lawd, ___. let me know.

* In the six-line stanzas, the fifth and sixth lines of text are sung to the same music as the third and fourth.

Chorus:
>Lawd, if I got my ticket, can I ride?
>Lawd, if I got my ticket, can I ride?
>Lawd, if I got my ticket, can I ride?
>Ride away to the heaven that mornin'.

1 Tell you one thing, it certainly is sho',
The Judgment's comin' an' I don't know;
Want to be ready when I'm called to go,
If anything lackin', Lawd, let me know. (*Chorus.*)

[33]

2 Hear a great talk of the Judgment Day,
   Got no time to projick away:
   Away by and by, without a doubt,
   Jehovah will order His angels out,
   Clean out the world and leave no sin.
   "Tell me, please, where have you been?" (*Chorus.*)

3 Hear big talk of the gospel train,
   "You want to get on it?" "Yes, that's my aim."
   Stand at the station and patiently wait,
   The train is coming and it's never late.
   So long coming that it worried my mind,
   Thought it wa'n't coming, but was just on time. (*Chorus.*)

CHOOSE YOU A SEAT 'N' SET DOWN

e′ to *f′♯*. No. 1317. Dock Reed, Henry Reed, Vera Hall, Livingston, Ala., 1937.

An ex-slave, an old Negro woman, talked to us of her life and her songs:

"I been drug about and put through the shackles, till I done forgot some my children's names. My husband died and left me with nine children, and none of 'em could pull the others out of the fire iffen they fell in. I had mo'n that, but some come here dead and some didn't. Dey ain't a graveyard in this here settlement where I ain't got children buried, and I got children dead in Birmingham and Bessemer.

"I mos' blind now and I can't hear good and I ain't never read no verse in no Bible in my life, 'cause I can't read. I sets 'cross the road here from the church and can't go 'cause I'm cripple and blin', but I hear 'em singin'."

Moderate ♩ =126

LEADER (MAN) WITH GROUP (MAN and WOMAN) *singing in unison and octave.*

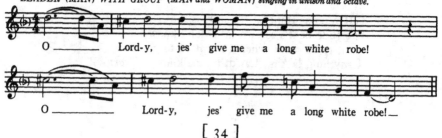

O ——— Lord-y, jes' give me a long white robe!

O ——————— Lord-y, jes' give me a long white robe! —

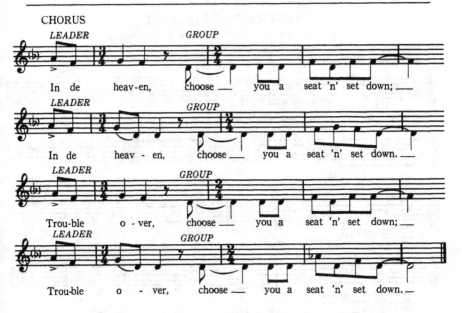

1 O Lordy, jes' give me a long white robe!
O Lordy, jes' give me a long white robe!

Chorus:
    In de heaven, choose you a seat 'n' set down;
    In de heaven, choose you a seat 'n' set down;
    Trouble over, choose you a seat 'n' set down;
    Trouble over, choose you a seat 'n' set down.

2 O Jesus, was my mother there?
O Jesus, was my mother there?

3 O Jesus, jes' give me a starry crown,
O Jesus, jes' give me a starry crown.

4 O Lordy, was my brother there?
O Lordy, was my brother there?

[35]

LOW DOWN CHARIOT

a'. No. 1315. Vera Hall and Dock Reed, Livingston, Ala., 1937. See Boa, No. 26.

Moderately fast ♩ = 72

WOMAN *

MAN (LEADER)
Oh, let - n me ride,__ oh, let - n me ride,__ Oh, let -

- n me ride,___ oh, let - n me ride,__ Oh, let -

- n me ride,__ oh, let - n me ride,__ Oh,___ Oh,

low down__ the char - iot, let - n me ride.___

* In group singing, the part sung here by the woman would be sung by the group.

1 Oh, let-n me ride, oh, let-n me ride,
   Oh, let-n me ride, oh, let-n me ride,
   Oh, let-n me ride, oh, let-n me ride,
   Oh, low down the chariot, let-n me ride.

2 Got a right to ride, oh, let-n me ride,
   Got a right to ride, oh, let-n me ride,
   Got a right to ride, oh, let-n me ride,
   Oh, low down the chariot, let-n me ride.

3 Got a ticket to ride, 7 My mother done rid,

4 I'm humble to ride,   8 Train's comin',

5 I'm beggin' to ride,   9 I'm a warrior,

6 I'm a soldier,   10 I'm prayin',

11 Prayin' to ride,

[36]

I. 2. WHITE RELIGIOUS SONGS

OVER JORDAN

(Wayfaring Stranger)

L. L. McDowell, Smithville, Tenn. By courtesy of Sidney Robertson and Charles Seeger. See Ja.2, p. 71; De, 169; Ja.1, pp. 250 ff. See No. 3223.

L. L. McDowell, Smithville, Tennessee, says that this is the tune sung by the old settlers of De Kalb County. Additional stanzas are made by changing the word "father" to "mother," "brother," "sister," etc.

Slow

I'm just a poor way-far-ing stran-ger, A-tra-veling through this world of woe, But there's no sick-ness, toil, nor dan-ger In that bright world to which I go. I'm go-ing there to meet my fa-ther, I'm go-ing there no more to roam, I'm just a-go-ing o-ver Jor-dan, I'm just a-go-ing o-ver home.

OH, LOVELY APPEARANCE OF DEATH

g'. No. 1491. Mr. and Mrs. Boyd Hoskins, Clay County,
Ky., 1937, and note from Ola E. Winslow, *American
Broadside Verse* (Yale Univ. Press).

Reverend George Whitefield, a distinguished follower of John Wesley, the founder of Methodism, ten years before his death wrote this song to be sung at his own funeral. Although he had been a minister of the Church of England and a graduate of Oxford, Whitefield became the first circuit rider in the American Colonies. His parish extended to the most remote settlement, and his preaching and influence established Methodism firmly. Benjamin Franklin estimated that Whitefield's magnetic and powerful voice could reach an audience of twenty thousand. He made seven trips from England to America, staying sometimes several years.

When Whitefield died in 1770, Phillis, a seventeen-year-old Negro girl only nine years out of Africa, who belonged to J. Wheatley of Boston, wrote a sixty-two-line "elegiac poem on the death of the celebrated Divine and eminent servant of Jesus Christ, the late Reverend and pious George Whitefield, Chaplain to the Right Honourable the Countess of Huntingdon, who made his exit from this transitory state to dwell in the celestial realms of bliss on Lord's Day, when he was seized with a fit of asthma at Newburyport near Boston, in New England.

*"He leaves this world for Heaven's unmeasured Height,
And worlds unknown receive him from our sight."*

The following version of George Whitefield's funeral hymn was sung for us by a deacon and a deaconess of the Hard-Shell Baptists in Clay County, Ky., in 1937.

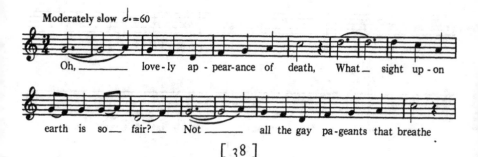

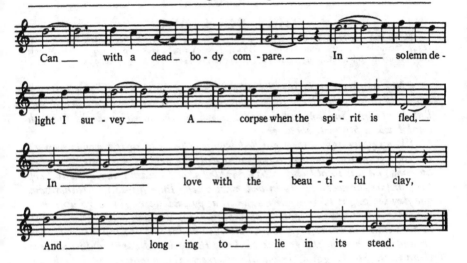

Can __ with a dead __ bo - dy com - pare. __ In __ solemn de -

light I sur - vey __ A __ corpse when the spi - rit is fled, __

In __ love with the beau - ti - ful clay,

And __ long - ing to __ lie in its stead.

1 Oh, lovely appearance of death,
What sight upon earth is so fair?
Not all the gay pageants that breathe
Can with a dead body compare.
In solemn delight I survey
A corpse when the spirit is fled,
In love with the beautiful clay,
And longing to lie in its stead.

2 Its languishing pain is at rest,
Its aching and aching are o'er;
The quiet immovable breast
Is pained by affliction no more.
The heart it no longer receives
Of trouble and torturing pain;
It ceases to flutter and beat,
It never shall flutter again.

THE ROMISH LADY

Music and text from Walker, William, *The Southern Harmony*, E. W. Miller, Philadelphia, 1854, facsimile reprint from Hastings House, New York, 1939. No. 1040. Mrs. Minnie Floyd, Murrells Inlet, S.C., 1937. See Ja.2, p. 27; Ed, p. 221; Sc.2, p. 176; Be, p. 450.

"*My mother taught me the tune to 'The Romish Lady' long before I knew all the words. I caught up the tunes easy when I was a little thing. But I couldn't find anybody could tell me all the words straight through until I was a big girl, about grown.*

"*Way years ago, a lady got bad burnt. She lived in the woods way up the road from us. She was burnt awful bad, the worst I ever saw. And her husband, he was so old and so bad crippled that he wasn't any good to help her; in fact, he was laid up in bed most of the time himself. Mother said one day we ought to go up there, and Pappy said we ought to go up there, too. We didn't have no money, nor nothing much to eat, except just enough to keep skin and bones together for all of us children. Well, Mother looked around, and she said she guessed anybody that was bad burnt could use some clean rags. So she got a big bundle of clean rags together, and I took 'em up there.*

"*Well, when I got there, it was the awfullest pitiful sight I ever saw. I was ashamed I didn't have no money nor even anything to eat with me. But as soon as ever the lady saw me, she said, 'The Lord sent you.'*

"*'No,' says I. 'Just my mother and daddy sent you some old clean rags.'*

"*'If they'd sent a ten-dollar bill, it couldn't be better,' she said like she meant it.*

"*Well, I stayed on that day to sorter clean up and cook 'em a little something to eat. Then they seemed to need somebody to nurse 'em so bad that I just stayed on for a spell. I was going to be married the next week, but I just put that off; and I stayed on there twelve weeks, all time putting off the wedding that much longer. And I guess it'd 'a' been just as well if I had put it off for always.*

"*The lady had a lot of books, most of 'em religious books and hymnbooks. One of 'em was called 'Christian Harmony Note Book,' as I recollect the name. It had 'The Romish Lady' in it. And that's where I learned the rest of the words. I had plenty of time to learn 'em and sing in the evenings. I don't know what I would have done without my tune singing, and the burnt lady said she didn't know what they would have done neither without me a-singing. I sure was glad to learn the rest of 'The Romish Lady.'*"

—Mrs. MINNIE FLOYD, Murrells Inlet, South Carolina.

Moderately slow ♩=60

There was a Rom-ish la - dy brought up in pop-er - y,

Her mo-ther al-ways taught_ her the priest she must o - bey;

"Oh, par-don me, dear mo - ther, I_ hum-bly pray thee now,

* 𝅝 = 4/4. See Walker, William, *Southern Harmony Songbook*, prefatory material.

For un-to these false i - - dols I can no long-er bow."

1 There was a Romish lady brought up in popery,
Her mother always taught her the priest she must obey;
"Oh, pardon me, dear mother, I humbly pray thee now,
For unto these false idols I can no longer bow."

2 Assisted by her handmaid, a Bible she conceal'd,
And there she gain'd instruction, till God his love reveal'd.
No more she prostrates herself to pictures deck'd with gold,
But soon she was betray'd, and her Bible from her stole.

3 "I'll bow to my dear Jesus, I'll worship God unseen,
I'll live by faith forever, the works of men are vain;
I cannot worship angels, nor pictures made by men,
Dear mother, use your pleasure, but pardon if you can."

4 With grief and great vexation, her mother straight did go,
To inform the Roman clergy the cause of all her woe;
The priests were soon assembled, and for the maid did call,
And forc'd her in the dungeon, to fight her soul withal.

5 The more they strove to fright her, the more she did endure,
Although her age was tender, her faith was strong and sure;
The chains of gold so costly they from this lady took,
And she with all her spirits the pride of life forsook.

6 Before the Pope they brought her, in hopes of her return,
And there she was condemned in horrid flames to burn.
Before the place of torment they brought her speedily,
With lifted hands to heaven she then agreed to die.

7 There being many ladies assembled at the place,
She raised her eyes to heaven and begg'd supplying grace.
"Weep not, ye tender ladies, shed not a tear for me—
While my poor body's burning, my soul the Lord shall see.

8 "Yourselves you need to pity, and Zion's deep decay;
Dear ladies, turn to Jesus, no longer make delay."
In comes her raving mother, her daughter to behold,
And in her hand she brought her pictures deck'd with gold.

9 "Oh, take from me these idols, remove them from my sight;
Restore to me my Bible, wherein I take delight.
Alas, my aged mother, why on my ruin bent?
'Twas you that did betray me, but I am innocent.

10 "Tormentors, use your pleasure, and do as you think best—
I hope my blessed Jesus will take my soul to rest."
Soon as these words were spoken, up steps the man of death,
And kindled up the fire to stop her mortal breath.

11 Instead of golden bracelets, with chains they bound her fast;
She cried, "My God give power, now must I die at last?
With Jesus and his angels forever I shall dwell.
God pardon priest and people, and so I bid farewell."

I. 3. THE HOLINESS PEOPLE

The "Holiness" preachers frankly tell their congregations that they want them to have a good time in church. As one said, "I believe God would like to look down and see his little children dancing before his altar like we are." It is in character for his wife to play a guitar or a piano and to lead and compose inspirational songs. Musical instruments—from fiddles to saxophones—are played in church and the hymns sung are the liveliest of revival tunes, Negro and white. Speaking in tongues, holy dancing, public confession of sin, handling of rattlesnakes and of fire, all these offer amusement and an opportunity for individual expression to the bitterly poor of America. Like the rural Negro church services, the Holiness meetings are a sort of American folk theater, and their recent mushroom growth in every part of the United States, across barriers of race and language, proclaims their firm basis in the folkways of America.

KEEP YOUR HANDS ON THAT PLOW

e♭. No. 1397. Elihu Trusty, Paintsville, Ky., 1937. See Sh, 2:292; Whi, p. 115. A hymn of the Holiness Church sung by the sect that believes in foot washing. Also sung as a Negro spiritual.

Moderate ♩=96

Got my hands on the gos-pel plow, Would-n't take noth-in' for my jour-ney now.___ Keep your hands on that plow,___ hold___ on. Hold on, ___ hold on, Keep your hands on that plow,___ hold___ on.

1 Got my hands on the gospel plow,
   Wouldn't take nothin' for my journey now.
   Keep your hands on that plow, hold on.

   Chorus:
   Hold on, hold on,
   Keep your hands on that plow, hold on.

2 Took Paul and Silas, put 'em in the jail,
   Had no one to go their bail.
   Keep your hands on the plow, hold on.

3 Paul and Silas, they begin to shout,
   Jail doors opened and they walked out.
   Keep your hands on the plow, hold on.

4 Peter was so nice and neat,
   Wouldn't let Jesus wash his feet.
   Keep your hands on the plow, hold on.

5 Jesus said, "If I wash them not,
   You'll have no father in this lot."
   Keep your hands on the plow, hold on.

6 Peter got anxious and he said,
   "Wash my feet, my hands and head."
   Keep your hands on the plow, hold on.

THE LITTLE BLACK TRAIN

*e′ to f′. No. 1394. Brother Elihu Trusty, Paintsville,
Ky., 1937. See Whi, p. 65; Sc.2, p. 260.*

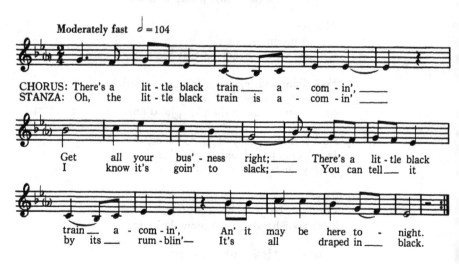

Moderately fast ♩ = 104

CHORUS: There's a lit - tle black train ___ a - com - in', ___
STANZA: Oh, the lit - tle black train is a - com - in' ___

Get all your bus' - ness right; ___ There's a lit - tle black
I know it's goin' to slack; ___ You can tell ___ it

train ___ a - com - in', An' it may be here to - night.
by its ___ rum - blin'— It's all draped in ___ black.

Chorus (intermittent through the song):
There's a little black train a-comin'—
Get all your business right;
There's a little black train a-comin',
An' it may be here tonight.

1 Oh, the little black train is a-comin',
I know it's goin' to slack;
You can tell it by its rumblin'—
It's all draped in black.

2 The train we are singin' about,
It has no whistle or bell,
And when you find your station
You are in heaven or hell.

[46]

3 There's a little black train and an engine,
  And one small baggage car;
  You won't need to have much baggage
  To come to the judgment bar.

4 O Death, why don't you spare me?
  I see my wicked plight.
  Have mercy, Lord, to hear me,
  Come and set me right.

5 Oh, Death had fixed the shackles
  Around his throat so tight,
  Before he got his business fixed,
  The train rolled in that night.

6 They are men and women
  What love their sport and game,
  Yet Death is ridin' with them
  Will take them just the same.

7 Go tell that barroom lady,
  All filled with worldly pride,
  That Death's black train's a-coming—
  Prepare to take a ride.

8 There's a rich old man in his darkness
  Says: "I have no such fears—
  I'll build my barns a little larger,
  For I'll live a million years."

9 So while he sat there plannin',
  The God of power and might
  Took the old fool to the judgment bar,
  So his soul's in the fire tonight.

HOLY GHOST

B, b. No. 1346. Mr. and Mrs. Crockett Ward and Mrs.
Thomas Rutherford, Galax, Va., 1937. See Whi, p. 97.

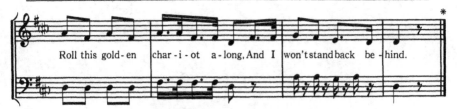

* The above notation is a transcription of the two parts heard on the record.

1 If this ain't the Holy Ghost, I don't know,
   If this ain't the Holy Ghost, I don't know,
   If this ain't the Holy Ghost, I don't know,
   And I won't stand back behind.

   Chorus:
       Roll this golden chariot along,
       Roll this golden chariot along,
       Roll this golden chariot along,
       And I won't stand back behind.

2 Effie'll beat the tambourine and I'll beat the drum,
   Effie'll beat the tambourine and I'll beat the drum,
   Effie'll beat the tambourine and I'll beat the drum,
   And I won't stand back behind.

II

SOCIAL SONGS

1. White Dance Tunes
2. Negro Game Songs
3. Bahaman Negro Songs
4. Lullabies
5. Whoppers
6. Courting Songs
7. Old-Time Love Songs
8. French Songs and Ballads from Southwestern Louisiana

II. 1. WHITE DANCE TUNES

Breakdown tunes and square dances have experienced a spectacular revival in the last ten years in the United States. They have furnished a ground upon which the whole population—American and recent American, old and young, rural and metropolitan—could meet on a common basis of recreational activity. As rural workers moved into the cities, barn dances have appeared on the radio and old-time sets have been called between fox-trots in beer parlors and dance halls. Middle-class people in the cities flock to square-dance classes and turn out in thousands to watch the dancing at folk festivals in every part of the country. Here first and second generation immigrants see something that they can immediately understand and participate in, since their own folk dances are not too different in design from those of rural America.

That there existed, on the other hand, a deep-seated Protestant prejudice against square-dancing is testified by Aunt Molly Jackson.

"When I was nine years old and we lived in East Burnstead, Kentucky, at a little coal-mining camp named Queen City, these Spivey children they wanted me to come and stay all night with them on Christmas Eve night because they was goin' to get enough together to have a square dance and a party of just children. So Charlie Spivey he come out to the house and said to my stepmother, 'Aunt Lizzybeth, can't Molly go an' stay all night with us—it's Christmas Eve night?'

"And she said, 'You'll have to go out to the commissary and ask her father.' So he went and asked my father, and my father said, 'No, she can't go.' And they come back and told a story, said my father had said 'yes, I could go.' So I went up and dressed and went to stay all night with the Spivey children; and when my father come home that night I was missin' and the dance was on, and I was a-dancin' in the dance. But I didn't know that I was dancin'; I thought it was a play we was a-playin' called 'Swing Your Partner.' They knowed that if they told me it was a dance that they was a-dancin' that I'd be afraid, so I wouldn't dance it. So John Spivey he was a-pickin' the banjo, he was the oldest one, he was fourteen, he was singin', callin' the sets. In the square dance back in them times they said,

"'Flies in the buttermilk—shoo, fly, shoo;
Gone again, skip to my Lou.'

And just as my father come in the door they called that part of the set.

*Well, he reached and got me by the back of my neck and he went to peckin'
me in the head with his fist and said, 'Gone again, skip to my Lou, my darlin',' and he carried me clean home that way. So then all the kids, ever'
time they see me come out in the yard, they'd scream, 'Gone again, skip to
my Lou,' and they kept me housed up for a month or more thataway, for
shame. They was teasin' me about the way my old man had hauled me out
of the first dance I had ever went to, and I never went to another dance in
my life until I was a married woman. I didn't even know how to dance till
after I was married, and then when Jim Stewart and I was married we
always attended every barn dance.*

"*At first when I begin to go with them to dances, just to keep from stayin'
at home by myself, I would be what they call a wallflower. I'd watch the
rest dance, but I wouldn't dance, because it was agin my father's will and I
was afraid he'd find it out; and I knowed he'd always said that if he'd find
out a child of his was goin' to a dance, if they was married or forty years old,
he'd whip 'em the same. But I delighted in it, and after a while I begin to
take chances; and after that Jim Stewart, my husband, and myself we went
a lot to private dances. He learned me all the different steps he danced,
which was thirty-nine different steps—Pigeon Wing, Railroad, Back Step,
Double Shuffle, Mustard Top, the Hound Dog, and a whole lot of others
I've forgot. My husband he beat music down with steel knittin' needles on
the strings and this makes very beautiful music. His family was all musicians and dancers, every one of 'em; his sister—and she was a large heavy
woman (she wore a number seven shoe and she weighed from 185 to 190
pounds)—she was noted to be the best dancer that attended the square dances
in those days.*"

BONYPARTE

*d, d'. No. 1568. W. M. Stepp, Salyersville, Ky., 1937.
Known sometimes as "Bonaparte's Retreat Across the Rocky
Mountains." The piece is descriptive—marching, wind
howling, etc.*

"*Did you ever read the history of Napoleon the Bonyparte? It must
have been a few hundred years or so ago, I couldn't tell you. He was a great
warrior, and I tell you what he used to do. If some country like Germany
would try to take some poor little country that was defenseless and make
'em do as they wanted 'em to do—you know, work for 'em and all that—
well, he'd go and he'd fight for that country, and he'd lick Germany. He
had a army of his own, you know. And that country would pay him, and
Germany also would have to pay him for his expenses. His army was*

located in France. He was a Frenchman—not the King of France, he went out for himself. That's all he ever done, was just watchin' countries and makin' his money that way."

CALLAHAN

a^b. No. 1537. Luther Strong, Hazard, Ky., 1937.

"I learned 'Callahan' from one of them Jackson County fellows playing the fiddle and singing it. I used to hear an old man by the name of Bob Lehr play it and sing it in Jackson County. This man, Callahan, he killed somebody. This old man seen him hung, this man Bob Lehr did.

"Tell you what he did, this Callahan. He was a fiddler, and when they was about to hang him, he took his fiddle and he offered anybody, any fiddler that would come up there and sit down with him and play that tune, he'd give them that fiddle. And they wouldn't do it and when his last minute was up and they was fixing to trip the gallows with him, why, he busted that fiddle all to pieces over that coffin. They was afraid to come up there and play with him, afraid some one would shoot them, and so he busted that fiddle all to pieces over the head of his own casket.

"It had been a feud. He had killed somebody in one of them feudses and they got him in jail. Bessie Larkin was a girl he married. They was engaged to be married, and he got into that trouble, and she married him after he got in jail and went on to jail with him. They lived together in jail, yes, sir, four or five months or maybe six or eight. She lived right there in the jail-house with him, married him in jail—she liked him. That was about thirty or maybe forty years ago in Manchester, down in Clay County. Ever since that time they've called this here tune 'Callahan.'"

> *What're you gonna do with the pretty Bessie Larkin,*
> *Whenever John Callahan's dead and gone?*
> *What're you gonna do with pretty Bessie Larkin?*
> *Oh, fare you well, my pretty little one,*
> *Oh, fare you well, my darling.*

Very fast ♩ = 160

D.S. 𝄋 3 times; 3rd time end at Fine

* In the first repetition of the tune, the four measures beginning at (a) are played twice, the succeeding four measures are omitted, and the remainder is played as written. In the second repetition, the four measures at (a) are played twice, the succeeding four measures are played as written, the four measures beginning at (b) are omitted, and the remainder is played as written. The four measures beginning at (b) were transcribed from the first repetition, which differs from the first playing chiefly in that the execution is clearer. The bowing in "Callahan" and "Bonyparte" could not be determined with sufficient accuracy to allow its notation.

HOP UP, MY LADIES

g. No. 1363. Acc. on guitar and banjo and sung by
Fields and Wade Ward, Galax, Va., 1937. Other titles:
"Hop Light, Ladies," "Miss McCloud's Reel."

Fast ♩ = 116 *increasing to* 120 *at end of second stanza*

Did you ev - er go to meet-in', Un - cle Joe, Un - cle Joe? Did you

ev - er go to meetin', Un-cle Joe? Did you ev - er go to meet-in', Un - cle

Joe, Un - cle Joe? Don't mind the wea - ther so the wind don't blow.

CHORUS

Hop up, my la - dies, three in a row, Hop up, my la - dies,

three in a row, Hop up, my la - dies, three in a row. Don't

mind the wea - ther so the wind don't blow.

1 Did you ever go to meetin', Uncle Joe, Uncle Joe?
Did you ever go to meetin', Uncle Joe?
Did you ever go to meetin', Uncle Joe, Uncle Joe?
Don't mind the weather so the wind don't blow.

Chorus:

      Hop up, my ladies, three in a row, (3)
      Don't mind the weather so the wind don't blow.

[58]

2 Will your horse carry double, Uncle Joe, Uncle Joe?

3 Is your horse a single-footer, Uncle Joe, Uncle Joe?

4 Would you rather own a pacer, Uncle Joe, Uncle Joe?

5 Say, you don't want to gallop,

6 Say, you might take a tumble,

7 Well, we'll get there soon as t'others,

DUCKS IN THE MILLPOND

c'♯. No. 1370. Acc. on guitar and sung by Fields Ward,
Galax, Va., 1937. Related to "Old Dan Tucker."

Ducks in the mill-pond, A-geese in the o-cean, A-hug them pret-ty girls If I take a no-tion. Lord, Lord,— gon-na get on a rink-tum, Lord, Lord,— gon-na get on a rink-tum.—

1 Ducks in the millpond,
A-geese in the ocean;
A-hug them pretty girls
If I take a notion.

Chorus:
Lord, Lord, gonna get on a rinktum,
Lord, Lord, gonna get on a rinktum.

2 Ducks in the millpond,
A-geese in the clover,
A-jumped in the bed,
And the bed turned over.

3 Ducks in the millpond,
A-geese in the clover,
A-fell in the millpond,
Wet all over.

[59]

4 Up the hickory,*
  Down the pine,
  Tore my shirt-tail
  Way up behind.

5 I looked down the road,
  Saw Sal a-comin',
  Thought to my soul
  I'd kill myself a-runnin'.

6 Monkey in the barnyard,
  Monkey in the stable,
  Monkey git your hair cut
  Soon as you are able.

7 Had a little pony,
  His name was Jack;
  Put him in a stable,
  And he jumped through a crack.

8 Chew my terbacker
  And spit my juice,
  Want to go to heaven,
  But it ain't no use.

* Stanzas 4–8 from Ray Wood (Raywood, Texas), *Mother Goose of the Ozarks.*

LYNCHBURG TOWN
(*A banjo tune*)

b. No. 1587. Acc. on banjo and sung by James Mullins,
Florress, Ky., 1937. See Whi, pp. 157, 178.

Fast ♩=144

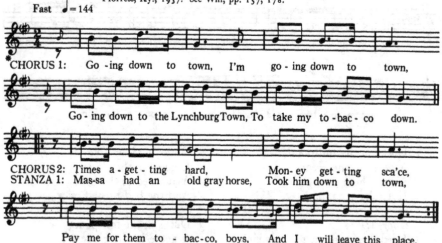

CHORUS 1: Go -ing down to town, I'm go - ing down to town,

Go - ing down to the Lynchburg Town, To take my to - bac - co down.

CHORUS 2: Times a - get - ting hard, Mon- ey get - ting sca'ce,
STANZA 1: Mas-sa had an old gray horse, Took him down to town,

Pay me for them to - bac-co, boys, And I will leave this place.
Sold him for a half a dol - lar And on-ly a quar-ter down.

* Choruses 1 and 2 are sung before each stanza. Stanzas are sung to the tune of either chorus.

Chorus 1:
> Going down to town,
> I'm going down to town,
> Going down to the Lynchburg Town,
> To take my tobacco down.

Chorus 2:
> Times a-getting hard,
> Money getting sca'ce,
> Pay me for them tobacco, boys,
> And I will leave this place.

1 Massa had an old gray horse,
> Took him down to town,
> Sold him for a half a dollar
> And only a quarter down.

2 Old massa had a brand-new coat
> And he hung it on the wall,
> A nigger stole old massa's coat
> And wore it to the ball.

3 Old massa to the sheriff wrote
> And sent it by the mail,
> Mr. Sheriff got old massa's note
> And put the thief in jail.

4 Old massa had a big brick house,
> 'Twas sixteen stories high,
> And every story in that house
> Was full of chicken pie.

5 Old massa was a rich old man
> He was richer than a king.
> He made me beat the old tin pan
> While Sary Jane would sing.

6 Old massa bought a yaller gal,
  He fotch her from the South,
  Her hair was wrapped so very tight
  That she couldn't shut her mouth.

7 Massa had an old black hen,
  She laid behind the door,
  Every day she laid three eggs
  And Sunday she laid more.

8 Massa had an old coon dog
  And he was a half a hound,
  He could run for an hour and a half
  And never touch the ground.

9 Somebody's stole my old coon dog,
  I wish they'd bring him back;
  He run the old ones over the fence
  And the little ones through the crack.

10 I went down to town
  And went into the store,
  And every pretty girl in that town
  Came running to the door.

11 Last time I saw my girl,
  She was standing in the door,
  Her shoes and stockings in her hand
  And her feet all over the floor.

12 I went down to town
  To get me a jug of wine,
  They tied me up to a whipping post
  And give me forty-nine.

13 I went down to town
  To get me a jug of gin,
  They tied me up to a whipping post
  And give me hell agin.

JINNY GIT AROUND
(*A banjo tune*)

bb. No. 1590. Acc. on banjo and sung by James Mullins, Florress, Ky., 1937.

Fast ♩ = 144 *increasing to* 160 *at end of recording*

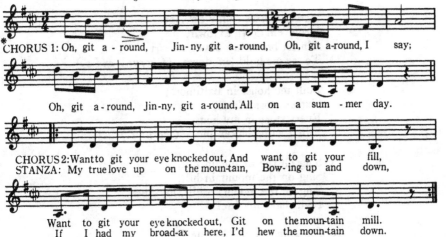

CHORUS 1: Oh, git a - round,   Jin-ny, git a-round,   Oh, git a-round, I   say;

Oh, git a - round, Jin-ny, git a-round, All   on   a   sum - mer   day.

CHORUS 2: Want to git your eye knocked out, And   want to git your   fill,
STANZA: My true love up   on the moun-tain,   Bow-ing up and   down,

Want to git your eye knocked out, Git   on the moun-tain   mill.
If   I had my   broad-ax   here, I'd   hew the moun-tain   down.

* The banjo interludes occur between chorus 2 and each succeeding stanza. The form of the song would appear, therefore, to be "stanza, chorus 1, chorus 2," in spite of the fact the song begins with chorus 1.

Chorus 1:
>Oh, git around, Jinny, git around,
>Oh, git around, I say;
>Oh, git around, Jinny, git around,
>All on a summer day.

Chorus 2:
>Want to git your eye knocked out,
>And want to git your fill,
>Want to git your eye knocked out,
>Git on the mountain mill.

1 My true love up on the mountain,
>Bowing up and down,
>If I had my broadax here,
>I'd hew the mountain down. (*Chorus 1 and 2.*)

[63]

2 Jaybird up in the acorn tree,
  Shaking acorns down,
  My true love in the sugar tree,
  Shakin' sugar down. (*Chorus 1 and 2.*)

3 Sixteen horses to my carriage,
  Drive 'em down to town;
  Almost break my dovey's heart
  To see me hold 'em down. (*Chorus 1 and 2.*)

4 Built me house in Baltimore,
  Sixteen stories high,
  Every story in my house
  Filled with chicken pie. (*Chorus 1.*)

5 Sing on the mountain hill,
  Sing on the mountain hill,
  Sing on the mountain hill, my love,
  I will have my fun.

6 I'm goin' up on Grabble Dick,
  I'm goin' up next Friday,
  I'm goin' up on Grabble Dick
  And marry Miss Betsy, Friday.

7 I will have my fun, my love,
  I will have my fun,
  Take my glass away from me,
  I don't want no more. (*Chorus 2.*)

8 Jaybird pull a two-ox load,
  Sparrow, why not you?
  My legs so long and slender, love,
  I'm feared I'll pull in two.

9 Feared I'll pull in two, my love,
  Feared I'll pull in two,
  Feared I'll pull in two, my love,
  Feared I'll pull in two.

[64]

10 Snowbird died with whooping cough,
   Crawfish died with colic,
   Jaybird died with a sick headache,
   Inquiring the way to the frolic. (*Chorus 1 and 2.*)

11 When I git one dram,
   Then I want two.
   When I get on a high lonesome
   I don't care what I do. (*Chorus 1 and 2.*)

KING WILLIAM WAS KING GEORGE'S SON *

g'. No. 1365. Mr. and Mrs. Crockett Ward, Galax, Va., 1937. See Bot, p. 227.

"It was mostly skippin' and swingin' each other around in those days, not this huggin'-up business like today. Of course the play parties was used a lot for courtin', you might say; but so was the Sunday singin's and camp meetin's, too, for that matter. When you get young people together they's goin' to be courtin'. Now I think a play party's a pretty good place for young folks to find out about each other, how they can get along with people, and if a girl's got any life about her, anything about her to like besides her looks. And a slicked-up boy now—many a girl's found out how little sense such a boy has got when she sees him alongside a bunch o' right clever fellers; or, maybe she's been a-holdin' his good looks against him, and she finds out he's got more sense than she thought he had and can hold with the smartest of 'em. There ain't no harm in a decent-conducted play party or singin' party, as I can see."

Moderately fast ♩ = 96

King Wil-liam was King George's son And from the
roy-al race he run, Up-on his breast he wore a
star To show to the world he was a man of war.____

* For directions see B. A. Botkin, *The American Play-Party Song*, p. 57.

1 King William was King George's son
And from the royal race he run,
Upon his breast he wore a star
To show to the world he was a man of war.

2 Go choose you East, go choose you West,
Go choose the one that you love the best;
If she's not here to take her part
Choose you another with all your heart.

3 Down on this carpet you shall kneel,
Sure as the grass grows in the field,
Hug her neat and kiss her sweet,
Then you may rise upon your feet.

HAD A LITTLE FIGHT IN MEXICO

e'ᵇ. No. 1351. Mrs. Carlos Gallimore and her sons, Dale and Gene, Galax, Va., 1937. See Bot, p. 232.

Directions: Couples line up and promenade through the first stanza and chorus. The girls pause at the second stanza, while the boys go forward, thus changing partners. The third stanza is dramatized in greeting the new partner. Stanzas 2 and 3 are inserted at the will of any couple who can get a following of voices.

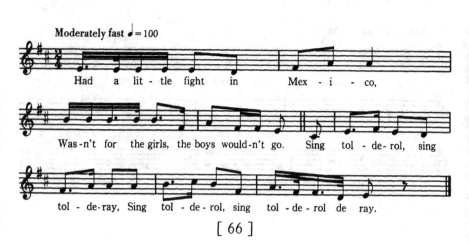

Moderately fast ♩ = 100

Had a lit - tle fight in Mex - i - co,

Was-n't for the girls, the boys would-n't go. Sing tol - de - rol, sing

tol - de-ray, Sing tol - de - rol, sing tol - de - rol de ray.

1 Had a little fight in Mexico,
    Wasn't for the girls, the boys wouldn't go.*

    Chorus:
        Sing tol-de-rol, sing tol-de-ray,
        Sing tol-de-rol, sing tol-de-rol-de-ray.

2 Come to the place where the blood was shed,
    The girls turned back and the boys went ahead.

3 And the girls and the boys where they did meet,
    They laughed and talked and kissed so sweet.

4 You better get up, you're mighty in the way,
    Choose you a partner and come along and play.

5 Oh, that little fight in Mexico,
    None was killed but John Taylor-o.

6 I had an old hat with a flop-down brim,
    It looked like a toad frog settin' on a limb.

7 I had an old cow and I milked her in a gourd,
    Set it in a corner and covered it with a board.

8 I want to go to Texas, and to Texas I'll go,
    And I'll vote for old John Tyler-o.

9 I went to the fight in Mexico,
    Fightin' for the gunboats all in a row.

        Repeat stanzas 2, 3, 4.

* Stanzas 4 and 5 from B. A. Botkin, *The American Play-Party Song*, p. 233; stanzas 6–9, from manuscript sent to John A. Lomax thirty years ago. This version is entitled "Old John Tyler" and gives 1841 as the date of the song.

THE BANK OF THE ARKANSAW

c' to bb. No. 1337. Mrs. Minta Morgan, Bells, Texas, 1937. See Lo.2, p. 261.

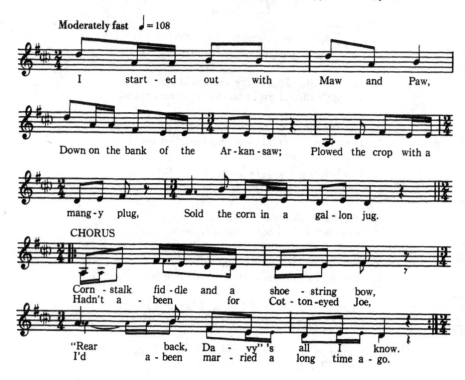

1 I started out with Maw and Paw,
   Down on the bank of the Arkansaw;
   Plowed the crop with a mangy plug,
   Sold the corn in a gallon jug.

Chorus:

> Cornstalk fiddle, and a shoestring bow,
> "Rear back, Davy" 's all I know.
> Hadn't a-been for Cotton-eyed Joe,
> I'd a-been married a long time ago.

[68]

2 Two little Indians and one old squaw,
  Settin' on the bank of the Arkansaw;
  Never put out a hook and line,
  Steal all the big fish off of mine.

3 Prettiest little girl I ever saw,
  Lived on the bank of the Arkansaw;
  Eyes were blue and her cheeks were red,
  She was sweet as gingerbread.

4 Mustang grape and the sweet pawpaw
  Grow on the bank of the Arkansaw;
  Every time a pretty girl wanted a beau,
  Up jumped Jimmy and away went Joe.

5 My best girl is hard to please;
  My best pants were up to my knees;
  I got the first good pair I saw
  Laying on the bank of the Arkansaw.

6 Jackson pushed his mother-in-law
  Over the bank of the Arkansaw;
  The old lady showed him how to swim—
  When she got out, she threw him in.

7 The old lady ran away with the law,
  Down on the bank of the Arkansaw;
  Fell in love with the popinjay,
  They'll be back about dinnertime o' day.

II. 2. NEGRO GAME SONGS

This group of gay, gamboling airs the Negroes learned directly from white singers. They have made a few characteristic changes—syncopations, introduction of earthy lines and of familiar words for unfamiliar ones. The eight melodies, gathered from across the whole South, have common family likenesses. They are related to the white play-party tunes on the one hand and to the Bahaman Negro songs on the other.

LADIES IN THE DININ' ROOM

f'². No. 88. Alabama Negro children, Atmore, Ala., 1934. See *Mem.*, 16:183.

* The above notation is a transcription of the two parts heard on the record.

A choose-your-love, kissing-game song.

    1 Ladies in the dinin' room,
      Sittin' by the fi-ah,
      Lost her slipper and she fell down,
      Raise your foot up high-ah.

    2 Choose the one the ring goes round,
      Choose the one with money,
      Choose the one they call Annie Lee,*
      Kiss your darlin' honey.

* Or the name of any one of the group of players.

[70]

YOU TURN FOR SUGAR AN' TEA

c'. No. 948. Annie Brewer, Montgomery, Ala., 1937.

Moderately fast ♩=63

You turn for sug-ar an' tea, I turn for can - dy;

Boys all love that sug-ar an' tea, Girls all love that can - dy.

You turn,— I turn,— You turn,— I turn.—

Players line up as for Virginia Reel. Couples advance, swing, turn, and promenade as the text indicates. Negro children use no very complicated figures, but their steps are often very intricate.

1 You turn for sugar an' tea,
   I turn for candy;
   Boys all love that sugar an' tea,
   Girls all love that candy.

   Chorus:
            You turn, I turn,
            You turn, I turn.

2 Some ladies love that sugar an' tea,
   Some ladies love candy,
   Some ladies wheel all around
   An' kiss their loves so handy.

3 Miss Brown * sure loves sugar an' tea,
   Miss Brown sure loves candy,
   Miss Brown sure can turn all around
   And kiss her true love handy.

* The name of any girl player.

4 Lead through that sugar and tea,*
  Oh, lead through that candy,
  You lead through that sugar and tea,
  And I'll lead through that candy.

* The last stanza from B. A. Botkin, *The American Play-Party Song*, p. 228.

JOHNNIE BOUGHT A HAM

d. No. 904. Myrtle and George Pinnacle, Murrells Inlet, S.C., 1937.

"Johnnie Bought a Ham" is a clapping game played like "Pease Porridge Hot." The Pinnacle children of Murrells Inlet, South Carolina, slap in syncopated rhythm. The climax is reached in the last three lines when they slap their partners' hands with as much force as possible, sometimes knocking them off balance.

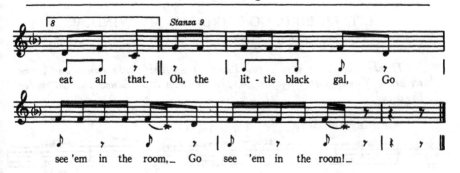

eat all that. Oh, the lit-tle black gal, Go

see 'em in the room,— Go see 'em in the room!—

1 Johnnie bought a ham,
Fried him in the pan,
Johnnie bought a ham from a
    Boston-mo,*
Sixteen story high, you know.

2 Mary and Mack,
Dressed in black,
Twenty-four buttons
Up and down her back.

3 Comb her hair,
Broke my comb,
I'll tell mamma
When she come home.

4 Mary Mack,
Dressed in black,
Silver buttons
All down her back.

5 Ast my mamma
For fifteen cents,
To see the elephant-ee
Jump the fence.

6 Jumped so high
Cleared the sky,
Never come back
Till the Fou'th o' July.

7 Away down
In Jaybird Town,
Folks have to work
Till the sun goes down.

8 Little piece o' meat,
Very fat,
Folks would grumble
If you eat all that.

9 Oh, the little black gal,
Go see 'em in the room,
Go see 'em in the room!

* Usually "Balti-mo'." Sometimes "Boston sto'."

[73]

LITTLE BIRD, GO THROUGH MY WINDOW

a. No. 1303. Eddie Nelson, Murrells Inlet, S.C., 1937.
See *JAFL*, 33:94; Ne, p. 118.

It takes six children to play. Three on each side take hands and make an arch. Then, couple by couple, the children drop hands and go under the arch.

1 Little bird, little bird, go through my window,
Little bird, little bird, go through my window,
Little bird, little bird, go through my window,
And buy molasses candy.

Chorus 1:
Go through my window, my sugar lump, (2)
And buy molasses candy.

[74]

2 Blue bird, blue bird, go through my window, (3)
And buy molasses candy.

Chorus 2:
Go through my window, my little bird, (2)
And buy molasses candy.

SALLY GO ROUND THE SUNSHINE

d'. No. 1303. Eddie Nelson, Murrells Inlet, S.C., 1937.

"I've played it different in different schools. One place we would catch hands and hold 'em up and go-in-and-out-the-window, you know. When we said 'Boom! Boom!' we would stop and catch somebody and he had to choose a partner, or sometimes we made him pay a fine.

"Then I've played it two rings, boys outside and girls inside, goin' different ways. 'Boom! Boom!' means stop and stomp your feet, and you have to take the partner you stop in front of.

"But I like it best just to have one ring and dance to the right for the sun and then to the left for the moon, then back again for the sunshine. Then stop 'Boom! Boom!' and scramble for partners. That just meant you could stand next to the girl you liked best when you played again—if you could get her, I mean."

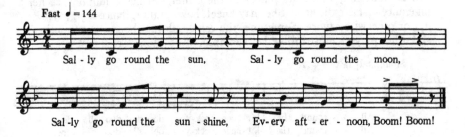

Fast ♩ = 144

Sal - ly go round the sun, Sal - ly go round the moon,

Sal - ly go round the sun - shine, Ev - ery aft - er - noon, Boom! Boom!

Sally go round the sun,
Sally go round the moon,
Sally go round the sunshine,
Every afternoon,
Boom! Boom!

[75]

DON'T YOU LIKE IT?

bb. No. 878. Annie Brewer, Montgomery, Ala., 1937.

Acted out by Annie Brewer, this is a prancing, teasing song with a challenge to a chase or a tussle.

Don't you like it? don't you take it? Here my col - lar, come and

shake it. You think you's big___ be-cause you been on the boat;

You passed by me like a she nan - ny goat.

COCKY DOODLE DOODLE DOO

f'#. No. 88. Group of Negro girls, Kirby Industrial School, Atmore, Ala., 1934.

March or skip while singing "All around the kitchen, etc." Then stand still as indicated, while the player in the center "makes a motion" as her ingenuity or taste dictates. She may kneel, bow, prance, dance a jig, "shake it," or otherwise cavort. Sometimes the center player chooses the "motion" and other players must follow her example, must "do it like this."

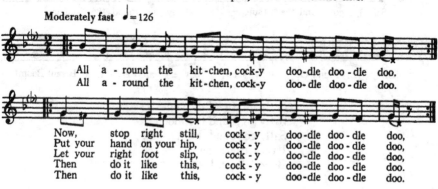

All a - round the kit - chen, cock-y doo - dle doo - dle doo.
All a - round the kit - chen, cock-y doo - dle doo - dle doo.

Now, stop right still, cock - y doo - dle doo - dle doo,
Put your hand on your hip, cock - y doo - dle doo - dle doo,
Let your right foot slip, cock - y doo - dle doo - dle doo,
Then do it like this, cock - y doo - dle doo - dle doo.
Then do it like this, cock - y doo - dle doo - dle doo.

[76]

1 All around the kitchen, cocky doodle doodle doo; (2)

2 Now, stop right still, cocky doodle doodle doo,
   Put your hand on your hip, cocky doodle doodle doo,
   Let your right foot * slip, cocky doodle doodle doo,
   Then do it like this, cocky doodle doodle doo. (2)

3 All around the kitchen, cocky doodle doodle doo; (2)

4 Now, stop right still, cocky doodle doodle doo,
   Put your hand on your hip, cocky doodle doodle doo,
   Let your right foot * slip, cocky doodle doodle doo,
   Then do it like this, cocky doodle doodle doo.

* Sometimes sung, "backbone," with appropriate movements.

KITTY, KITTY CASKET

f♯. No. 88. See previous song. See Ne, p. 168.

"Kitty, Kitty Casket" is a drop-the-handkerchief play song which seems to combine parts of two ring-games, "Itisket Itasket" and "Lost My Handkerchief." In east Texas, Alabama, and Mississippi we have heard Negro school children sing:

> *Lost my handkerchief yesterday,*
> *I found it today, I found it today,*
> *It was all full o' mud and I tossed it away;*
> *I tossed it away, an' I tossed it away.*

"Tossed it away" is the signal for the player with the handkerchief to drop it behind a child in the ring. "Throwed" and "dashed" are preferred by some children. An east Texas group sings,

> *It was all muddied up and I dashed it away,*
> *Dish-ma, dash-ma, dish-ma, dash-ma, dish-ma, dash-ma, etc.,*

the chant continuing until the chase is well under way.

[77]

Newell * says that the game played in England to the tune of "Itisket, Itasket" is called "Drop-Glove," also in some places "Lost Letter." He cites the following American version, presumably as sung by white children at play:

> *Itisket, Itasket, A green and yellow basket,*
> *I sent a letter to my love, And on my way I dropped it.*

Edna Potter † in her collection of game songs for American children closes her version with

> *A little boy came along, And put it in his pocket.*

In 1938 swing versions of the tune became popular under the title, "Atisket, Ataket." In these versions composers, singers, and arrangers used their ingenuity in setting down elaborate details about the finder of the letter as well as the desperate feelings of the loser. Though the children would not admit it, we suspected that these swing versions through the radio and the nickel-in-the-slot phonographs had influenced the east Texas group ‡ of little Negro girls who sang as they played Drop-the-Handkerchief:

> *Atisket, Ataket, A green and yellow basket.*
> *I wrote a letter to my love, And on the way I dropped it,*
> *I dropped it, I dropped it, Yes, on my way I dropped it.*
> *Sure, one of you have picked it up, And put it in your pocket.*
> *It's you, it's you, it's you, it's you!*

On the other hand "Kitty, Kitty Casket," sung to us in Alabama in 1934, carries its own evidences of originality.

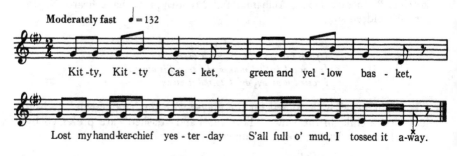

Moderately fast ♩=132

Kit-ty, Kit-ty Cas-ket, green and yel-low bas-ket,

Lost my hand-ker-chief yes-ter-day S'all full o' mud, I tossed it a-way.

* W. W. Newell, *Games and Songs of American Children*, p. 169.
† Edna Potter, *This Way and That*, No. 3.
‡ Liberty School, Newton, Texas.

II. 3. BAHAMAN NEGRO SONGS

The Bahama Islands are of coral and limestone, part of a system of coral reefs off the east coast of Florida. Covered with a sparse growth of evergreen, aromatic bush, they float low and dark green on the brim of the most brilliant and iridescent blue sea in the world. The soil makes a thin covering over the limestone and coral, and the life of the Negro inhabitant is a bitter struggle, even in that heavenly climate, for food and clothing. The men are sponge fishers and farmers at the same time. They cut back the brush with machetes to find some little pothole in the coral in which to plant a banana sprout, some yams or corn. They harvest their stunted orange trees and fish while the children hunt for the red and purple crabs along the sandy paths. After the evening meal in the nights of the full moon the young people gather on the beach and build a little fire of coconut leaves. Over this they heat the goatskin head of their drum, made at home out of a wooden sugar pail. When the drummer brings it to the right pitch, the long-legged, barefoot girl, who is the leading singer, begins,

> "*Wind blow east, wind blow west,*
> *Wind blow the* Settin' Star *right down in town.*"

The girls join with her and the couplet is repeated. They clap their hands with the music and begin to swing their hips. The boys join in the refrain,

> "*The wind blow the* China *right down in town.*"

Over and over they sing as the drum begins to touch the senses with its delicate and subtle rhythms, preparing the young people for the dance. Then out into the center of the singing circle leaps a young boy, his hat on the back of his head, his arms stiff out from his body. Fingers spread wide, legs bowed, his whole body is crouched like a black eagle about to fly. He whirls and stamps his feet, and with the triple rhythm of the drum his body freezes for instants in taut angular postures. Then he whirls and stops with both feet planted flat, his belly out before one of the girls in the circle. She takes his place in the center of the ring then, and dances. The high shrill singing, the clapping, never stop, as the voice of the drum summons the dancers in and out of the ring. Behind the group of lithe, moving shadows that sing, the flames of the little pile of coconut leaves flicker and die, and the sea near by whispers unconcernedly in the moonlight, because it has been to many jumping dances and will see many more.

THE WIND BLOW EAST

d, d', f'♯. No. 485. Group of men and women, with
drum accompaniment. Nassau, Bahamas, 1935.

A West Indian hurricane howls through the islands leaving three Bahaman sloops, the *Sunshine,* the *China,* and the *Setting Star* right down in town.

* The above notation is a transcription of the principal (continuous) voice parts heard on the record. The chorus is repeated many times between stanzas (6, then D.C.; 9½, then D.C.; 1½, end). In this song and in "Biddy, Biddy," the drum rhythms are those of the first stanza and chorus; they tend to become more complex as the songs proceed. Predominating pitches on the drum approximate I and V.

1 Oh, the wind blow east,
  The wind blow west,
  The wind blow the *Sunshine*
  Right down in town.

  Chorus:
    Oh, the wind blow the *China*
    Right down in town,
    Oh, the wind blow the *China*
    Right down in town.

2 Oh, the wind blow east,
  The wind blow west,
  The wind blow the *Settin' Star*
  Right down in town.

  Alternate Chorus:
    Oh, the wind blow the *Sunshine*
    Right down in town,
    Oh, the wind blow the *Sunshine*
    Right down in town.

BIDDY, BIDDY

f, f', a'. No. 485. See previous record. See Ne, p. 150.

In mosquito season children and grown-ups squat around smudge fires in the open, roast crabs, and "talk ol' story." This is the time of "B' Booky," "B' Rabby," and "Little Jack," "a little piece of dirt out of the alley" who always marries Princess Greenleaf in the end. Often the hero wins his desire by singing a song or playing his little "tune-tune," and almost all the stories have as a part of their fairy texture some little fragmentary, but compelling tune. Some of these tunes have English, some African backgrounds. "Biddy, Biddy," an English derivative, is sometimes sung as a jumping dance song.

* See footnote to the music of "The Wind Blow East."

1 Biddy, Biddy, hold fast my gold ring,
Hey, Mamma, hoo-ay,
Never get-a London back again,
John saw the island.

2 You drink coffee and I drink tea,
Hey, Mamma, hoo-ay,
Never get-a London back again,
John saw the island.

NEVER GET A LICKIN' TILL I GO DOWN TO BIMINI

f. No. 434. Acc. and sung by a street band with mandolin, guitar, and tenor banjo, Nassau, Bahamas, 1935.

When the tourist boats and the tourist planes dock in Nassau, they are
met by one or several of the town's street bands. These bands (banjo, one
or two guitars, mandolin, and rattle) sing and play Bahaman versions of
American jazz tunes of ancient vintage and fresh-improvised, hot arrangements of Bahaman folk-dance tunes. At night they go over the hill and
improvise even hotter arrangements for the "round dances"—fox trots,
one-steps, etc.—which have recently been increasing in popularity in the
islands. The following tunes, examples of this "sophisticated" genre, are
signposts of future development in Bahaman folk music.

Oh, when I go down to Bimini,
Never get a lickin' till I go down to Bimini.
Bimini gal is a rock in the harbor,
Never get a lickin' till I go down to Bimini.

[83]

MARRIED MAN GONNA KEEP YOUR SECRET

c′. No. 420. Elizabeth Austin and a group of women with clapping accompaniment, New Bite, Cat Island, Bahamas, 1935.

Most Bahaman dance songs are faintly, if not markedly, scandalous. Like Haitian Mardi Gras songs, they serve, without naming names, to retail gossip about or to poke fun at an enemy or some person who has acted shamefully or ridiculously. The satire, however, is softened by the kittenish giggles of the young girls who do the singing.

o, Hi - li - li - lee - o, Hi - li - li - lee -

o, Hi - li - li - lee - o. 2. Sin - gle boy gon-na talk a-

last time

o, Hi - li - whee

* The above notation is a transcription of the three clearest and most continuous parts heard on the record. The first and second parts are at times reinforced in the upper octave. The third part, crooned softly, differs with each singing of stanza and chorus. The clapping doubles speed toward the end of the recording.

1 Married man gonna keep your secret,
Hi-li-li-lee-o.
Married man gonna keep your secret,
Hi-li-li-lee-o.

Chorus:
>Hi-li-li-lee-o,
>Hi-li-li-lee-o,
>Hi-li-li-lee-o,
>Hi-li-li-lee-o.

2 Single boy gonna talk about you.
Hi-li-li-lee-o.
Single boy gonna talk about you,
Hi-li-li-lee-o.

Chorus:
>Hi-li-li-lee-o, etc.

A WASP BITE NOBI ON HER CONCH–EYE

e. No. 434. See "Bimini Gals."

A wasp bite Nobi on her conch-eye,
A wasp bite Nobi on her conch-eye,
Oh, run here, Mamma, come hold the light,
See these Germans go'n' fight tonight,
Wasp bite Nobi on her conch-eye.

[86]

DON'T YOU HURRY WORRY WITH ME

f. No. 434. See previous song.

Don't you hur-ry wor - ry with me, Don't you hur-ry wor - ry with me,

Don't you hur-ry wor - ry with me, I'm gon-na pack up your eyes with sand.

1 Don't you hurry worry with me,
Don't you hurry worry with me,
Don't you hurry worry with me,
I'm gonna pack up your eyes with sand.

2 If you tell me that again, (3)
I'm gonna pack up your eyes witn sand.

3 Mr. Munson he get broke, (3)
I'm gonna pack up your eyes with sand.

4 Don't you hurry worry with me, (3)
I'm gonna pack up your eyes with sand.

ROUND THE BAY OF MEXICO

F, a. No. 516. Henry Lundy, Nassau, Bahamas, 1935.
See Co, pp. 84, 91; Boa, p. 129; Co, p. 261; also "Santy
Anno," this volume, p. 206.

Bahaman Negro men are reputed to be the finest small-boat sailors in the world. Certainly, when one sees a twenty-five-foot boat, with one tattered and rotten sail, bringing oranges, bananas, corn, sugar cane, sponges, twenty goats, a cow, and six or eight human beings into Nassau harbor, after a journey across several hundred miles of open sea, one tends to believe this. The men spend half their lives on the sea, navigating their reef-filled courses at night with catlike calm and sureness, and their demeanor aboard their little craft is full of the grave beauty and the quiet dignity of the blue sea itself.

In August, when the hurricane season approaches, they pull their sloops up on the beach out of reach of the storms. The whole village descends to the beach, lays hold of the rope, and, as the "launching song" is raised, heaves together. These songs are fragmentary variants of well known sea shanty tunes, and sung as they are, in harmony, substantiate Joanna Colcord's statement that "first among the shanty singers" were the American Negroes.

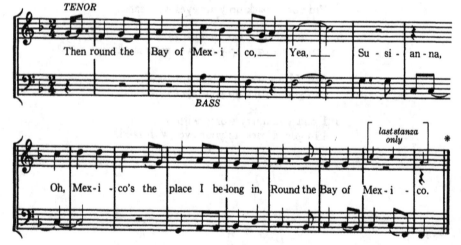

Moderate ♩ = 84

TENOR

Then round the Bay of Mex-i - co,___ Yea,___ Su - si - an-na,

BASS

Oh, Mex-i - co's the place I be-long in, Round the Bay of Mex-i - co.

last stanza only

*

* The above notation is a transcription of the two parts heard on the record.

Chorus:
>> Then round the Bay of Mexico,
>> Yea, Susianna,
>> Oh, Mexico's the place I belong in,
>> Round the Bay of Mexico.

1 Oh, why those yaller gals love me so,
>> Yea, Susianna,
> Is 'cause I don't talk everything that I know,
>> Round the Bay of Mexico.

2 Then when I was a young man in my prime,
>> Yea, Susianna,
> Oh, I knock those young gals, two at a time,
>> Round the Bay of Mexico.

3 Those Nassau gals ain't got no comb,
>> Yea, Susianna,
> They comb their hair with a whipper backbone,
>> Round the Bay of Mexico.

WHEN DE WHALE GET STRIKE

f♯. No. 512. David Pryor, Nassau, Bahamas, 1935. See
"Greenland Whale Fishery," p. 214.

Moderate ♩ = 92

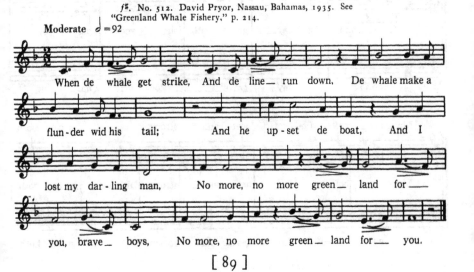

When de whale get strike, And de line— run down, De whale make a
flun-der wid his tail; And he up-set de boat, And I
lost my dar-ling man, No more, no more green— land for—
you, brave— boys, No more, no more green— land for— you.

DIG MY GRAVE

A♭, a♭, c'. No. 502. Group of Andros Island men,
Nassau, Bahamas, 1935. See Mem. III, p. 37.

The present popularity of close-harmony anthem singing among Bahaman Negro men is due, probably, to its fairly recent introduction from the United States, which the Bahaman thinks of as a land of milk and honey and millionaires. In the evenings on the sponging grounds south of Andros, on Sundays on the water front, these groups gather, each about a leader who improvises ballads about the last hurricane, about Noah or Job, while the group fills in sad harmony—early English with a dash of barber-shop—behind him. "Dig My Grave," thus improvised by a group of men from Andros Island, is, we feel, one of the finest of Negro spirituals.

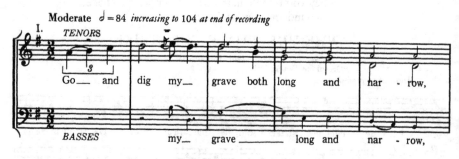

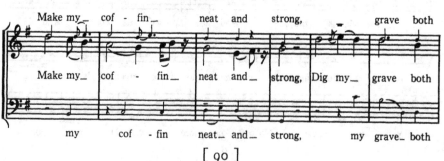

long and nar - row, Make my— cof - fin— neat and strong.

long and nar - row, Make my— cof - fin— neat and strong.

long and nar - row,— Make my cof - fin both neat and strong.

II.

Oh, two two to my feet, Now

Two two to my head,

Two two to my feet, Now, but

Two two, my Lord, Two two to my feet,

two two to car - ry me, Lord, when I die. — Fine

two two to car - ry me, Lord, when I__ die.

(Bass takes the melody)
Two two to car - ry me to heav - en when I __ die.

IIIA.

Oh, well, my

Now__ my__ soul's go'n'- ta shine__ like__ a star,

Lord, Lord, oh, well, my

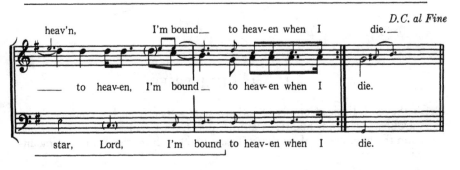

* The above notation is a transcription of the principal (continuous) voice parts heard on the record. Sections IIIA and IIIB are sung over and over, varying widely at each singing.

1 Go and dig my grave both long and narrow,
  Make my coffin neat and strong,
  Dig my grave both long and narrow,
  Make my coffin neat and strong.

2 Two two to my head, two two to my feet,
  Two two to carry me to heaven when I die.

3 Now my soul's go'n' ta shine like a star,
  Oh, well, my soul's go'n' ta shine like a star,
  My Lord-a, my soul's go'n' ta shine like a star, Lord,
  I'm bound to heaven when I die.

4 My little soul's go'n' ta shine like a star,
  Twinkle like a twinkle-in' little star,
  My soul's bound to heaven,
  I'm bound to heaven when I die.

II. 4. LULLABIES

Seven lullabies from five Southern states—two from low-country South Carolina, two from middle Alabama, one from Creole New Orleans, one from the pine woods of southeast Texas, and one from the Tennessee mountain country.

MAMMA'S GONE TO THE MAIL BOAT

b. No. 1033. "Mom" Tina Russell, Negro. Murrells Inlet, S.C., 1937.

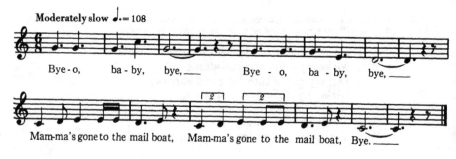

1 Bye-o, baby, bye,
  Bye-o, baby, bye,
  Mamma's gone to the mail boat,
  Mamma's gone to the mail boat,
  Bye.

2 Go to sleepy, baby, bye, (2)
  Father's gone to the mail boat, (2)
  Bye.

OL' HAG, YOU SEE MAMMY?

e♭. No. 909. Aunt Stella Horry, Negro, Murrells Inlet, S.C., 1935.

Ol' hag, you see Mam-my? No,_____ no. Ol' hag, you see Mam-my? No, no. Mam-my car-ry bub-by, go-in' to i - lant,_____ Pap-py go-in' to sea sho',_____ Row -boat__ for cat -fish, row-boat.

1 Ol' hag, you see Mammy?
No, no.
Ol' hag, you see Mammy?
No, no.
Mammy carry bubby goin' to ilant,*
Pappy goin' to seasho'.
Row boat for catfish, row boat.

* Island.

DADDY SHOT A BEAR

g. No. 948. Annie Brewer, Montgomery, Ala., 1937.
Patting song.

Dad -dy shot a bear, Dad - dy shot a bear, Shot him through the key - hole An' nev - er touch a hair.

Daddy shot a bear,
Daddy shot a bear,
Shot him through the keyhole
An' never touch a hair . . .

On and on as long as the baby likes it.

HUSH, LI'L' BABY

eb. No. 878. Annie Brewer, Montgomery, Ala., 1937.
See Sh, 2:342.

Hush, li'l' ba-by, don' say a word, Mam-ma's gon-na buy you a mock-in' bird.

1 Hush, li'l' baby, don' say a word,
Mamma's gonna buy you a mockin'bird.

2 If that mockin'bird don' sing,
Mamma's gonna buy you a diamond ring.

3 If that diamond ring turn brass,
Mamma's gonna buy you a lookin' glass.

4 If that lookin' glass gets broke,
Mamma's gonna buy you a billygoat.

5 If that billygoat won' pull,
Mamma's gonna buy you a cart and bull.

6 If that cart and bull turn over,
Mamma's gonna buy you a dog named Rover.

7 If that dog named Rover won' bark,
Mamma's gonna buy you a horse and cart.

8 If that horse and cart fall down,
You'll be the sweetest girl in town.

[96]

CRABE DANS CALALOU

f#. No. 889. Ernestine Laban and Amelie Alexandre,
New Orleans, La., Lafont Catholic Home, 1937.

This Creole Negro lullaby from New Orleans is sung in an almost iden-
tical form in Haiti. It was probably brought to New Orleans by the slaves of
those French planters who escaped to Louisiana after the successful revolt of
the Haitian Negroes.

Moderately fast ♩ = 104

Fais do - do, mon fils, Cra - be dans ca - la - lou, Fais do - do, mon

fils, Cra - be dans ca - la - lou. *Fine* Pa - pa,___ li

cour - i la ri - vière, Ma - man,___ li cour - i pê - cher crabe. *D.C. al Fine*

1 Fais dodo, mon fils,
Crabe dans calalou;
Fais dodo, mon fils,
Crabe dans calalou.

Papa, li couri la rivière,
Maman, li couri pêcher crabe.

2 Fais dodo, mon fils,
Crabe dans calalou;
Fais dodo, mon fils,
Crabe dans calalou.

Papa moin couri la rivière,
Maman moin couri pêcher crabe.

1 Go to sleep, my son,
Crabs are in the pot;
Go to sleep, my son,
Crabs are in the pot.

Paw, he's gone to the riverside,
Maw, she's gone off a-catching
crab.

2 Go to sleep, my son,
Crabs are in the pot;
Go to sleep, my son,
Crabs are in the pot.

My paw's down at the riverside,
My maw's gone off a-catching
crab.

3 Dodo, ma fille,
  Crabe dans calalou;
  Dodo, ma fille,
  Crabe dans calalou.

3 Sleep, baby mine,
  Crabs are in the pot;
  Sleep, baby mine,
  Crabs are in the pot.

MARY WAS A RED BIRD

c'♯. No. 2662. Henry Truvillion, Newton, Texas, 1939, assisted by Ruby Lee Truvillion, 8 years. "An old slavery-time song, come down through our white folks an' our family to me, Henry Truvillion, Jr., and my little girl, Ruby Lee."

Moderately fast ♩ = 63

Ma - ry wore her red dress,— red dress,— red dress,

Ma - ry wore her red dress — All day long.

1 Mary wore her red dress, red dress, red dress,
  Mary wore her red dress
  All day long.

2 Mary wore her red hat, red hat, red hat,
  Mary wore her red hat
  All day long.

3 Mary wore her red shoes, etc.

4 Mary wore her red gloves, etc.

5 Mary made a red cake, etc.

6 Where'd you git yo' shoes fum, etc.

7 Got 'em fum de dry goods, etc.

[98]

8 Where'd you git yo' butter * fum, etc.

9 Got it fum de grocy, etc.

10 Where'd you git yo' gloves fum, etc.

11 Got 'em fum de dry goods, etc.

12 Mary was a red bird, red bird, red bird,
Mary was a red bird
All day long!

* "If the baby don' go to sleep by now, you can jes' keep on an' on, th'ough all de ingreemunts o' de cake."

COTTON EYE JOE

Margaret Valiant and Tannis Tugwell, 1937. They learned the song from a mountain woman in Tennessee. See Lo.2, p. 262; Whi, p. 359; Sc.1, p. 69. See No. 1619.

1 Where did you come from,
Where did you go?
Where did you come from,
Cotton Eye Joe?

2 Come for to see you,
Come for to sing,
Come for to show you
My diamond ring.

II. 5. WHOPPERS

Away out yonder in Arizony
Where it ain't rained since Noah
And it's so dry you have to prime yourself to spit,
And it's so dry the grass widows can't take root,
Thar's a wonderful forest whar the trees is a-growin'
Jest the same as they did centuries and centuries ago,
But a-a-all pewtrified, ladies and gentlemen,
A-a-all pewtrified.
And the roots of them thar trees is a-growin' way down in the ground,
A-spreadin' out and a-takin' holt on the dirt,
Jest the same as they did centuries and centuries ago—
But a-a-all pewtrified, ladies and gentlemen, all pewtrified.
And the branches of them thar trees is a-growin' full of twigs and leaves
*   and birds' nests,*
Jest the same as they did centuries and centuries ago;
And flyin' around them thar branches and through the pewtrified air
Is a number of pine hens,
Sand-hill cranes,
White-necked ravens,
And yellow-headed blackbirds,
All a-singin' their beautiful songs jest as they did centuries and centuries
*   ago,*
But a-a-all pewtrified, ladies and gentlemen,
A-a-all pewtrified.

Now when I give a lecture on Arizony up to Boston last week and told
*   this interestin' scientific fact,*
Some unbelievin' miscreant sings out,
"What about the law of gravitation?"
And I sings out right back at him,
"Seems to me that anybody with the sense of a coyote'd know that away
*   out there in Arizony*
This here new law of gravitation hain't worked for centuries and cen-
*   turies,*

But is like everythin' else aout there—
A-a-all pewtrified, ladies and gentlemen,
Completely pewtrified."

—Contributed by John A. Lomax, Jr.

BILLY BARLOW

d. No. 740B2. Acc. on guitar and sung by Bud Wiley,
Zweifel Ranch, Fort Spunky, Texas, 1935.

Moderately fast ♩.= 84

"Let's go hunt-in'," says Risk-y Rob, "Let's go
hunt-in'," says Rob-in to Bob, "Let's go hunt-in'",says Dan'l and
Joe, "Let's go hunt-in'," says Bil-ly Bar - low.

1 "Let's go huntin'," says Risky Rob,
  "Let's go huntin'," says Robin to Bob,
  "Let's go huntin'," says Dan'l and Joe,
  "Let's go huntin'," says Billy Barlow.

2 "What shall I hunt?" says Risky Rob, etc.
  "Hunt for a rat," says Billy Barlow.

3 "How shall I get him?" says Risky Rob, etc.
  "Go borry a gun," says Billy Barlow.

4 "How shall I haul him?" says Risky Rob, etc.
  "Go borry a cart," says Billy Barlow.

[101]

5 "How shall we divide him?" says Risky Rob, etc.
  "How shall we divide him?" says Billy Barlow.

6 "I'll take shoulder," says Risky Rob,
  "I'll take side," says Robin to Bob,
  "I'll take ham," says Dan'l and Joe,
  "Tail bone mine," says Billy Barlow.

7 "How shall we cook him?" says Risky Rob, etc.
  "How shall we cook him?" says Billy Barlow.

8 "I'll broil shoulder," says Risky Rob,
  "I'll fry side," says Robin to Bob,
  "I'll boil ham," says Dan'l and Joe,
  "Tail bone raw," says Billy Barlow.

THE CROOKED GUN

b. No. 1301. Tune and some stanzas, Mrs. Minnie Floyd, Murrells Inlet, S.C., 1937. Other stanzas from Barbara Bell, Minneapolis, Minn. See Sh, 2:217.

1 One pleasant summer morning it came a storm of snow,
  I picked up my old gun and a-hunting I did go.
  I came across a herd of deer and I trailed them through the snow,
  I trailed them to the mountains where straight up they did go.

2 I went up yonder river that ran up yonder hill,
  And there I spied a herd of deer, and in it they did dwell;
  Soon as the buck they saw me, like devils they did run
  To the bottom of the river and squat upon the ground.

3 Then I went under water, five hundred feet or more.
  I fired off my pistols, like cannons they did roar.
  I fired away among the buck, at length I killed one;
  The rest stuck up their brustles, and at me they did come.

4 Their horns being in full velvet, as high as Egypt's mass,
  And they did through my body like streaks of lightning pass.
  When they had thus quite riddled me that bulldogs might run through,
  I being so enraged then, my naked sword I drew.

5 I fought them with my broadsword, six hours I held them play,
  I killed three hundred and fifty, and the rest they ran away.
  I gathered up my venison, and out of waters went;
  To seek and kill all those that fled, it was my whole intent.

6 Just as I stood a-gazing, the sun came rolling by;
  I gathered up my venison, jumped on as he drew nigh.
  He carried me all 'round this world, all 'round the swelling tide;
  The stars they brought my venison, and so merrily I did ride.

7 Just as the sun was going down, he gave a sudden twirl,
  And I could hold on no longer, so I fell in another world,
  As Providence provided, I fell upon the moon,
  And in the course of a day or so he brought me safe at home.

8 I gathered up my money for venison and for skin;
  I carried it into my barn, it wouldn't half go in.
  The rest I gave unto the poor, bright guineas out of hand.
  Now don't you think that I can live a noble gentleman?

THE RAM OF DARBY

d. No. 2358. Tune, John Norman, Munising, Mich., 1938. Text, Pete Harris, Richmond, Texas; Jesse Harris, Livingston, Ala.; Mrs. Minnie Floyd, Murrells Inlet, S.C.; Mrs. Minta Morgan, Bells, Texas. See Hu, p. 273; Sh, 1:184; Ga.2, p. 460; *PTFLS*, No. 5, p. 157; Be, p. 224, also *Didn't He Ramble*—Will Handy (sheet music). W. C. Handy says this is an arrangement of a current folk song.

1 As I went down to Darby-town
  All on the market day,
  I saw the biggest ram, sir,
  That ever fed on hay.

  Chorus:
      Didn't he ramble?
      He did ramble,
      He did ramble till those butchers cut 'im down.

[104]

2 This ram was fat behind, sir,
  This ram was fat before,
  This ram was ten rod high, sir,
  (I'm sure he was no more).

3 This ram did have four feet, sir,
  And on them he did stand,
  And every hoof he had, sir,
  It covered an acre of land.

4 The horns upon this ram, sir,
  They grew so very high
  That every time he would rattle them
  They would rattle against the sky.

5 The wool upon this ram's back
  It grew so mighty high,
  The eagles built their nests there
  And the young ones dast not fly.

6 Oh, the wool that's on this ram, sir,
  Was dragging on the ground,
  They took it to the weaver
  And it weighed five thousand pound.

7 The wool growed on this ram's belly,
  It growed so short and thick,
  It caused the girls in Darby
  A season for to pick.

8 The hair growed on this ram's sides,
  It grew so long and thin,
  It caused the girls in Darby
  A season for to spin.

9 Oh, this ram he had two horns, sir,
  They reached up to the moon,
  A man went up in January
  And never got down till June.

[105]

10 The ram had a hollow jaw tooth
   Held sixty bushels of corn,
   The man he took the hollow jaw tooth
   For to make him a blowin' horn.

11 That ram he had long, long hair
   Reached way down to the ground,
   The devil stole a strand of hair
   And made his wife a gown.

12 The ram he had a great long tail
   Reached way down to hell,
   Every time he wagged the tail
   He rang that hotel bell.

13 This ram he had two horns, sir,
   And they were made of brass,
   One come out of po' ol' head
   And the other come out of his yup se doo-la lolly.

14 The man that butchered this ram
   Was a-scairt of his life,
   He sent to Philadelphy
   And got him a four-foot knife.

15 The man that butchered this ram, sir,
   Got drownded in the blood,
   The man that held the basin
   Got washed away in the flood.

16 The blood did run twenty-four mile, sir,
   (I'm sure it was no more).
   It turned an overshot mill, sir,
   That never was turned before.

17 His head was in the meat market,
   His tail was in the street,
   All the ladies come along
   Says, "Here's your market meat."

18 Took all the boys in our town
To roll away his bones,
Took all the girls in our town
To roll away his yup se doo-la lolly.

19 The man who owned this ram
Was considered very rich,
Or the man who told this story
Was a lyin' son of a yup se doo-la lolly.

THE LADY WHO LOVED A SWINE

e'b. No. 2590. Mrs. K. B. Jones, Houston, Texas, spring, 1939.

Moderately fast ♩.=104

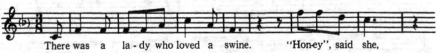

There was a la-dy who loved a swine. "Hon-ey", said she,

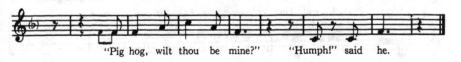

"Pig hog, wilt thou be mine?" "Humph!" said he.

1 There was a lady loved a swine.
"Honey," said she,
"Pig hog, wilt thou be mine?"
"Humph!" said he.

2 "I'll build thee a silver sty,
Honey," said she,
"And in it thou shalt lie."
"Humph!" said he.

3 "I'll pin it with a silver pin,
"Honey," said she,
"That thou may'st go out and in."
"Humph!" said he.

[107]

4 "Wilt thou have me now?" said she.
  "Honey," said she.
  "Speak or my heart will break."
  "Humph!" said he.

TOLL-A-WINKER

f'. No. 64. Gant family, Austin, Texas, 1934. See Hu, p. 275; JAFL, 4:269.

When ____ I was a lit-tle boy as fat as I could roll,

(whistle _____) When I was a lit-tle boy as

fat as I could roll, They put me on a box car, and there we had a show.

Toll-a - wink-er, toll - a - wink -er, tum - tol - ly- aye.

1 When I was a little boy as fat as I could roll, *(whistle)*
  When I was a little boy as fat as I could roll,
  They put me on a boxcar, and there we had a show.
  Toll-a-winker, toll-a-winker, tum-tolly-aye.

2 Long come Johnny and he passed me by, *(whistle)*
  Long come Johnny and he passed me by,
  His feet on the ground and his head in the sky.
  Toll-a-winker, toll-a-winker, tum-tolly-aye.

3 He bantered me for wrestle and I hopped, jumped, and run, *(whistle)*
  He bantered me for wrestle and I hopped, jumped, and run,
  Beat him at his game and shot him with a gun.
  Toll-a-winker, toll-a-winker, tum-tolly-aye.

4 Grabbed him by his feet and slung his head down, (*whistle*)
Grabbed him by his feet and slung his head down,
Gave him such a sling till I slung him over town.
Toll-a-winker, toll-a-winker, tum-tolly-aye.

5 The people all around saw the deed I done, (*whistle*)
The people all around saw the deed I done,
They sentenced me to ten thousand ton.
Toll-a-winker, toll-a-winker, tum-tolly-aye.

6 Had a little dog his name is Don, (*whistle*)
Had a little dog his name is Don,
His legs went to feet and his body went to tongue.
Toll-a-winker, toll-a-winker, tum-tolly-aye.

7 Have a little box about three feet square, (*whistle*)
Have a little box about three feet square,
When I go to travel I put him under there.
Toll-a-winker, toll-a-winker, tum-tolly-aye.

8 When I go to travel I travel like an ox, (*whistle*)
When I go to travel I travel like an ox,
And in my vest pocket I carry that box.
Toll-a-winker, toll-a-winker, tum-tolly-aye.

9 Had a little hen her color was fair, (*whistle*)
Had a little hen her color was fair,
Sat her on a bomb and she hatched me a hare.
Toll-a-winker, toll-a-winker, tum-tolly-aye.

10 The hare turned a horse about six foot high, (*whistle*)
The hare turned a horse about six foot high,
If a man beats this he'll have to tell a lie.
Toll-a-winker, toll-a-winker, tum-tolly-aye.

THE MARROWBONE ITCH *

*e. No. 1427. Acc. on guitar by Farmer Collett, sung
by Mike Brock, Middle Fork, Leslie County, Ky., 1937.*

*"My mother used to say that head lice, bedbugs, and the seven-year itch
were not a disgrace to have, but a disgrace to keep."*

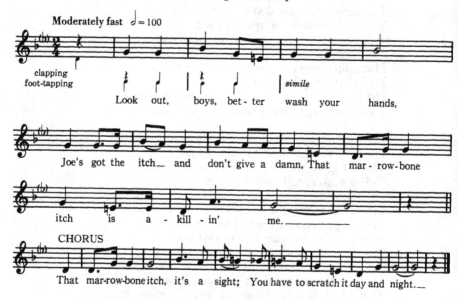

1 Look out, boys, better wash your hands,
  Joe's got the itch and don't give a damn,
  That Marrowbone itch is a-killin' me.

Chorus:
  That Marrowbone itch, it's a sight;
  You have to scratch it day and night.

2 There's poor old Eph, he's a-looking mighty blue,
  He's got the itch and Roberta have too.
  That Marrowbone itch is a-killin' me.

* Pronounced "Mar'bone eetch."

3 When you take the itch, your hands do crack,
   Judy has got it and so has Jack.
   That Marrowbone itch is a-killin' me.

4 When you go to Spruce Pine, better take you a cob,
   Billy's got the itch and so has Bob.
   That Marrowbone itch is a-killin' me.

   Shouted:
      Killin' me too, boys!

5 Itch is a-leavin' the Marrowbone Valley,
   Hiram's got it and so has Sally.
   That Marrowbone itch is a-killin' me.

OLD BLUE

*a*b. No. 671. Acc. on guitar and sung by Carl Roberts, Zweifel Ranch, Fort Spunky, Texas,
1935. Other stanzas from Hu, p. 201. See also Whi, p. 207.

1 I raised a dog and his name was Blue,
   And I betcha five dollars he's a good one, too.

   Chorus 1:
      Saying, "Come on, Blue, boo-hoo."

2 Shouldered my ax and I tooted my horn,
Gonna get me a possum in the new ground corn.

Chorus 1:
    Saying, "Come on, Blue, boo-hoo."

3 Old Blue treed, I went to see,
There sat the possum on a 'simmon tree. (*Chorus 1.*)

4 That possum clumb down on a swingin' limb,
Blue barked at the possum, possum growled at him. (*Chorus 1.*)

5 He grinned at me, I looked at him,
I shook him out, Blue took him in. (*Chorus 1.*)

6 Got that possum and I put him in a sack,
Next thing I knew I had him on my back. (*Chorus 1.*)

7 Baked that possum good and brown,
And I lays them sweet potatoes round and round.

Chorus 2:
    Saying, "Come on, Blue, you kin have some, too."

8 "Blue, what makes your eyes so red?"
"I've run them possums till I'm almost dead." (*Chorus 2.*)

9 When old Blue died, he died so hard
That he shook the ground in my back yard.

Chorus 3:
    Saying, "Go on, Blue, I'm comin', too."

10 Old Blue died, I laid him in the shade,
I dug his grave with a silver spade. (*Chorus 3.*)

11 I let him down with a golden chain,
Link by link slipped through my hand. (*Chorus 3.*)

12 There is only one thing that bothers my mind,
Blue went to heaven, left me behind. (*Chorus 3.*)

13 When I get there, first thing I'll do,
Grab me a horn and blow for old Blue. (*Chorus 3.*)

WUNST I HAD AN OLD GRAY MARE

a to *b*. No. 1483. Ella Sibert, Horse Creek, Clay County, Ky., 1937. See Sh, 2:326.

1 Wunst I had an old gray mare, (2)
And her back wore out and her belly bare.

Chorus:
      Taddle diddle dink dink, taddle diddle day;
      Taddle diddle dink dink, taddle diddle day.

2 Then I turned her down the creek,
Purpose of a little green grass to eat.

3 Then I took her darned old tracks,
And I found her in a mudhole flat of her back.

4 Then I feelding very stout,
Took her by the tail and I hoist her out.

5 Then I thought it was no sin,
I hoist up my knife and I skinned her skin.

[113]

6 Then I put it in some moose,
  Purpose of to make my winter's shoes.

7 Then I hung it in the loft;
  'Long come a rogue and stoled it off.

8 Darn the rogue that stoled it off;
  Left my toes all out to the frost.

HOG ROGUES ON THE HARRICANE

e♭. No. 1517. Theophilus G. Hoskins, Hyden, Ky., 1937.

"This is Tom Hardy and Lishe Morgan's hog song. There was some hog rogues down the river here, and they was accused of stealing hogs, and old Tom Morgan, he made that song. It was on some of our people, and he was our people, too; but he made the song. Some of them wanted to kill him over it, and some of them said, 'Let him go, he's all right,' said, 'He's a purty good feller.' I learned that when I was about five years old, and I'm fifty-eight now. That's been about fifty-three years ago, I guess."

Moderately fast, somewhat free ♩ = 72 *increasing to* 80 *at end of recording*

Oh, con - cern - ing of some gen - tle - men who lived down be - low,

They fol - lered hog - steal - in' wher - ev - er they did go.

Oh, some - times they had ba - con, and some - times none.

They mount - ed on their hors - es, and they shoul - dered up their guns.

1 Oh, concerning of some gentlemen who lived down below,
They follered hog-stealin' wherever they did go.
Oh, sometimes they had bacon, and sometimes none.
They mounted on their horses, and they shouldered up their guns.

2 Straightway to the Harricane,* straightway they did steer,
To skeer up the wild hogs and run out the deer.
Oh, when they got there they listened awhile,
Looking at each other, beginning to smile.

3 They said, "It's the old spotted sow and the blue listed boar,
The very same hogs we fought † here before."
Oh, the old spotted creature was a-lying in her bed,
She heard every word the damned villyans said.

4 Oh, the old spotted sow made a leap for to run,
She soon was stopped by the cracking of a gun.
They blew for old Trimble Foot very loud and shrill,
He overtook the boar at the foot of the hill.

5 If you don't believe me, they're guilty of a heap,
They stole nine head of Wash Morgan's sheep.
You remember last Wednesday before,
From old Billy Sachs took a half a dozen more.

6 Oh, trouble and vexation wherever you may be,
Trouble and vexation wherever you shall see.
Oh, the whips begin to crack and the pigs begin to squeal,
Up come Bob and Stokes a-walking on their heels.

* Harricane or Hurricane Creek, Leslie County, Kentucky.
† Pronounced to rhyme with "spout."

COD LIVER ILE

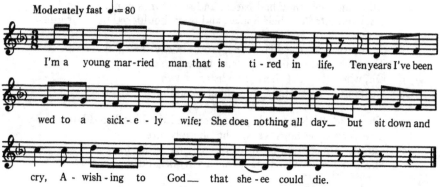

♭. No. 1770. Acc. on guitar and sung by Burl Ives, New York City, 1938. See Gr, p. 316.

Moderately fast ♩.=80

I'm a young mar-ried man that is ti-red in life, Ten years I've been wed to a sick-e-ly wife; She does nothing all day— but sit down and cry, A-wish-ing to God— that she-ee could die.

1 I'm a young married man that is tired in life,
Ten years I've been wed to a sickly wife;
She does nothing all day but sit down and cry,
A-wishing to God that she could die.

2 A friend of me own came to see me one day
And said that me wife was a-fadin' away.
He afterwards told me that she would get strong
If I got her a bottle from Doctor Dearjohn.

3 I bought her one bottle, 'twas just for to try,
And the way that she drank it you'd swear she was dry;
I bought her another which vanished the same,
Till I think she's got cod liver ile on the brain.

Chorus:
"Oh, doctor, oh, doctor, oh, dear Doctor John,
Your cod liver ile is so pure and so strong
I'm afraid to me life I'll go down in the sile
If me wife don't quit drinking your cod liver ile."

4 She likes it so much that there is no doubt
Me wife she got fat and terrible stout,
And when she got stout, of course, she got strong,
And then I got jealous of Doctor Dearjohn. (*Chorus.*)

[116]

5 Me house it resembles a big doctor's shop
With bottles and bottles and bottles on top,
And then in the morning when the kettle does bile
I'll swear it be singing of cod liver ile. (*Chorus.*)

TOM BOLYN

f. No. 1438. Eliza Pace, Hyden, Ky., 1937. Other stanzas from Fl.1, p. 177. See also Sh, 2:202; for exhaustive discussion, Ga.1, 211; Be, p. 501.

Moderately fast, somewhat free ♩.= 96

Tom Bo - lyn was Scotch-man born, His shoes wore out and his stock-ings were torn, The calf of his leg come down to his shin, "I'm a hell of a fell-low," says Tom Bo - lyn.

1 Tom Bolyn was Scotchman born,
His shoes wore out and his stockings were torn,
The calf of his leg come down to his shin.
"I'm a hell of a fellow," says Tom Bolyn.

2 Tom Bolyn had no boots to wear,
He bought him a goatskin to make him a pair,
The woolly side out and the skinny side in.
"Cool in the summer," says Tom Bolyn.

3 Tom Bolyn bought him an old gray mare,
Her sides was sore, her feets was bare;
Away he went through thick and thin.
"I'm going a-courting," says Tom Bolyn.

4 He rode over to a Dutchman's hall,
There he got down amongst them all—
"Come in, come in, I bid you come in."
"I've come here a-courting," says Tom Bolyn.

5 "Come in, come in, you welcome guest,
Take which of my daughters that you like best."
"I'll take one for love and the other for kin,
I'll marry them both," says Tom Bolyn.

6 After the wedding we must have a dinner;
They had nothing to eat that was fit for a sinner,
Neither fish, flesh, food, nor no such a thing—
"It's a hell of a dinner," said Tom Bolyn.

7 And after the dinner, we must have a bed;
The floor it was swept and the straw it was spread;
The blankets was short and besides very thin,
"Stick close to my back," said Tom Bolyn.

8 But his wife's mother said the very next day,
"You will have to get another place to stay—
I can't lie awake and hear you snore;
You can't stay in my house any more."

9 Tom Bolyn got into a hollow tree,
And very contented seemed to be;
The wind did blow and the rain beat in.
"This is better than no house," said Tom Bolyn.

10 Tom Bolyn, his wife and wife's mother,
They all went over the bridge together,
The bridge it broke, they all went in,
"First to the bottom," said Tom Bolyn.

*　　*　　*

"A man staked his old bell cow in the pasture. A full-grown mosquito came along and et the cow, then started ringing the bell for the calf."

"*Back in Tennessee where I learned the songs I sing, the singin' bees were just courtin' bees. The boys and girls would meet 'round at the neighbors' houses and sing in between the courtin'. The one who knew the most songs was always the most popular.*"   —MRS. MINTA MORGAN.

THE BACHELOR'S LAY

c′ to *b*. No. 1337. Mrs. Minta Morgan, Bells, Texas, 1937. See *JAFL*, 25:281; Cox, p. 468; Be, p. 263.

Moderately fast ♩. = 84

Stanzas 1,2,3,6

As I___ was travel-ling one morn-ing in May,   I heard an old

bache-lor be - gin-ning a lay;   "Oh, I can't tell why the

rea-son may be That none of those girls won't mar - ry me.

Stanzas 7,8,9,10

"I've sailed on the main and I've fol - lowed the coast,   No con-quest in

love can I hon - est - ly boast;   And I can't tell why the

rea-son may be That none of those girls won't mar - ry me."

1 As I was traveling one morning in May,
   I heard an old bachelor beginning a lay:
   "Oh, I can't tell why the reason may be
   That none of those girls won't marry me.

2 "I've courted the rich and I've courted the poor,
   I've often been snubbed at the meetinghouse door,
   And I can't tell why the reason can be
   That none of those girls won't marry me.

3 "I've offered them silver, I've offered them gold,
   And many fine stories to them I have told,
   But gold and silver won't do, you now see,
   For none of the girls have married with me.

4 "Nine good horses I've rode to death,
   I've rode them till they had no breath;
   And five new saddles wore out to the tree,
   Yet none of the girls have married with me.

5 "I've been through the mountains, I've traversed the plains;
   I courted the misses, I've courted the dames;
   And I can't tell why the reason may be
   That none of those girls won't marry me.

6 "I've traveled by land and sailed by sea,
   Ten thousands of miles those girls to see,
   And I can't tell why the reason can be
   That none of those girls won't marry me.

7 "I've sailed on the main and I've followed the coast,
   No conquest in love can I honestly boast;
   And I can't tell why the reason may be
   That none of those girls won't marry me.

8 "I've asked them to tell me what stood in the way;
   They've all of them answered, 'I'd rather not say';
   And I can't tell why the reason may be
   That none of those girls won't marry me."

                    *   *   *

9 I thought to myself that while passing along
   I'd make a reply to the bachelor's song:
   "Oh, sir, I can tell you just what you must do
   If you want a young lady to marry you.

10 "Go shave off your whiskers and powder your hair,
   Go dress yourself up with the greatest of care,
   Put on a broadsword and bright buckles, too,
   If you want a young lady to marry you."

11 Now this is the hook and the catch of a bachelor's life,
   Cheer up, young man, and get you a wife,
   Make no delay, by which you get none,
   For this is the way the old bachelor done.

KATY DOREY

c'. No. 828. Aunt Molly Jackson, New York City,
1935. See Sh, 2:119; Ga.2, p. 393.

"*The larger children would sing these little funny songs and us smaller children would hear 'em, and we'd get together and sing 'em and make a big laugh out of 'em. This particular Sunday we was all down under a big shade tree swingin' on the limb and a-singin' one.*

"*My grandfather hollered over to my father and said what was he a-doin' settin' over there not correctin' his children and them a-singin' sich rough songs as that. And my father he hollered back over to my grandfather and he said, 'If that's all that you've got to do,' he says, 'is to be out,' he says, 'a-payin' attention,' he says, 'to what babies and children says,' he says; 'if you don't want these little children,' says, 'to sing these things and do these things,' says, 'correct your children that's much larger and older than them an' stop them singin' these songs before them and then,' says, 'I'll ashore you,' says, 'that my babies and Rance Rollins's babies won't be a-singin' these songs they learned from the bigger kids,' he says.*"

—AUNT MOLLY JACKSON.

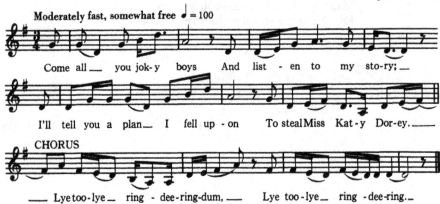

Moderately fast, somewhat free ♩ = 100

Come all — you jok-y boys And list-en to my sto-ry; —

I'll tell you a plan — I fell up-on To steal Miss Kat-y Dor-ey. —

CHORUS

— Lye too-lye — ring-dee-ring-dum, — Lye too-lye — ring-dee-ring. —

1 Come all you joky boys
  And listen to my story;
  I'll tell you a plan I fell upon
  To steal Miss Katy Dorey.*

* In other versions, "Kittie Morey," or "Katy Morey."

[122]

Chorus:
>   Lye too-lye ring-dee-ring-dum,
>   Lye too-lye ring-dee-ring.

2 I went down to Katy's house,
   Just like a clever feller;
   I told her that the peaches and plums
   Was getting ripe and meller.

3 I told her that I suited her,
   I was not trying to flatter;
   I told her that her sister Sal
   Knowed nothing of the matter.

4 I did not have to ask her twice,
   She put on her best bonnet.
   My heart was beating very fast,
   As 'cross the fields we ran it.

5 "It's now we're here alone,
   And no one knows the matter;
   It's you must die or else comply,
   For I've no time to flatter."

6 Katy seemed quite pleased, my hand she squeezed:
   "There's but one thing I fear, sir,
   Is that my father may come this way,
   And he would find us here, sir.

7 "But if you'll climb the highest tree,
   That rises in this bower,
   And if my father keeps away,
   We'll spend a happy hour."

8 Katy stood at the foot of the tree,
   Until I had ascended:
   "It's you may get down the way you got up,
   For now your fun is ended."

[123]

9 "You look just like an owl," she said,
"Your company I shun, sir;
You may eat your plums and suck the stones,
For I am going to run, sir."

10 Away Katy heeled it over the plain,
And left me here distracted;
I ripped, I swore, my shirt I tore,
To think how I had acted.

11 About three months from that day
Kate and I got married.
And about three months after that
A lovely son she carried.

12 It's time to hush up foolish song,
It's time to quit all rhyming;
But ever' time this baby squalls,
Begod, I think of climbing.

JOHNNY McCARDNER

a. No. 1534. Tune and part of text from Hazel Hudson, Hazard, Ky. Other stanzas from No. 1698 and from Cox, p. 511; Be, p. 248.

Fast ♩ = 108

Last Sa-tur-day night I called at the house And in-to the win-dow I crept like a mouse; I o-pened the door and I made it straight-way Right in-to the room where the girls all stay—And it's hard times.

1 Last Saturday night I called at the house
   And into the window I crept like a mouse;
   I opened the door and I made it straightway
   Right into the room where the girls all stay—
   And it's hard times.

2 Such a laughing and chattering as we did keep,
   We woke the old widow up out of her sleep,
   "O daughter, O daughter, O daughter," said she,
   "What impudent scoundrel is this before me?"
   And it's hard times.

3 "O widow, O widow, you'd better keep calm *
   Until you find out just who I am;
   It's Johnny McCardner, I go by the name,
   A-courting your daughter for the purpose I came"—
   And it's hard times.

4 "Oh, you are so old, and she is so young,
   You will get suited and she will get stung;
   You are so old and she is so young—"
   She up with the broomstick and at me she come—
   And it's hard times.

5 Out of the window in the ice and the snow,
   I mounted my horse and away I did go;
   The blood it run down my shins in great grooves,
   For I never had been beaten with a broomstick before—
   And it's hard times.

6 Come all ye young men, take warning from me,
   Be careful when girls you go for to see;
   Or else like me you'll meet with your doom,
   Get beat like the devil and flogged with the broom—
   And it's hard times.

* Pronounced to rhyme with "dam."

LOLLY TOO-DUM

f♯. No. 1384. Abner Boggs, Harlan County, Ky., 1937.
Other stanzas from Mrs. Emma Dusenberry, Mena, Ark.
See Hu, p. 280; Sh, 2:159; Be, p. 266.

One familiar form of folk song carries forward its theme by question and reply of two actors, usually a boy and a girl—a form often used a generation ago in courting bees, neighborhood concerts and on the amateur stage. In America such songs were sometimes called "answer-back" songs. A popular duet of this type began:

TOMMY: *Pretty, pretty Polly Hopkins, howdy do, howdy do?*
POLLY: *I'm none the better, Tommy Tompkins, for seeing you, for seeing you.*

Moderately fast ♩ = 69

As I went out one morn-ing to breathe the morn-ing air,

Lol-ly too-dum, too-dum, lol-ly too-dum day.

As I went out one morn-ing to breathe the morn-ing air,

I heard a dear old mo-ther say-ing, "O my daugh-ter fair,"

Lol-ly too-dum, too-dum, lol-ly too-dum day.

[126]

1 As I went out one morning to breathe the morning air,
  Lolly too-dum, too-dum, lolly too-dum day.
  As I went out one morning to breathe the morning air,
  I heard a dear old mother saying, "O my daughter fair,"
  Lolly too-dum, too-dum, lolly too-dum day.

2 "You better go wash them dishes, and hush your flattering tongue,
  Lolly too-dum, too-dum, lolly too-dum day.
  You better go wash them dishes, and hush your flattering tongue;
  You know you want to marry, and that you are too young,"
  Lolly too-dum, too-dum, lolly too-dum day.

3 "Oh, pity my condition just as you would your own,
  For fourteen long years I've lived all alone."

4 "Supposing I was willing, where would you get your man?"
  "Why, Lordy mercy, Mammy, I've picked out handsome Sam."

5 "Supposing he would slight you, just as you done him before?"
  "Why, Lordy mercy, Mammy, I could marry forty more."

6 "There's peddlers and tinkers and boys from the plow,
  Oh, Lordy mercy, Mammy, the fit comes on me now."

7 "Oh, now she is married and well for to do,
  Six married daughters, now I'm on the market too."

8 "Why, Lord sakes, Mammy, it's who would marry you?
  There's no man alive would want a wife as old as you."

9 "There's doctors and lawyers, and men of all degree,
  And some wants to marry, and some will marry me."

10 "Now I am married, it's well for to be,
  Ha, ha, ha, you jolly girls, the fit is off of me!"

WHERE HAVE YOU BEEN, MY GOOD OLD MAN? *

d'. No. 1546. Hazel Hudson, Hazard, Ky., 1937. See Sh, 2:338.

Moderately fast ♩ = 108

So— where have you been, my good old man? Oh,— where have you been, my hon-ey-lov- ey dove?— So where have you been,my good old man? You're the best old man— in the world. Been to the store.

1 WOMAN: So where have you been, my good old man?
　　　　　Oh, where have you been, my honey-lovey dove?
　　　　　So where have you been, my good old man?
　　　　　You're the best old man in the world.
　MAN: Been to the store.

2 WOMAN: So what did you git me, my good old man?
　　　　　Oh, what did you git me, my honey-lovey dove?
　　　　　So what did you git me, my good old man?
　　　　　You're the best old man in the world.
　MAN: Got you a dress.

3 WOMAN: How much did it cost, my good old man? etc.
　MAN: Cost five dollars.

4 WOMAN: Ain't you 'fraid it'll break you up? etc.
　MAN: Don't care if it do.

5 WOMAN: What do you want for your supper? etc.
　MAN: Five bushels of eggs.

6 WOMAN: Ain't you 'fraid it'll kill you? etc.
　MAN: Don't care if it do.

* As arranged by Amadeo de Phillipi this melody was used as the theme of the American School of the Air Series on Folk Music, 1939–40.

7 WOMAN: Where you want to be buried? etc.
  MAN: In the chimney corner.

8 WOMAN: Ain't you 'fraid of snuffin' ashes? etc.
  MAN: Don't care if I do,
          So long as I'm near you.

JENNIE JENKINS

*a*b. No. 1345. Acc. on guitar and mandolin and sung by Mr. and Mrs. E. C. Ball, Rugby, Va., 1937. See Sh, 2:371; Fl.1, pp. 164 ff.

Moderately fast ♩ = 104

1 MAN: Will you wear white, O my dear, O my dear?
          Oh, will you wear white, Jennie Jenkins?
  WOMAN: I won't wear white,
          For the color's too bright,
          I'll buy me a fol-de-roldy-tildy-toldy, seek-a-double,
          use-a-cause-a-roll-the-find-me.
  MAN: Roll, Jennie Jenkins, roll.

2 MAN: Will you wear blue, my dear, O my dear?
        Oh, will you wear blue, Jennie Jenkins?
  WOMAN: I won't wear blue,
        The color's too true, etc.

3 MAN: Will you wear red, my dear, O my dear?
        Oh, will you wear red, Jennie Jenkins?
  WOMAN: I won't wear red,
        It's the color of my head, etc.

4 MAN: Will you wear black, my dear, O my dear?
        Oh, will you wear black, Jennie Jenkins?
  WOMAN: I won't wear black,
        It's the color of my back, etc.

5 MAN: Will you wear purple, my dear, O my dear?
        Oh, will you wear purple, Jennie Jenkins?
  WOMAN: I won't wear purple,
        It's the color of a turkle, etc.

6 MAN: Will you wear green, my dear, O my dear?
        Oh, will you wear green, Jennie Jenkins?
  WOMAN: I won't wear green,
        For it's a shame to be seen, etc.

*   *   *

"Women don't like these songs about 'Don't believe in a woman, you're lost if you do.' Women don't like such songs because they cause people to lose confidence in women. I mind me of another they sing, 'When I Was Single'; and that song is another song against the morals of women, and no woman don't like that song.

"Men don't like for women to sing songs like—'They're confined and slaved by their husbands.' They think that causes their women to lose confidence in them. Of course, they don't always get mad; it's owin' to what place they're at. Say, if they're at a party or a dance and it's played, they just pretend to ignore it. Like the song, 'Come All You Fair and Tender Ladies, Be Careful How You Court Young Men.' A lot of times

a woman would be singing that and they'd say, 'Oh, sing something else, for there's no truth in that.' Songs that women makes up about men, about their husbands and about their sweethearts and things like that, they think that we've given them the wrong kind of a deal and it's not justice and it's not right and they protest and everly have as far back as I can remember."

—AUNT MOLLY JACKSON.

MARRIED ME A WIFE

e'. No. 648. Acc. on guitar and sung by Gant family, Austin, Texas, 1936.

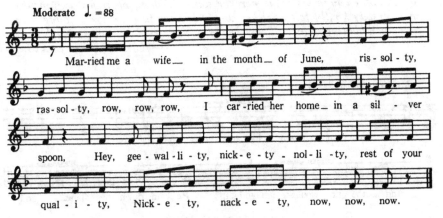

1   Married me a wife in the month of June,
    Rissolty, rassolty, row, row, row,
    I carried her home in a silver spoon,
    Hey, gee-wallity, nickety-nollity, rest of your quality,
    Nickety, nackety, now, now, now.

2   She combed her hair but once a week,
    She says that combs are all too cheap.

3   She sweeps the floor but once a year,
    She says that brooms are all too dear.

4   She churns her milk in the old man's boot,
    For the sake of a dasher she uses her foot.

5   The butter is made of old grizzly gray,
    The milk takes legs and walks away.

[131]

OLD SHOES AND LEGGIN'S

f. No. 1355. Uncle Alex Dunsford, Galax, Va., 1937.
Other stanzas from Angie Clark, Mullins, S.C. See Sh.2,
93; Cox, p. 492; Be, p. 264.

*"He was an old rich man that had plenty of money and plenty of gold
and silver, and this girl's mother wanted her to be nice to him and try to
keer fer him because he was a wealthy man; and the girl—he simply didn't
appeal to her, and naturally she didn't want him at any cost.*

*"In the mountains you'd sing this song any time that the mother begin
to talk to the daughters about marryin' some old man, when probably maybe
they already kindly felt like they was in love or fancyin' some young man
in the neighboring county. Then they sang it as a kind of protest song."*

—Aunt Molly Jackson.

1 A man that was old came a-courtin' one day
   And the girls wouldn't have him;
   He came down the lane and walked on a cane,
   With his old shoes on and his leggin's.

2 Mamma told me to open the door,
   I shan't have him;
   I opened the door and shoved him to the floor,
   With his old shoes on and his leggin's.

[132]

3 My mother, she told me to give him a chair,
  For the girls wouldn't have him;
  I gave him a chair and he looked mighty quare,
  With his old shoes on and his leggin's.

4 My mother she told me to hang up his hat,
  Oh, but I wouldn't have him!
  I hung up his hat and he kicked at the cat,
  With his old shoes on and his leggin's.

5 My mother she told me to give him some meat,
  Oh, but I wouldn't have him!
  I gave him some meat and oh, how he did eat,
  With his old shoes on and his leggin's.

6 Mamma told me to bake him a pie,
  Oh, but I wouldn't have him!
  I baked him a pie and he swore he ate a fly,
  With his old shoes on and his leggin's.

7 My mother she told me to give him a hoe,
  Oh, but I wouldn't have him!
  I gave him a hoe and he jumped Jim Crow,
  With his old shoes on and his leggin's.

8 Mamma told me to bake him a cake,
  Oh, but I wouldn't have him!
  I baked him a cake and he swore he ate a snake,
  With his old shoes on and his leggin's.

9 My mother she told me to give him a saw,
  Oh, but I wouldn't have him!
  I gave him a saw and he played "Rye Straw,"
  With his old shoes on and his leggin's.

10 My mother she told me to put him to bed,
   Oh, but I wouldn't have him!
   I put him to bed and he stood on his head,
   With his old shoes on and his leggin's.

11 Mamma told me to saddle his horse,
Oh, but I wouldn't have him!
Saddled his horse and he went North,
With his old shoes on and his leggin's.

12 My mother she told me to send him away,
For the girls wouldn't have him;
I sent him away and he left us to stay,
With his old shoes on and his leggin's.

BLUE BOTTLE

e'. No. 1359. Acc. on guitar and sung by Mrs. Carlos
Gallimore, Galax, Va., 1937. See Sh, 1:341; Hu, p. 174.

Moderately fast ♩=96

When I was a bach-e-lor, brisk and young,

Court-ed a la-dy with a flat-ter-ing tongue;

Kiss-es I gave her were a hun-dred and ten.

I promised to mar-ry, but I did-n't tell her when,

I promised to mar-ry, but I did-n't tell her when.

1 When I was a bachelor, brisk and young,
  Courted a lady with a flattering tongue;
  Kisses I gave her were a hundred and ten.
  I promised to marry, but I didn't tell her when,
  I promised to marry, but I didn't tell her when.

2 Monday morning I married me a wife,
  Thinking I'd live a happier life.
  Fiddlin' and dancin' and all the fine plays,
  How happy we were in all those days,
  How happy we were in all those days!

3 Tuesday morning I carried her home,
  I thought to my soul I had a wife of my own.
  She curled her nose and scold and scold;
  If ever I heard the like before. (2)

4 Wednesday morning I went to the wood,
  Thinkin' to my soul she would never be good,
  Cut me a lash where the willows grow green,
  Think she's the toughest that ever I seen. (2)

5 Thursday morning I lashed her well,
  Cuffed her more than tongue can tell;
  "If this is the best that you're goin' to do,
  The devil may have you tomorrow before two." (2)

6 Friday morning at break of day
  On her death pillow she was scolding away;
  Ruffets and the Cuffets and the little devils came,
  And carried her away to the home of the same. (2)

7 Saturday morning as I lay alone,
  I had no wife, no bride of my home;
  My blue bottle is my best friend,
  My week's sorrow has now an end. (2)

DEVILISH MARY

e. No. 18. Jesse Stafford, Crowley, La., 1934. Other stanzas from Mrs. S. P. Griffin, Newberry, Fla. See Sh, 2:200.

"There was a woman that we called her 'Puss Erving', had a son named Dock, and we called him 'Puss's Dock.' He and his wife lived in adjoinin' rooms with me. These mining shacks were built with four rooms on Four Mile Creek, and two families lived in these houses with a bedroom and kitchen for each family.

"He got to singin' against her one mornin', and he had the blues because he was forty-one dollars in debt, and he was a-making his song. He was settin' with the baby—they just had one child; they was young people—he was a-settin' by the stove and a-nussin' the baby and he was a-singin':

> *"'Oh, I'm forty-one dollars in debt*
> *To the old Durell Coal Company;*
> *I'm going back to Rock Holt*
> *And leave old Nettie standin' in the mud up to her knees.'*

That was his wife. She started to sing back at him,

> *"'Oh, yes, I'm going back to Rock Holt, Kentucky,*
> *And I'll swing those pretty boys around and around.'*

He throwed the baby down on the bed and smacked her plumb across the house, and they got into a fight over that; and me and Jim Stewart we run in, and I pulled him one way and he pulled her another, and we stopped the fight. But when we run in he had her right by the hair pullin' her right down. They'd very often get to singin' against each other and get mad and get into a fight that way." —Aunt Molly Jackson.

Moderately fast ♩ = 126

Stanza 1

I went up to Lon-don Town To court a fair young la - dy; I in - quired a - bout her name And they

[136]

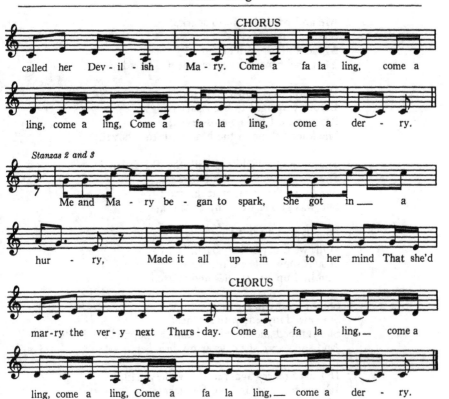

1 I went up to London Town
To court a fair young lady;
I inquired about her name
And they called her Devilish Mary.

Chorus:
Come a fa la ling, come a ling, come a ling,
Come a fa la ling, come a derry.

[137]

2 Me and Mary began to spark,
   She got in a hurry,
   Made it all up into her mind
   That she'd marry the very next Thursday.

3 We hadn't been married but about two weeks
   Before we ought to been parted;
   Every time I looked cross-eyed,
   She knocked me in the head with the shovel.

4 She washed my clothes with the old soapsuds,
   She filled my bath with switches,
   She let me know right at the start
   She was gonna wear my britches.

5 One day I said to Mary,
   "Oh, we'd better be parted."
   Just as soon as I said the word,
   Bundled up her clothes and started.

6 She filled my heart with sadness,
   She sewed my side with stitches,
   She jumped and she kicked and she popped her heels,
   And she swore she'd wear my britches.

7 If I ever marry again in this wide world,
   It'll be for love, and not for riches;
   Marry a little girl about two feet high
   So she can't wear the britches.

DO COME BACK AGAIN

e′. No. 1362. Mrs. W. P. Davis, Galax, Va., 1937. See
Sh, 2:96 ff.

*"This is a mighty sorrowful soundin' song," said Mrs. Alice Williams
of Ashland, Kentucky, "but I like it. It's the one that Canas used to sing
when he came over the mountain a-courtin' me. He made it sound as mournful as he could so's to make me pity him."*

"Did you pity him?"

"Well, I reckon so; I been married to him thirty year."

Moderate ♩ = 138

Once I knew a lit-tle girl, and I loved her as__ my__ life;

Free - ly would I have giv-en her my hand and my heart

To__ have made__ her my__ wife.

1 Once I knew a little girl, and I loved her as my life;
  Freely would I have given her my hand and my heart
  To have made her my wife.

2 I took her by the hand and I led her to the door,
  I embraced her in my arms and I asked her once more,
  Oh, I asked her once more.

3 She looked up in my face with scorn and disdain,
  And the answer that she gave me was, "You can't come back again,
  No, you can't come back again."

4 I stayed away six weeks; this gave her cause to complain,
And she wrote me a letter saying, "Do come back again,
Oh, do come back again!"

5 I wrote her an answer, it was just to let her know
That young men often venture where they ought not to go,
Where they ought not to go.

6 Come, all ye young men, take warning by me:
Never place your affections on a green growing tree,
On a green growing tree.

7 The leaves they will wilt, and the roots they will decay,
And the beauty of a fair young maid will soon fade away,
Oh, will soon fade away.

MY OLD TRUE LOVE

f'♯. No. 1341. Mrs. Gladys Helen Davis and Mrs.
Flossie Ellen Evans, Galax, Va., 1937. See Sh, 2:113 ff.;
Cox, p. 413.

*"Sometimes people do kill themselves for love, of course. I remember
one time Big John told the girl he was engaged to that he was a-goin' over
to _____ to get whisky. Now she knew he had a child by another woman
over there, and she thought that he was a-goin' to see her. So before he
started out, she sat down in his lap and grabbed his pistol and throwed it in
her breast. When it shot, she jumped so her head nearly touched the ceiling.
Big John never got over it."* —AUNT MOLLY JACKSON.

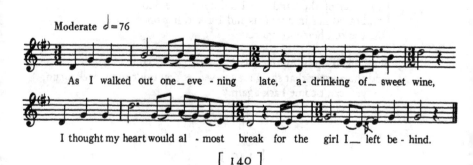

Moderate ♩=76

As I walked out one _ eve - ning late, a - drink-ing of _ sweet wine,

I thought my heart would al - most break for the girl I _ left be - hind.

[140]

1 As I walked out one evening late, a-drinking of sweet wine,
  I thought my heart would almost break for the girl I left behind.

2 Farewell, farewell, my old true love, farewell, farewell for a while;
  I go away, I come again, if it be ten thousand miles.

3 Ten thousand miles, my old true love, I hope that never will be;
  For the parting with you, my old true love, will be the death of me.

4 Weep not for me, my old true love, though far from home I be;
  I flatter myself I never shall need for friends to comfort me.

5 I would to God I never been born, or died when I was young,
  Or never had seen your rosy red cheeks, or heard your flattering tongue.

6 When I forsake you, my old true love, the rocks shall meet the sun;
  The fire shall freeze like ice, my dear, the raging sea shall burn.

7 Oh, who will shoe your feet, my dear, or who will glove your hand,
  Or who will kiss your rosy red lips when I am in a foreign land?

8 My father will shoe my feet, my dear, my mother will glove my hand,
  My rosy red lips will never be kissed till you return again.

FARE YE WELL, MY DARLIN'

*d' to d'♭. No. 1302. Mrs. Minnie Floyd, Murrells Inlet,
S.C., 1937. Text rearranged. See Co, p. 215; Be, p. 380.*

*"I went back to Kentucky in 1934 and met this girl named Anna. I asked
her if she'd ever gotten married and she said, No. Since her sweetheart was
killed in the World War, she never could find no one no more that she could
really keer for."*

Moderately slow ♩=88

So fare ye well, my darl - in', so fare ye well, my dear,

Don't_ grieve for my long ab - sence, while I am pres - ent here.

Since it is _ my mis - for - tune a sol - dier for to be,

Oh, try to live con - tent - ed and do _ not grieve for me.

1 So fare ye well, my darlin', so fare ye well, my dear,
   Don't grieve for my long absence, while I am present here.
   Since it is my misfortune a soldier for to be,
   Oh, try to live contented and do not grieve for me.

2 She wrung her lily-white hands and so mournful she did cry,
   "You've enlisted as a soldier and in the war you'll die.
   In the battle you'll be wounded and in the center be slain;
   It'll burst my heart asunder if I'll never see you again."

[142]

3 "I'm going away tomorrow to tarry for a while,
   So far from my dear darling, it's about five hundred mile,
   I hope the time is comin' that I and you shall meet,
   With words and looks or kisses we will each other greet."

4 Where the cannons are loudly roaring, and bullets by showers fall,
   And drums and fifes are beating to drown the wounded man's call,
   Stand steady by your captain, let bombs and grapeshot fly,
   Trust in God, your Saviour, but keep your powder dry.

I'VE RAMBLED THIS COUNTRY BOTH EARLYE AND LATE

f♯. No. 1596. James Mullins, Morgan County, Ky., 1939. See Cr, p. 94; Be, p. 194.

I've ram-bled this coun-try both ear-lye__ and late,
Hard was my for-tune and sad__ was my__ fate:
I came un-to my love's door ex-pect-ing to get in;
In-stead of see-ing pleas-ure, my trou-bles just be-gin.

1 I've rambled this country both earlye and late,
  Hard was my fortune and sad was my fate:
  I came unto my love's door expecting to get in;
  Instead of seeing pleasure, my troubles just begin.

[143]

2 I stood there one hour as patient as Job,
  Calling to Pretty Polly, "Come open the door."
  I saw another man enjoying of my room,
  I walked away by the light of the moon.

3 I took to my heels just as hard as I could go,
  I rambled way down in the far shady grove,
  And there I set down with a bottle in my hand,
  Drinking of brandy and thinking of that man.

4 So earlye next morning Pretty Polly passed me by
  With her red rosy cheeks and her black sparkling eyes;
  Her eyes they were so black and her hair were of the same,
  I'm wounded in my heart: did you ever feel that pain?

5 I wish I were a fisherman on yon riverside,
  Pretty Polly my object come floating down the tide;
  I'd throw my net around her, I'd bring her to the shore,
  And have Pretty Polly to weep for no more.

6 Green grows the laurel and so does the rue,
  Sugar is sweet, but not like you;
  And since it is no better, I'm glad it is no worse,
  Brandy in my bottle and money in my purse.

EAST VIRGINIA

a^b. No. 1601. Acc. on banjo and sung by Walter Williams, Salyersville, Ky., 1937. See Sh, 2:232.

"*Lots of young men would take their banjos along when they was courtin', but they was others that was too bashful. They was good banjo players you could set down under the shade of an apple tree or by the side of a barn by themselves and they could play wonderfully; but to put 'em before people, they was shy and ashamed and they couldn't play nothin'.*"

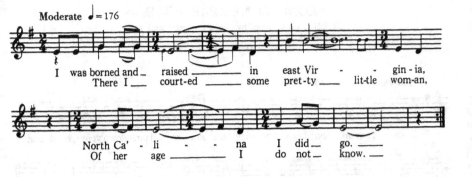

Moderate ♩ = 176

I was borned and raised in east Vir - gin - ia,
There I court-ed some pret-ty lit-tle wom-an,

North Ca' - li - na I did go.
Of her age I do not know.

1 I was borned and raised in east Virginia,
North Ca'lina I did go.
There I courted some pretty little woman,
Of her age I do not know.

2 Well, her eyes of a dark brown color,
Oh, her cheeks of a rosy red;
On her breast were square white lilies
To show the tears that she had shed.

3 On her feet she wears little slippers,
On her hair she wears a bow;
Oh, the way I love that brown-eyed darling,
Nobody on earth shall never know.

4 For when I'm asleep I'm dreaming of you,
When I'm awake I see no rest;
Moments seem to me like hours,
With ache and pain all through my breast.

5 I've got a wife and two little babies,
All at home, they're all at home.
Oh, the section boss paid me forty-two dollars,
All in gold, sir, all in gold.

[145]

LONG LONESOME ROAD

e'b. No. 1368. Acc. by the Bogtrotters and sung by
Fields Ward, Galax, Va., 1937. See Od.2, p. 46; Sc.1,
p. 73. (See also "Look Down That Lonesome Road.")

Oh,— look up and down that long, lonesome road, Hang down your head and cry, —— my love,— Hang down your— head and — cry.

1 Oh, look up and down that long, lonesome road,
   Hang down your head and cry, my love,
   Hang down your head and cry.

2 Oh, I wish to the Lord I had never been born,
   Or died when I was a baby, my love,
   Or died when I was a baby.

3 No, I wouldn't be here eatin' this cold corn bread,
   Or soppin' in this salty gravy, my love,
   Or soppin' in this salty gravy.

4 You caused me to weep, you caused me to mourn,
   You caused me to leave my home, my love,
   You caused me to leave my home.

5 I'll never hold those red rosy cheeks
   Or hear that flattering tongue, my love,
   Or hear that flattering tongue.

6 Oh, I wish I had some pretty little girl
   To tell my secrets to, my love,
   To tell my secrets to.

7 This little girl I'm goin' with,
   Tells everything I do, my love,
   Tells everything I do.

8 If you don't quit those rough, rowdy ways,
   Goin' be in some county jail, some day,
   Goin' be in some county jail.

9 Oh, look up and down that long, lonesome road,
   Hang down your head and cry, my love,
   Hang down your head and cry.

"Talkin' about brogans, they was a lasty shoe and a cheap shoe. The first pair I ever had I borrowed from my mammy because my first boy friend had asked me to go to church and I was ashamed to go without shoes. These old brogans was patched up with ground hog's hide because his hide was awful strong, strong enough for shoestrings. When I walked into the church house with my sweetheart, one of the Bowlins, I got the ring of the preacher's voice, and it was my daddy. My daddy was set against the whole Bowlin race, and I knew he'd kill me if he found me with Alf. He had done already said, 'I'll kill my child and bury her before I'll let her blood be mixed with a Bowlin's.' So when I heard my daddy's voice, I took off those old patched brogans and ran all the way home in my bare feet."

LITTLE BONNY

*d'. No. 1370. Acc. on guitar and sung by Fields Ward,
Galax, Va., 1937.*

A modern tune of the kind that can be easily accompanied with a couple of chords on a guitar, it is likely to be heard anywhere there is mountain music—over the radio and on "hill-billy" records. "Long Lonesome Road" belongs to the same category.*

Moderate ♩.=69

HORUS: Good - bye, lit - tle Bon-ny, good - bye, _____ Good-bye, lit - tle
TANZA: I asked your _ mam-ma for _ you; _____ I asked your _

Bon-ny, good - bye. _____ I'll see you a - gain, but the
pa - pa, _ too. _____ They both said, _ "No, lit - tle

Lord _ knows when. Good - bye, _ lit - tle Bon -ny, good - bye. _____
Bon-ny can't _ go." That's all _ that I can _ do. _____

Chorus:

> Goodbye, little Bonny, goodbye,
> Goodbye, little Bonny, goodbye.
> I'll see you again, but the Lord knows when.
> Goodbye, little Bonny, goodbye.

1 I asked your mamma for you;
  I asked your papa, too.
  They both said, "No, little Bonny can't go."
  That's all that I can do.

2 My trunk is packed and gone,
  My trunk is packed and gone,
  My trunk is gone and I'm alone.
  Goodbye, little Bonny, goodbye.

* For other tunes of the same type, the same provenience and the same vintage, see also "Chilly Winds" and "As I Went Out for a Ramble."

[148]

II.   7. OLD-TIME LOVE SONGS

Ask a Southern ballad singer for "Barbara Allen" or "Lord Lovell" or another of the old ballads, and he will be likely to say, "Why, that's nothing but an old *love song*." This means: (1) The plot is, usually, a love story and was felt by the singers to have a close relationship with their lives and loves. (2) Strictly religious singers would not sing it or tolerate its being sung in their homes. (3) It was sung at "courtin' " parties, or in circumstances in which the song had a meaningful connection with the emotions of the singer. The people of America who preserved these songs and the rural people who still sing them have never felt that these ancient ballads, called by scholars English and Scottish popular ballads, were particularly ancient; nor have they valued them as such. Instead, as we have tried to point out in our notes, they have kept these songs because they felt the near and moving reality of them.

OLD BANGHAM

No record. Adelaide Hemingway, Washington, D.C., 1939. See "Sir Lionel," Child No. 18; Sh, 1:54; Da, p. 125; Be, p. 29.

"My grandmother learned to sing 'Old Bangham' from her mother, who had traveled out to the Sioux Indian country from her girlhood home in western Massachusetts. She was a Longley, and the song must have been brought from England when the family came to Massachusetts in the early 1630's. In 1866 my grandmother sailed round the Cape of Good Hope in one of the last clipper ships to come to the Far East. She brought the song to the dry plains of North China, to her new home at Kalgan, the gateway to Mongolia, where she sang it to her six children, lulling them to sleep many a time as they swung along in a mule litter or jolted over the rough roads in a Peking cart.

"As a little girl I also was sung to sleep by the minor tones of 'Old Bangham' as our cart went bump, bump *over even rougher Shansi roads which brought us gradually nearer to supper and bed in a willow-shaded Chinese inn or at home in our mission compound."*

Moderate

Old Bang-ham did a-hunt-ing ride, Der-rum, derrum, der-rum, Old Bang-ham did a-hunt-ing ride, kim-my qua, Old Bangham did a-hunt-ing ride, A sword and pis-tol by his side, Der-rum, kim-my quo-qua. ___

1 Old Bangham did a-hunting ride,
  Derrum, derrum, derrum,
  Old Bangham did a-hunting ride,
  Kimmy qua,
  Old Bangham did a-hunting ride,
  A sword and pistol by his side,
  Derrum, kimmy quo qua.

2 He rode unto the riverside,
  And there a pretty maid he spied.

3 "Fair maid," said he, "will you marry me?"
  "Oh, no," said she, "for we can't agree."

4 "There lives a bear in yonder wood,
  He'll grind your bones and suck your blood."

5 He rode unto the wild bear's den,
  There lay the bones of a hundred men.

6 Old Bangham and the wild bear fought,
  By set of sun the bear was naught.

7 He rode unto the riverside
  And there a pretty maid he spied.

8 "Fair maid," said he, "will you marry me?"
  "Oh, yes," said she, "for now we agree."

THE MERMAID

bb. No. 1438. Eliza Pace, Hyden, Ky., 1937. See Child No. 289; Sh, 1:292.

Aunt Lize Pace, eighty years odd, is the wittiest and gayest lady in Leslie County, Kentucky. She lives with her daughter in an old log cabin on the bank of the Clear Fork and, when Lize is not inching along over her cane to the post office or entertaining some neighbor's child at her front door, she has her face in a book, her old eyes following a story of adventure in the Klondike or on the sea.

"Years ago when that funny old Englishman* come over the mountains and wrote down these old love songs I know, I could sing like a mocking- bird, and wasn't no step I couldn't put my foot to in a dance. I didn't keer for nothin', and I was happy as a lark all day. But now I'm a-gittin' deef and erbout lame, and I can't stir around for my livin' like I used to. The government sends me my old-age money, but it's shore hard to support a family on three dollars a month, now, ain't it? That's what makes it so I can't remember that last verse to this here pretty song. Anyhow, I do pretty well for sich an old woman—don't I, now?"

Moderate, somewhat free ♩=112

As — I went out one — eve - ning, Far — out of sight of the land, There I saw a mer-maid a - sit-ting on a rock With a comb and a glass in her hand.

     1 As I went out one evening,
      Far out of sight of the land,
      There I saw a mermaid a-sitting on a rock
      With a comb and a glass in her hand.

* The English collector Cecil J. Sharp.

[151]

2 A-combing down her long yellow hair,
Her skin was like a lily so fair,
Her cheeks were like two roses and her eyes were like the stars
And her voice was like the nightingale's air.

3 This little mermaid swum into the deep,
The winds begin fur to blow,
The hail and the rain was so dark in the air,
We'll never see the land any more.

4 At last come down the captain of our ship,
With a plumb and a line in his hand;
He plumbed the sea to see how fur it was
To a rock or else to the sand.

5 He plumbed her behind and he plumbed her before
And the ship kept turning around,
The captain cried out, "Our ship will be wrecked
When the needle swings straight around.

6 "Then throw out your loading as fast as you can,
The truth to you I will tell,
This night we all must start
To heaven or else to hell."

TEE ROO

· *a.* No. 61. Foy and Ado Gant, Austin, Texas, 1934.
See "The Farmer's Curst Wife," Child No. 278; Sh,
1:275; Da, p. 505; Be, p. 94.

"A lot of times it was sung by the farmers to skeer their wives up a little bit when they'd been quarrelin' and raisin' sand around, to make 'em afraid the same thing might happen to them. You know them old religious women, they're awful afraid of the devil. Yes, they's plenty of them believe that the devil come and called on the old man one mornin' when he was startin' out to plow and sacked her up and took her away and the farmer wouldn't accept her at all when he brought her back." —Aunt Molly Jackson.

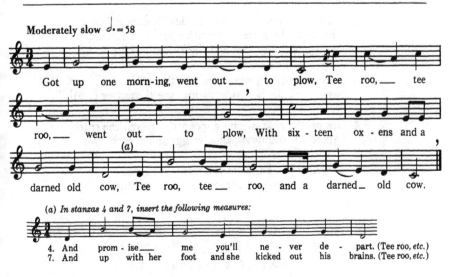

Moderately slow ♩.=58

Got up one morn-ing, went out __ to plow, Tee roo, __ tee

roo, __ went out __ to plow, With six-teen ox-ens and a

(a)
darned old cow, Tee roo, tee __ roo, and a darned __ old cow.

(a) *In stanzas 4 and 7, insert the following measures:*

4. And prom-ise __ me you'll ne - ver de - part. (Tee roo, *etc.*)
7. And up with her foot and she kicked out his brains. (Tee roo, *etc.*)

1 Got up one morning, went out to plow,
   Tee roo, tee roo, went out to plow,
   With sixteen oxens and a darned old cow,
   Tee roo, tee roo, and a darned old cow.

2 Up stepped the old devil sayin', "How do you do?
   There's one in your family that I must have."

3 "Oh, please don't take my oldest son,
   There's work on the place that's got to be done."

4 "It's all I want's that wife of yours."
   "Well, you can have her with all of my heart,
   And promise me you'll never depart."

5 He picked her up upon his back,
   He looked like an eagle skeered off of the rack.

6 He carried her on about half of the road,
   He says, "Old woman, you're a devil of a load."

[153]

7 He carried her on to the old devil's door,
   There stood a little devil with a ball and a chain,
   And up with her foot and she kicked out his brains.

8 Nine little devils went climbing the wall,
   Saying, "Take her back, daddy, she'll murder us all."

9 Got up the next morning, peeped through the crack,
   I spied the old devil come wagging her back.

10 And now you know what a woman can do,
   She can whup out the devil and her husband too.

SWEET WILLIAM

B. No. 1357. Fields Ward, Galax, Va., 1937. See "Earl
Brand," Child No. 7; Sh, 1:14 ff.

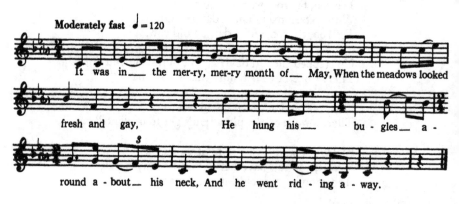

1 It was in the merry, merry month of May,
   When the meadows looked fresh and gay,
   He hung his bugles around about his neck,
   And he went riding away.

2 He rode till he came to Fair Ellen's house;
   He knocked and he tingled at the ring.
   "Asleep or awake, Fair Ellen," I said,
   "Pray arise and let me in."

3 Fair Ellen arose and she slipped on her clothes
   To let Sweet William in;
   No one was so ready as Fair Ellen herself
   To arise and let him in.

4 Then he mounted her upon the milk-white horse,
   Himself on the iron-gray;
   He hung his bugles around about his neck,
   And they went riding away.

5 They rode till they came in three miles of the place,
   They stopped and they looked all around;
   They looked and they saw some seven iron men
   Come hasting over the ground.

6 "Get down, get down, Fair Ellen," I said,
   "And take my steed in hand,
   Till I go back to yonder spring
   And stop those seven iron men."

7 She stood till she saw her six brothers fall;
   Her father, he fell so near.
   "Sweet William," I said, "come and stop your case,
   For you seem almost too severe."

8 She took a handkerchief from her side,
   'Twas made of linen so fine;
   She took and she wiped his bleeding, bleeding wound,
   For the blood ran as red as any wine.

9 Then he mounted her upon the milk-white steed,
   Himself on the iron-gray;
   He hung his bugles around about his neck,
   And they went riding away.

[155]

10 They rode till they came to his mother's house;
   He knocked and he tingled at the ring.
   "Asleep or awake, dear mother," I said,
   "Pray arise and let me in."

11 His mother arose and she slipped on her clothes
   To let Sweet William in;
   No one was so ready as his mother herself
   To arise and let him in.

12 "Dear mother," I said, "come and bind up my head,
   You never shall bind it any more."
   Sweet William, he died of the wound that he bore,
   And Fair Ellen, she died also.

BLACK JACK DAVY

b. No. 72. Gant family, Austin, Texas, 1934. See "The Gypsy Laddie," Child No. 200; Sh, 1:233; Hu, p. 118; Be, p. 73.

One morning I called on the Gant family at ten o'clock. Mrs. Gant met me at the door dressed in her early morning wrapper.

"The children are all asleep," she whispered apologetically, "and haven't gone to school today. Last night we all got to singing and dancing. We didn't go to bed until two o'clock this morning. The children stayed up, too, so I'm letting the whole bunch sleep until dinnertime."

The Gants were east Texas people from the sandy, square-dancing, razorback country that stretches into Arkansas, through northern Louisiana, Mississippi, and Alabama to the mountains. The Gants had followed cotton into Oklahoma, then down into the Panhandle and, in drought and years of bad prices, had moved on. In Oklahoma they learned new songs, new Gants were born, and some of the young ones began to pick the guitar. In the Panhandle they learned cowboy songs, the oldest daughter was married and had her first baby, and Adoniram began to pick the guitar. Dispossessed again, they came to Austin, the capital, looking for something to do. When there were no more jobs, they got a little food from the Relief and lived in a shack on the bank of the Colorado River.

The Gants were from the square-dancing, ballad-singing country, and on Saturdays there was always a dance at their house. On other week nights some of the boys would drop in to pick Ether's guitar, and there would be singing on the porch.

"Working on the highway, earning three dollars a day."

And when no one was sick and the girls didn't have dates, there might be a singing at home: Mrs. Gant, who taught them their songs and their love of singing, and who knew the saddest songs; the oldest daughter, Glyda, who pretended to turn her nose up at the ballads but could sing "The Old Lady from Tennessee" better than anybody else in the family; Foy, who could pick the guitar as well as a man and used to remind them of their tunes; Ella, who was twelve and knew all the old tunes, especially the "funny ones"; the three boys, who mostly sang the blues, the cowboy songs, and the jailhouse ballads; Mr. Gant, who had one song, "Bangum and the Boar," over which his rights were almost personal; and then on the beds, leaning against someone's knee or breast, the tow-headed Gant kids, listening, falling asleep, and waking up to listen again.

"The singing kept us so happy, we just couldn't go to sleep," smiled Mrs. Gant.

Gant songs in this book: "Tee Roo," "Adieu to the Stone Walls," "Black Jack Davy," "When First to This Country a Stranger I Came."

Moderately fast ♩ = 72

Black Jack Da - vy came a - rid - in' through the woods, Sing - ing songs so gay,___ Sang so loud he made the wild - woods ring, Charmed the hearts of a la - dy, Charmed the hearts of a wife.

(a) *In stanza 2, insert the following measures:*

Said, "Where is ___ my wife?"

1 Black Jack Davy come a-ridin' through the woods,
Singing songs so gayly,
Sang so loud he made the wild woods ring,
Charmed the hearts of a lady,
Charmed the hearts of a wife.

2 The old man came in that night,
Inquiring for his lady,
Said, "Where is my wife?"
The servant spoke before he thought,
"She's gone with the Black Jack Davy,
She's gone with the Black Jack boy."

3 "Go saddle me up my milk-white horse,
Saddle him slow and easy,
I'll ride all night till the broad daylight
And overtake my lady,
And overtake my wife."

4 He rode all day and he rode all night,
Till he came to the edge of the water;
There he looked on the other side,
There he spied his darling,
There he spied his wife.

5 "Will you forsake your house and home?
Will you forsake your baby?
Will you forsake the one you love
To roam with the Black Jack Davy?
To roam with the Black Jack boy?"

6 "Yes, I'll forsake my house and home;
Yes, I'll forsake my baby.
And I'll forsake the one I love
To roam with the Black Jack Davy,
To roam with the Black Jack boy."

7 "Will you pull off your snow-white gloves
  Made of Spanish leather,
  Give to me your lily-white hand,
  Bid farewell forever,
  Bid farewell goodbye?"

8 "Yes, I'll give up my snow-white gloves,
  Made of Spanish leather,
  Give you my lily-white hand,
  Bid farewell forever,
  Bid farewell goodbye."

9 "Last night I lay in my own feather bed,
  By the side of my little baby;
  Tonight I'll lay in the mud and rain,
  By the side of Black Jack Davy,
  By the side of the Black Jack boy."

THE IRISH LADY

e♭ to d♭. Tune and first stanza. No. 1608. Capt. P. R. Nye, Akron, Ohio; other stanzas, No. 1302B. Mrs. Minnie Floyd, Murrells Inlet, S.C., 1937. See "Pretty Sally," Cox, p. 366; "The Brown Girl," Child No. 295; Sh, 1:366; Be, p. 111.

"Maybe they did die of broken hearts in the old days when they used to think that if they didn't get the man they wanted they were ruined forever. Nowadays they have learned that if they don't get one man, they'll get another one."

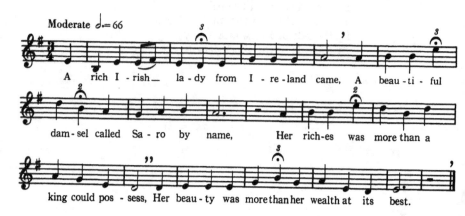

1 A rich Irish lady from Ireland came,
A beautiful damsel called Saro by name,
Her riches was more than a king could possess,
Her beauty was more than her wealth at its best.

2 A lofty young gentleman a-courtin' her came,
A-courtin' this damsel called Saro by name,
"O Saro, O Saro, O Saro," said he,
"I fear that my ruin forever you'll be.

[160]

3 "I fear that my ruin forever you'll prove
Unless you turn all your hatred to love."
"No hatred to you nor to no other man,
But this, for to love you is more than I can.

4 "So end all your sorrow and drop your discourse,
I never will have you unless I am forced."
Six months had appeared and five years had passed,
I heard of this damsel's misfortune at last.

5 She lay wounded by love and she knew not for why
And sent for this young man who she once did deny.
By her bedside those words they was said,
"There's a pain in your side, love, there's a pain in your head."

6 "Oh, no, kind sir, the right you've not guessed,
The pain that I feel here sits all through my breast."
"Am I your doctor and am I your cure?
Am I your pertector you sent for me here?"

7 "You are my doctor and you are my cure;
Without your pertection I'll die, I am sure."
"O Saro, O Saro, O Saro," said he,
"Don't you remember when I first courted thee?

8 "I asked you in kindness, you answered in scorn,
And now I'll reward you for the time past and gone."
"Time past and gone I hope you'll forgive
And grant me some longer in comfort to live."

9 "I'll never forgive you as long as I live;
I'll dance on your grave, love, when you're laid in the ground."
Off of her fingers gold rings she pulled three,
Said, "Take them and wear them while you're dancing on me."

10 "Adieu to my friends, adieu, all around,
Adieu to my true love, God make him a crown;
I'll freely forgive him although he won't me,
My follies ten thousand times over I see."

THE LADY OF CARLISLE

d'. No. 1587. Acc. on guitar and sung by Basil May,
Salyersville, Ky., 1937. See Sh, 1 :396; Ma, p. 82. Also
Robert Browning's "The Glove."

*"My mother sang lots of love songs but never when my pa was around.
She always waited until she went to see her people, and then she would get
together with her sisters who was great singers."*

Moderate ♩ = 100

1. Down in Car - lisle____ there lived a ____ la - dy, Being most
2. Un - less it was ____ a man of ____ hon - or, A man of

beau - ti - ful and gay; ____ She was _ de - ter - mined _ to live a
hon - or and high de - gree; ____ Then ap - proached ____ two lov - ing

Stanza 1

la - dy, No man on earth could her be - tray, ____
sol - diers, This fair la - dy for to_ see; ____

Stanzas 2,3,4,7,9

Stanzas 5,8,10,11

5. trav - el Till they come_ to the li - ons' den. ____
8. wo - men, But I will not give _ my _ life for _ love." _

Stanza 6

6. ho - ur This young la - dy lies speech-less on the ground. _

1 Down in Carlisle there lived a lady,
   Being most beautiful and gay;
   She was determined to live a lady,
   No man on earth could her betray,

2 Unless it was a man of honor,
   A man of honor and high degree;
   Then approached two loving soldiers,
   This fair lady for to see;

3 One being a brave lieutenant,
   A brave lieutenant and a man of war;
   The other being a brave sea captain,
   A captain on a ship that was *Kong Kong Kar*.

4 Up spoke this fair young lady,
   Saying, "I can't be but one man's bride;
   If you come back tomorrow morning
   And on this case we will decide."

5 She ordered her a span of horses,
   A span of horses at her command;
   Down the road the three did travel
   Till they come to the lions' den.

6 There she stopped and there she halted
   These two soldiers stood gazing around,
   And for the space of half an hour
   This young lady lies speechless on the ground.

7 And when she did recover,
   Threw her fan down in the lions' den,
   Saying, "Which of you to gain a lady
   Will return my fan again?"

8 Then up stepped this brave lieutenant,
   Raised his voice both loud and clear,
   "I know I am a dear lover of women,
   But I will not give my life for love."

9 Then up stepped this brave sea captain,
Raised his voice both loud and high,
"I know I am a dear lover of women;
I will return her fan or die."

10 Down in the lions' den he boldly entered,
The lions being both wild and fierce;
He marched around and in among them,
Safely returned her fan again.

11 And when she saw her true love coming,
Seeing no harm had been done to him,
She threw herself against his bosom,
Saying, "Here is the prize that you have won."

THE LAME SOLDIER

d to *e♭*. Nos. 1727, 1728. Mrs. Oscar Parks, Deuchars, Ind., 1938.

There was a lame sol - dier in time of the war, He
had a lame leg and his face were a scar, He marched up the
street— in Dub-lin so fair, And in— his arms— an in - fant bear.

1 There was a lame soldier in time of the war,
He had a lame leg and his face were a scar,
He marched up the street in Dublin so fair,
And in his arms an infant bear.

2 "Pretty Peggy, pretty Peggy, would you agree
To leave your old husband and baby to be,
To leave your old husband and baby to be,
And go with a soldier and sail on the sea?"

3 Pretty Peggy, pretty Peggy, she did agree
To leave her old husband and baby to be,
To leave her old husband and baby to be,
And go with the soldier and sail on the sea.

4 John bridled his horses and away he did ride,
Expecting to see Peg down by the seaside,
But when he got there it was late in the day—
And Peg and her soldier had sailed far away.

5 They had not been sailing more than two weeks or three,
Till Peg and her soldier they two disagreed;
He kicked her and he cuffed her and he called her whore,
He bid her adieu to her own country.

6 Now, when Peg got back it was late in the night,
Because she was ashamed to be seen in daylight,
She crept to the window to listen awhile,
To hear her old husband sing to her dear child.

7 "Rock-a-bye, baby, and don't you cry,
Your mamma's gone and left you and I cannot tell why;
But if she comes back here, she can't stay with me,
She may go with her soldier and sail on the sea."

8 "Open my door and let me in,
And I will never be called a false wench again."
"Go way from my door and leave me alone,
Go sail with your soldier, he'll find you a home."

[165]

WILLY REILLY

d to *c*. No. 1008. Capt. P. R. Nye, Akron, Ohio, 1937.
See Gr, p. 184; Cox, p. 336; Cr, p. 152; Be, p. 289.

"This was a favorite for a gathering on our boat in my childhood youth. My parents sang it times without number on request, along with many others." —CAPTAIN PEARL R. NYE, *of the Ohio Canal.*

The fullest American version of this Irish ballad appears, fifty-seven stanzas long, in Helen Creighton's *Songs and Ballads from Nova Scotia.* It was often printed in songsters in the early part of the nineteenth century.

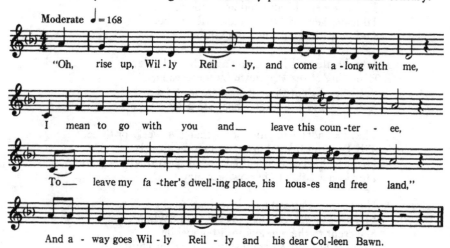

Moderate ♩ = 168

"Oh, rise up, Wil-ly Reil-ly, and come a-long with me,

I mean to go with you and__ leave this coun-ter - ee,

To__ leave my fa-ther's dwell-ing place, his hous-es and free land,"

And a - way goes Wil-ly Reil-ly and his dear Col-leen Bawn.

1 "Oh, rise up, Willy Reilly, and come along with me,
   I mean to go with you and leave this coun-ter-ee,
   To leave my father's dwelling place, his houses and free land,"
   And away goes Willy Reilly and his dear Colleen Bawn.

2 They go by hill and mountain and by yon lonesome plain,
   Through shady groves and valleys, all dangers to refrain;
   But her father followed after with a well armed band,
   And taken was poor Reilly and his dear Colleen Bawn!

[166]

3 It's home then she was taken and in her closet bound,
   Poor Reilly all in Sligo jail lay on the stony ground,
   Till at the bar of justice before the judge he'd stand,
   For nothing but the stealing of his lovely Colleen Bawn.

4 "Now in the cold, cold iron, my hands and feet are bound,
   I'm handcuffed like a murderer and tied unto the ground;
   But all the toil and slavery I'm willing to withstand,
   Still hoping to be succored by my dear Colleen Bawn."

5 The jailer's son to Reilly goes and thus to him did say:
   "Oh, get up, Willy Reilly, you must appear today,
   For great Squire Foillard's anger you never can withstand,
   I'm afraid you'll suffer sorely for your dear Colleen Bawn."

6 Now Willy's dressed from top to toe, all in a suit of green,
   His hair hangs o'er his shoulders most glorious to be seen;
   He's tall, so straight and comely, as any could be found,
   He's fit for Foillard's daughter, was she heiress to a crown.

7 "This is the news, young Reilly, last night that I did hear,
   The lady's oath will hang you, or else will set you free,"
   "If that be so," says Reilly, "her pleasure I will stand,
   Still hoping to be succored by my dear Colleen Bawn."

8 The judge he said: "This lady being in her tender youth,
   If Reilly has deluded her, she will declare the truth."
   Then like a moving beauty bright before him she did stand,
   "You're welcome then, my heart's delight, and my dear Colleen Bawn."

9 "Oh, gentlemen," Squire Foillard said, "with pity look on me,
   This villain came among us to disgrace our family;
   And by his base contrivances this villainy was planned,
   If I don't get satisfaction, I'll quit this Irish land."

10 The lady with a tear began, and thus replièd she:
    "The fault was none of Reilly's, the blame lies all with me,
    I forced him for to leave his place and come along with me,
    I loved him out of measure, which wrought our destiny."

[167]

11 Out spoke the noble Fox, at the table he stood by,
"Oh, gentlemen, consider on this extremity;
To hang a man for love is a murder, you may see,
So spare the life of Reilly, let him leave this coun-ter-ee."

12 "Good my lord, he stole from her, her diamonds and her rings,
Gold watch and silver buckles and many precious things,
Which cost me in bright guineas more than five hundred pounds,
I'll have the life of Reilly should I lose ten thousand pounds."

13 "Good my lord, I gave them him as tokens of true love,
And we are a-parting I will them all remove,
If you have got them, Reilly, pray, send them home to me."
"I will, my loving lady, with many thanks to thee."

14 "There is a ring among them I allow yourself to wear,
With thirty locket diamonds well set in silver fair,
And as a true-love token wear it on your right hand,
That you'll think of my broken heart when you're in a foreign land."

15 Then out spoke noble Fox: "You may let the prisoner go,
The lady's oath has cleared him, as the jury all may know;
She has released her own true love, she has renewed her name,
May her honor bright gain high estate and her offspring rise to fame!"

JOHN RILEY

bb. No. 1504. Mrs. Lncy Garrison, Providence, Laurel
County, Ky., 1937. See "George Reilly," Sh, 2:22; Cox, p. 323.

1 As I walked out one summer's evening
  To take the cool and pleasant air,
  'Twas there I spied a fine young lady
  And she looked to me like a lily fair.

2 I stepped up to her and kindly asked her
  If she would be a poor sailor's wife,
  "Oh, no, kind sir, I don't want to marry,
  I'd rather live a single life."

3 "What makes you so far from all human nature?
  What makes you so far from all womankind?
  You are young, you are youthful, fair, and handsome;
  You can marry me if you're so inclined."

4 "The truth, kind sir, I'll plainly tell you:
  I could have been married three years ago
  To one John Riley who left this country
  Has been the cause of my grief and woe."

5 "Don't think upon Riley and do forget him
  And go with me to a distant shore,
  And we'll sail over to Pennsylvany,
  Adieu to Riley forever more."

6 "I'll not go with you to Pennsylvany,
  Neither with you to a distant shore,
  For my heart is with Riley and I can't forget him,
  Although I may never see him any more."

7 Now when he saw that she loved him truly,
  He gave her kisses two or three,
  Saying, "I am Riley, your long lost lover,
  Who has been the cause of your misery."

8 "If you be he and your name is Riley,
   I will go with you to a distant shore,
   And we'll sail over to Pennsylvany.
   Adieu, young friends, forever more."

9 They locked their hands and their hearts together
   And to the church house they did go,
   And they got married to one another,
   They're living together, doing well.

LILY MUNRO

B♭. No. 1340. Uncle Alex Dunford, Galax, Va., 1937.
See Sh, 1:385; Be, p. 171; "Jackaro," "Jackie Fraisure,"
"Jack Munro," etc., Cox, p. 330. Tune, see "The Rich
Old Lady," p. 176.

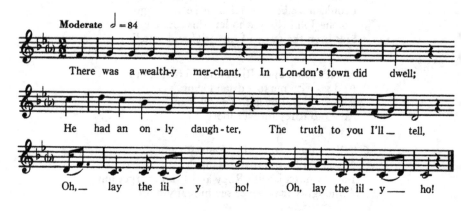

1 There was a wealthy merchant,
   In London's town did dwell;
   He had an only daughter,
   The truth to you I'll tell,
   Oh, lay the lily ho!
   Oh, lay the lily ho!

2 Her sweetheart went a-sailin'
   With trouble on his mind,
   A-leavin' from his country
   And his darling love behind,
   Oh, lay the lily ho!
   Oh, lay the lily ho!

3 His sweetheart dressed herself all up
   In man's array,
   And to the war department
   She then did march away,
   Oh, lay the lily ho!
   Oh, lay the lily ho!

4 "Before you come on board, sir,
   Your name we'd like to know!"
   A smile played over her countenance,
   "They call me Lily Munro,"
   Oh, lay the lily ho!
   Oh, lay the lily ho!

5 "Your waist is slim and slender,
   Your fingers they are small,
   Your cheeks too red and rosy
   To face a cannon ball,"
   Oh, lay the lily ho!
   Oh, lay the lily ho!

6 "My waist I know is slender,
   My fingers they are small,
   But it would not make me tremble
   To see ten thousand fall."
   Oh, lay the lily ho!
   Oh, lay the lily ho!

7 The drum began to beat,
   The fife began to play;
   Straightway to the field of battle
   They all did march away,
   Oh, lay the lily ho!
   Oh, lay the lily ho!

[171]

8 And when the war was ended,
This girl she searched the ground
Among the dead and wounded
Until her love she found,
Oh, lay the lily ho!
Oh, lay the lily ho!

9 This couple they got married,
So well they did agree;
This couple they got married
And why not you and me?
Oh, lay the lily ho!
Oh, lay the lily ho!

*　　*　　*

"*Back out West, a girl used to ask a boy into the parlor and sit down at the organ—the mournfullest instrument there ever was, I guess—and play 'em 'The Dyin' Cowboy' on and on. One of these here organs you had to pump. Some big old fat girls would pump till they'd get out of breath. While they'd puff, the boy would sweat.*

"*I don't know why they figured such a mournful song was good for courting. Anyhow it worked. Softened 'em up, I reckon.*"

PRETTY POLLY

d. No. 1346. Acc. on guitar and sung by Mr. and Mrs. E. C. Ball, Rugby, Va. Other stanzas from Aunt Molly Jackson, New York City. See Cox, p. 308; Ca, p. 74. See also Nos. 823 and 1348.

"*He wanted her to marry him and she refused him; but he kept on naggin' at her till finally she promised. Then he thought she was just puttin' it off from time to time so he decided to kill her. There's a lot of people like that—jealous-hearted, I call 'em.*" —AUNT MOLLY JACKSON.

* The guitar accompaniment (continuous throughout the song) interpolates here, in each stanza:

1 I courted pretty Polly the livelong night,
I courted pretty Polly the livelong night,
Then left her next morning before it was light.

2 "Pretty Polly, pretty Polly, come go along with me,
Pretty Polly, pretty Polly, come go along with me,
Before we get married, some pleasure to see."

3 She got up behind him and away they did go,
Over the hills to the valleys below.

4 They went a little farther and what did they spy?
A new-dug grave and a spade lying by.

5 "Willie, O Willie, I'm afraid of your way,
I'm afraid you will lead my poor body astray."

6 "Pretty Polly, pretty Polly, you're thinking just right,
I dug on your grave the best part of last night."

[173]

7 He threw her onto the ground, and she broke into tears,
 She threw her arms around him and trembled with fear.

8 "O Willie, please Willie, please spare my sweet life,
 How an you kill a girl that was to be your wife?"

9 "There's no time to talk now, there's no time to stand,"
 He drew out his knife all in his right hand.

10 He stabbed her to the heart, her heart's blood it did flow,
 And into the grave pretty Polly did go.

11 He threw a little dirt over her and started for home,
 Leaving no one behind but the wild birds to mourn.

12 A debt to the devil poor Willie must pay,
 For killing pretty Polly and running away.

THE LEXINGTON MURDER

a. No. 1369. Acc. on guitar and sung by Fields Ward,
Galax, Va., 1937. See: Sh, 1:402; Cox, p. 90; *JAFL,*
39:125; Be, p. 133.

"I guess she was in a family way and he didn't want to marry her."

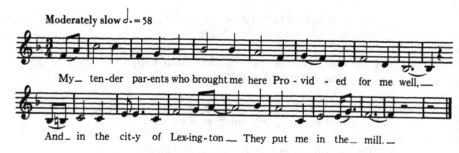

Moderately slow ♩. = 58

My— ten-der par-ents who brought me here Pro - vid - ed for me well,—

And— in the cit-y of Lex-ing-ton— They put me in the— mill. —

1 My tender parents who brought me here
   Provided for me well,
   And in the city of Lexington
   They put me in the mill.

2 'Twas there I spied a fair young miss,
   She had dark rolling eyes,
   I asked her if she would marry me,
   And she believed my lies.

3 Three weeks ago last Saturday night,
   Of course it was the day,
   The devil put it in my heart
   To take her sweet life away.

4 I went down to her sister's house
   At eight o'clock last night;
   And she, the poor girl, seemed to think
   At her I had a slight.

5 I asked her if she would take a walk
   A little way with me,
   That we might have a little talk
   About our wedding day.

6 We walked along both side by side
   Till we come to a silent place;
   I took a stick from off the fence
   And struck her in the face.

7 She fell down on her bended knee
   And loud for mercy did cry,
   "For heaven's sake, don't murder me,
   I'm unprepared to die."

8 I heeded not her mercy cry,
   But struck her all the more,
   Till I saw the innocent blood appear
   That I could never restore.

[175]

9 I run my hands in her coal-black hair,
    I swung her round and round;
    I threw her in a clear water stream
    That flowed through Lexington.

10 As I went down to my workshop,
    I met my servant, John;
    He asked me why I looked so pale
    And yet so very worn.

11 "And what is the cause of all that blood
    Upon your hands and clothes?"
    The answer was that I replied,
    " 'Twas the bleeding of my nose."

12 I lit my candle and went to my room
    And thought that I would rest,
    It seemed to me that flames of fire
    Were burning in my breast.

13 Young men, young men, take warning from me,
    And if your sweetheart's true,
    Don't ever let the devil get
    The upper hand on you.

THE RICH OLD LADY

e^b to f. No. 204. James Baker (Iron Head), Sugarland,
Texas, 1934. See Sh, 1:348; Cox, p. 464. Tune, see "Lily
Munro," p. 170.

A few variants and fragments of British ballads, such as this one, have
been found among Southern Negroes. On the whole, however, this tradition was absorbed and creatively used by the Negro people rather than per-
petuated in terms of specific songs. The incisive and clean-cut story-telling
technique, the use of incremental repetition, the handling of dramatic dialogue, the stanza form to be found in "John Henry," "Po' Laz'us,"
"Frankie," and others, were, in all likelihood, indirectly derived from the

classical English and Scottish tradition; but to this already rich technique, the Negro brought a genius for direct, introspective penetration into the emotions of his characters, and a wealth of melodic and thematic ideas of his own.

James Baker, whose prison nickname is Iron Head, knew four or five songs and ballads of British derivation. As he sang, he closed his eyes and sat stiff and straight in his chair in the posture of the traditional ballad singer; but his melodies, though basically British, had been decorated in a fashion that made them not only a very individual, but a most exquisite British song set.

Moderately fast, free ♩ = 92

Once I_ knowed old_ la-dy, Round Ten-nes-see did dwell, _____

She had a lov-in'_ hus-band,_ But she loved o-ther mens as well._

CHORUS

Love my darl-in'-o, _____ I_ love my darl-in'- o. __

1 Once I knowed old lady,
Round Tennessee did dwell,
She had a lovin' husband,
But she loved other mens as well.

Chorus:
Love my darlin'-o,
I love my darlin'-o.

2 "I'm goin' down to the doctor's shop
Just as straight as I can go,
See if I can't find sumpen 'roun' that place
That'll run my husband blind."

[177]

3 She only found two marrowbones,
   An' she told him to eat them all,
   Says, "Now, I'm blin', my dear young wife,
   An' I jes' can't see at all.

4 "Honey, I would go and drown myself
   If I only knew the way."
   Says, "Now, my dear, come and go with me,
   Mother's 'fraid you'll run astray."

5 Goes way down by the riverside,
   For to see her old man drown.
   "My dear kind wife, I cannot drown,
   Unless you shove me in."

6 She gits way back, takes a little runnin' start,
   Gonna shove her old man in;
   Old man jumps just a little one side,
   An' a-headlong she jumps in.

7 She whoops and she hollers,
   Just as loud as any woman could squall;
   Old man know his sweet wife's dyin',
   An' cannot see at all.

8 Old man bein' so kind-hearted,
   Knowin' too his sweet wife could not swim,
   Reached right down and git a long pole
   And he shoves her further in.

9 Come all you young, hasty women,
   An' take warnin' after me,
   Don't never try to drown a po' old man
   That's blind so he cannot see.

Chorus:
     Love my darlin'-o,
     I love my darlin'-o.

II. 8. FRENCH SONGS AND BALLADS FROM SOUTHWESTERN LOUISIANA

The towns on the east-west highway between New Orleans and the Texas border, the swamps along the coast, and the broad rice, cane, and cotton fields to the north and south of this highway have been until the last twenty years predominantly French-speaking. The people still have their own lore, their own patois, their own balladry, their own music, their own way of life, all rooted in the Norman-French culture they brought with them from Nova Scotia nearly two hundred years ago.

The tradition of folk music that this region has fostered, has received little or no attention.* As always, the townsfolk are a little ashamed of their country neighbors and their country neighbors' music. The boys and girls who come to college from the Cajun country are ashamed of being called "Cajuns." Meantime the ballad singers are still singing their ancient Norman ballads at country weddings, the *fais-dodo* bands creating their wild and fertile music at the rural dances. The songs in this section, the second collection of the kind, so far as we know, that has been published anywhere, will indicate, better than we can, what a rich storehouse of folk music is the Cajun country of southwestern Louisiana.

* A notable exception to this general neglect is the work of Miss Irène Thérèse Whitfield, Ph.D., of Louisiana State University, whose thesis on Acadian songs is shortly to be published. We wish to extend our thanks to Miss Whitfield for her invaluable work in making the preliminary transcriptions and translations of the songs in this section. Her collection, *Louisiana French Folk Songs*, has been published recently by the Louisiana State University Press.

SEPT ANS SUR MER

(Seven Years at Sea)

c'. No. 31. Julien and Elida Hofpauir, New Iberia, La.,
1 34. See BaS, p. 125; Ba, p. 27.

"Perhaps no other sailor's chantey can compare with 'Seven Years at Sea' for fame and historical interest. It is one of the most extensively traveled songs of European folk repertoires. Best known on the shores of Brittany and Poitou where it seems to have originated, it has spread across France and followed the seacoast into neighboring countries, north and south. It occurs in Icelandic, Danish, Norwegian, Catalan, Portuguese, Spanish and Swiss versions. . . . Thackeray adapted it for a humorous rhyme entitled 'Little Billee.'" *

Moderate ♩.=84

On a rest - é —— six ans — sur mer —

Sans pou - voir —— bord - er la — terre.

1 On a resté six ans sur mer
  Sans pouvoir border la terre.†

2 Au bout de la septième année
  On a manqué de provisions.

3 On a mangé souris et rats
  Jusque le touvre du navire.

4 On a tiré la courte paille
  Pour voir lequel qui s'rait mangé.

* Marius Barbeau, *Folk-Songs of French Canada*, p. 125.
† Repeat couplet to form each stanza.

5 "En voilà, p'tit Jean, s'il tombait-z-au cas,
　Ça serait p'tit Jean qui serait mangé.
　Ô voilà, p'tit Jean, qu'il tombe sur toi,
　Ça serait p'tit Jean qui serait mangé.

6 "O p'tit Jean, ça fait du mal."
　Il crie, "Courage, mes camarades."

7 "Je vois la terre sur toutes côtés,
　Trois pigeons blancs qui s'a voltigé.

8 "Je vois aussi trois filles du père
　Que se promenaient au bord du rivage.

9 "O si jamais je mets pieds sur terre
　La plus jolie je l'épouserai."

———

1 On stormy seas we six years sailed,
　And never once green land we hailed.*

2 The bitter seventh year came on,
　We found our stores at last were gone.

3 We ate the mice, we ate the rats,
　And through the hold we ran like cats.

4 And then at lots we took a try
　To see which one of us would die.

5 "Look, little John, if chance does will,
　It's you we'll take, it's you we'll kill.
　Look, little John, so chance does will,
　It's you we'll take, it's you we'll kill."

* Repeat couplet to form each stanza.

6 "Too bad, little John," they cried,
   "Oh, courage, comrades," he replied,

7 "For I see land on every side
   And three white pigeons toward us fly."

8 "And I see lovely sisters three
   Come walking down all by the sea;

9 "And if I set my foot on land
   I'll ask the fairest for her hand."

BLANCHE COMME LA NEIGE

(White As Snow)

d'b. No. 32. Julien and Elida Hofpauir, New Iberia,
La., 1934. See BaS, p. 40.

"Scholars are agreed in their estimate of 'White As Snow' . . . as one
the outstanding folk ballads in the French language." †

Moderate ♩ = 84

Le— plus— jeune— des— trois, L'a pris par sa main blan - che—

"Mon-tez, mon - tez, la bel - le, Des-sur mon che-val gris;

On log - it chez mon pè - re, Je vous a -mèn-er - rai."

* Stanza 4 begins here. The fourth line of text in this stanza is sung to the same music as the third line.

† Barbeau, *op. cit.*, p. 40.

1 Le plus jeune des trois,
L'a pris par sa main blanche—
"Montez, montez, la belle,
Dessur mon cheval gris;
On logit chez mon père,
Je vous amènerrai." } bis

1 The youngest of all three took her white hand and said, "Fair damsel, mount my gray horse and I will take you to the house of my father where we will stay together."

2 Quand-e la bell'-z-entend,
Elle s'est mite à pleurèze,—
"Soupez, soupez, la belle,
Prenez, oui, z-appétit,
Auprès du capitaine
Vo' passerez la nuit." } bis

2 When the damsel heard these words, she began to weep, and he said, "Eat, fair damsel, be of good cheer, for this night you will stay with a fine captain."

3 Quand-e-la bell'-z-etend
La belle est tombée morte, —
"Sonnez, sonnez, les cloches,
Tambours, violons, marchez,
M'amillionette est morte
J'en ai le cœur dolent." } bis

3 When the damsel heard these words, she fell to the ground like one dead, and he said, "Ring the bells, play drums and violins; my little sweetheart is dead and I have a doleful heart."

4 "Et où l'enterreront-ils?"
"Dedans l' jardin d' son père,
Sous les trois feuilles de lys;
Nous prierons Dieu, chers frères,
Qu'elle aille en Paradis." } bis

4 And they said, "Where shall she be buried?" "In the garden of her father beneath the three leaves of the lily. We pray to God, dear brothers, that she may fly to Paradise."

5 Au bout-e de trois jours
La bell' frappe à la porte,
"Ouvrez, ouvrez, la porte,
Cher père et bien-aimé,
J'ai fait la mort trois jours
Pour sauver mon honneur." } bis

5 When three days had passed, the damsel knocked on the door of her father's house and said, "Open the door, dear and beloved father, for three days ago I chose death to save my honor."

JE CARESSERAI LA BELLE PAR AMITIÉ
(I'll Give My Love a Light and Friendly Kiss)

d'b. No. 14. Elida Hofpauir, New Iberia, La., 1934.
See BaS, p. 201.

(a) *In stanza 2,*
insert here the following measure:

(lun) - di, lun - (di)

1 J'ai fait une belle trois jours, trois jours, mais c'est pas longtemps.
J'irai la voir lundi, lundi pour la caresser.
Je caresserai la belle par amitié,
Je caresserai la belle par amitié.

2 Si tu viendrais me voir lundi, lundi pour me caresser,
Je me mettrais malade, malade, mais dedans mon lit.
Alors, t'auras qu'une amitié pour moi,   (bis)

3 Si tu t' mettrais malade, malade, mais dedans ton lit,
Je me mettrais médecin, médecin, c'est pour te guérir.
Je guérirai la belle par amitié,   (bis)

4 Si tu t' mettrais médecin, médecin, c'est pour me guérir,
Je me mettrais poisson, poisson dans une rivière.
Alors, t'auras qu'une amitié pour moi,   (bis)

[184]

5 Si tu t' mettrais poisson, poisson dans une rivière,
  Je me mettrais pêcheur, pêcheur, c'est pour te pêcher.
  Je pêcherai la belle par amitié,   (bis)

6 Si tu t' mettrais pêcheur, pêcheur, c'est pour me pêcher,
  Je me mettrais oiseau, z-oiseau dans un grand bois.
  Alors, t'auras qu'une amitié pour moi.   (bis)

7 Si tu t' mettrais oiseau, z-oiseau dans un grand bois,
  Je me mettrais chasseur, chasseur, c'est pour te chasser.
  Je chasserai la belle par amitié,   (bis)

8 Si tu t' mettrais chasseur, chasseur, c'est pour me chasser,
  Je me mettrais une sœur, une sœur dans un couvent.
  Alors t'auras qu'une amitié pour moi, (bis)

9 Si tu t' mettrais une sœur, une sœur mais dans un couvent,
  Je me mettrais un prêtre, un prêtre, c'est pour te confesser.
  Je confesserai la belle par amitié,   (bis)

10 Si tu t' mettrais un prêtre, un prêtre pour me confesser,
   Je me mettrais mari, mari dans le purgatoire.
   Alors t'auras, etc.,

11 Si tu t' mettrais mari, mari dans le purgatoire,
   Je me mettrais St. Pierre et St. Paul pour ouvrir les portes.
   J'ouvrirai les portes par amitié, etc.,

12 Si tu t' mettrais St. Pierre et St. Paul pour ouvrir les portes,
   Je me mettrais un ange, un ange dedans le ciel,
   Alors t'auras, etc.,

13 Si tu t' mettrais un ange, un ange dedans le ciel,
   Je me mettrais lumière, lumière pour t'éclairer,
   J'éclairerai la belle par amitié, etc.,

1 Three days ago I found my love, and it's not so long,
I'll visit her on Monday, Monday to kiss her sweet.
I'll give my love a light and friendly kiss,
I'll give my love a light and friendly kiss.

2 If you come to see me on Monday, Monday to kiss me sweet,
I'll turn into a queasy wench and I'll seek my bed.
My goodness, what a friend of mine you'll be! (2)

3 If you turn into a queasy wench and you seek your bed,
I'll turn into a doctor then for to hold your hand.
I'll hold your hand in a light and friendly way. (2)

4 If you turn into a doctor then for to hold my hand,
I'll turn into a silver trout and I'll swim away.
My goodness, what a friend of mine you'll be! (2)

5 If you turn into a silver trout and you swim away,
I'll turn into a fisherman for to fish you out.
I'll fish you out in a light and friendly way. (2)

6 If you turn into a fisherman for to fish me out,
I'll turn into a nightingale and I'll fly away.
My goodness, what a friend of mine you'll be! (2)

7 If you turn into a nightingale and you fly away,
I'll turn into a hunter then, for to hunt you down,
I'll hunt you down in a light and friendly way. (2)

8 If you turn into a hunter then, for to hunt me down,
I'll turn myself into a nun and pray for your soul.
My goodness, what a friend of mine you'll be! (2)

9 If you turn yourself into a nun and pray for my soul,
I'll turn myself into a priest for to hear your sins.
I'll hear your sins in a light and friendly way. (2)

10 If you turn yourself into a priest, a priest for to hear my sins,
I'll turn myself into a husband way down in Hell,
My goodness, what a friend of mine you'll be. (2)

[186]

11 If you turn yourself into a husband way down in Hell,
I'll turn me into Saints Peter and Paul for to ope' the gates,
I'll kiss my love in a light and friendly way. (2)

12 If you turn you into Saints Peter and Paul for to ope' the gates,
I'll turn into an angel, sir, and live in heaven,
My goodness, what a friend of mine you'll be. (2)

13 If you turn yourself into an angel and live in heaven,
I'll turn myself into the sun for to make you shine,
I'll make you shine in a light and friendly way. (2)

QU'AVEC–VOUS, OUI, BELLE BLONDE
(What's Wrong, Little Blonde)
g to a♭. No. 17. Jesse Stafford, Crowley, La., 1934.

This enigmatic tune, which sometimes sounds medieval and sometimes like an early blues, was sung by a Cajun-speaking lanky, blond farmer near Crowley, named Jesse Stafford. He began with "Trois jolis tambours," and before he was through had recorded "Frankie and Johnny," "Weevily Wheat," "Devilish Mary," "I'm Alone in This World," "The Roving Cowboy," and this song of rum and wickedness.

Moderate ♩.=112

Je m'en-dors, je m'en-dors, et j'ai soif et j'ai faim, Le sol - eil est cou-

ché tu viens loin — d'la mai - son. Qu'a-vez - vous, oui, belle blon-de? Qu'a-vez-

vous, oui, belle brune? C'est tout pour la blonde et c'est ri - en pour la brune.

1 Je m'endors, je m'endors, et j'ai soif et j'ai faim,
Le soleil est couché, tu viens loin d' la maison.
Qu'avez-vous, oui, belle blonde? Qu'avez-vous, oui, belle brune?
C'est tout pour la blonde et c'est rien pour la brune.

2 O les gens de Crowley sont toujours dans l' chemin,
Sont toujours dans l' chemin-z-à chercher-z-à malfaire,
Avec le jug au plombeau-z-et le ferail à la poche,
Sont toujours dans l' chemin-z-à rechercher-z-à malfaire.

3 Je m'endors, je m'endors, et j'ai soif et j'ai faim,
Le soleil est couché, tu viens loin d' la maison.
Bye-bye, oui, belle blonde; bye-bye, oui, belle brune.
C'est tout pour la blonde et c'est rien pour la brune.

———

1 I am sleepy, I'm tired, and I'm hungry and dry,
And the sun has gone down and you've gone far from home.
What's wrong, little blonde? What's wrong, little brune?
I go for the blonde, and the brune I pass by.

2 Oh, Crowley's the town where the bums hang around,
Always travelin' the road, a-lookin' for fun,
With a jug in their hands and brass knucks in their pants,
Always travelin' the road, a-lookin' for fun.

3 I am sleepy, I'm tired, and I'm hungry and dry,
And the sun has gone down and you've gone far from home.
Bye-bye, little blonde; bye-bye, little brune.
I go for the blonde, and the brune I pass by.

LE PETIT MARI
(The Bantam Husband)
bb. No. 16. O. Dupont, Kaplan, La., 1934.

In Kaplan, a little town just west of Abbeville, Louisiana, we asked for old songs. We were sent to old Mr. ———, who was night watchman at a warehouse down by the depot. When we had convinced him that we were not teasing him, he agreed to sing but asked that we bring the ——— brothers down to help him out, and begged us not to forget "un 'tit whisky," for he was an old man. The ——— brothers, young men in their twenties, and the " 'tit whiskey" were both found in an hour or so. We hung up a lantern in the warehouse and set up our machine. Soon, in spite of the bats, the mosquitoes, and the stifling Louisiana summer night, old Mr. ——— was leading the brothers through the bottle of whisky and the old wedding songs of Kaplan. Among many others, they sang that night the ballad of "The Bantam Husband," one of the subtlest and gayest ballads in any language.

Mon père m'a don - né - t-un pe - tit ma - ri, O mon
Dieu, quel homme et quel pe - tit homme, Mon père m'a don - né - t-un pe -
tit ma - ri, O mon Dieu, quel homme et quel pe - tit homme.

1 Mon père m'a donné-t-un petit mari,
O mon Dieu, quel homme et quel petit homme,
Mon père m'a donné-t-un petit mari,
O mon Dieu, quel homme et quel petit homme.

[189]

2 Je l'ai mis couché dans mon grand lit,

3 Je l'ai perdu dans la paillasse.

4 J'ai allumé la chandelle pour le trouver.

5 La paillasse a pris feu.

6 Je l'ai trouvé du tout grillé.

7 Je l'ai exposé dans une soucoupe

8 Le chat est venu, l'a pris pour un rat.

9 O chat, ô chat, laisse mon mari.

------

1 My father, he gave me a bantam man,
Oh, my Lord, a manikin, not a man,*
My father, he gave me a bantam man,
Oh, my Lord, a manikin, not a man.

2 I laid him down in my corn-shuck bed,
Oh, my Lord, a manikin, not a man,
I laid him down in my corn-shuck bed,
Oh, my Lord, a manikin, not a man.

3 I lost him down in the quilts and sheets.

4 I lit me a candle to find him there.

5 The candle set the shucks on fire.

6 When I found him at last, he was toasted well.

7 I laid him out in a saucer of glass.

8 The cat took my manikin for a rat.

9 "O kitty," I cried, "let my husband be."

* Or, "Oh, my Lord, a bantam little man."

LES CLEFS DE LA PRISON
(The Keys of the Jail)
ab. No. 31. Elida Hofpauir, New Iberia, La., 1934.

So far as we know, this is an indigenous song. Its clipped, colloquial style, its syncopation, its lines from "The Boston Burglar" indicate its fairly recent origin. The precision of phrasing, the lighthearted bitterness of the lines, and the remarkably deft use of dialogue remind one of Villon. A swift and acid dialogue between a condemned man and his father and mother, it stands alone of its kind among American folk songs.

Fast ♩ = 88

THE BOY
Chère mom! ____ On vient m'don-ner les ____ clefs, ____ Les
clefs de la ____ pri - son, Les clefs de la pri - son. ____

HIS MOTHER
Gar' - tu! Com-ment dis - tu ____ te ____ donne ____ Les clefs de
la pri - son, ____ En quant les of - fi - ciers ____ Les a cro - chées dans l'cou, ____
____ Les a cro - chées dans ____ l'cou. ____

*

* This tune fits the first stanza only. The extra syllables in succeeding stanzas are sung, not by crowding them into the given tune, but by inserting extra beats or measures into the tune where needed. The tonal and rhythmic patterns of these inserted portions are drawn from preceding measures or fragments of them; no new melodic material is introduced.

1 THE BOY:
  Chère mom!
  On vient m' donner les clefs,
  Les clefs de la prison,
  Les clefs de la prison.

2 HIS MOTHER:
  Gar'-tu!
  Comment dis-tu—te donne
  Les clefs de la prison,
  En quant les officiers
  Les a crochées dans l' cou,
  Les a crochées dans l' cou.

3 THE BOY:
  Chère mom!
  Ils vont m' venir chercher,
  Mais à neuf heures à soir,
  Mais oui, c'est pou' me pend',
  Mais à dix heures en nuit,
  Mais à dix heures en nuit.

4 Chère mom!
  C'est ce qui m' fait plus d' peine,
  C'est de savoir ma mort
  Aussi longtemps d'avance,
  Aussi longtemps d'avance.

5 (Son père,
  Mais qui s'est mis à genoux
  En s'arrachant les cheveux,
  En s'arrachant les cheveux.)

6 HIS FATHER:
  Gar'-tu!
  Comment j'ai pu t' quitter
  C'est pou' t'en aller
  Mais dans un 'grand' prison.

1 THE BOY:
  Mama, they're gonna give me
  the keys to this jail, yes, the
  keys to this old jailhouse.

2 HIS MOTHER:
  What do you mean, give you
  the keys to this old jail, when
  the turnkeys have got them
  hung around their necks, yes,
  right around their necks.

3 THE BOY:
  Mama, I mean they're coming
  to get me about nine this evening, yes, and they're gonna
  hang me, about ten tonight, I
  mean, about ten tonight.

4 Mama, what makes me so damn
  sorry, is to know so far ahead
  of time, yes, so awful far ahead
  of time, that I'm gonna die.

5 (Look at his old father, he's
  down on his knees, tearing out
  his old gray locks, yes, tearing
  them out.)

6 HIS FATHER:
  Look here, now, how in the
  world could I leave you when
  you were going off to that big
  old prison pen!

7 THE BOY:
Cher pop!
Comment tu voulais j' fais
Et quand les officiers
Etaient autour de moi
Avec les carabines,
Avec les carabines?

8 Chère mom!
C'est ce qui m' fait plus d' peine
C'est de savoir ma mort
Aussi longtemps d'avance,
Aussi longtemps d'avance.

9 O mom!
Ils vont m' venir chercher
Mais à neuf heures à soir,
Mais oui, c'est pou' me pend',
Mais à dix heures en nuit,
Mais à dix heures en nuit.

10 Chère mom!
Oui, c'est, c'est toi qui m'amène,
Oui, oui, mon corps au terre
Avec mon beau ch'val cannelle,
Avec ma bell' voiture noire,
Avec les quat' roues rouges,
Avec les quat' roues rouges.

7 THE BOY:
Dear papa, what did you want
me to do when those police were
standing all around, with their
rifles in their hands, yes, with
their rifles in their hands?

8 Dear mama, what makes me so
damn sorry is to know so far
ahead of time, yes, so far ahead
of time, that I'm gonna die.

9 Mama, they're gonna come and
get me just about nine this evening, yes, and hang me about
ten tonight, I mean just about
ten tonight.

10 Dear mama, it's gotta be you
who takes me, yes, I mean,
takes my body down, with my
pretty light bay horse, and my
pretty black carriage, with those
four red wheels, I mean, with
those four red wheels.

BELLE

e^b. No. 11. Mr. Bornu, Kaplan, La., 1934.

The influence of the Westerns and of jazz is plain to be seen in this modern chronicle of the Cajun country. When a man is ready to sacrifice his cow pony (named, of all things, Henry) for his true love, he is, according to the philosophy of the wild young boys of southwestern Louisiana, a completely devoted lover.

1 Mais si j' une belle ici, Belle,
   C'est par rapport à toi, Belle,
   Mais si j' une belle ici, Belle,
   C'est par rapport à toi, Belle.

1 If I've a babe in town, Babe,
   It's just when you're around, Babe,
   If I've a babe in town, Babe,
   It's just when you're around, Babe.

2 J'ai pris ce char ici, Belle,
   Pour m'en aller au Texas, Belle,
   J'ai pris ce char ici, Belle
   Pour m'en aller au Texas, Belle.

2 I caught a long slow freight, Babe,
   Bound out for Texas state, Babe,
   I caught a long slow freight, Babe,
   Bound out for Texas state, Babe.

3 Y avait just' trois jours, Bel-
   Le, que j'étais là-bas, Belle,
   J'ai r'çu-z-une lettre de toi, Belle,
   Que t'étais bien malade, Belle.

3 Three days I hung around, Babe,
   That lonesome Texas town, Babe,
   You wrote you's sick in bed, Babe,
   Rags wrapped all round your head, Babe.

4 Que t'étais bien malade, Belle,
   En danger de mourir, Belle,
   J'ai pris ce char encore, Belle,
   Pour m'en r'venir ici, Belle.

5 Quand j'arrivais à toi, Belle,
   T'étais sans connaisance, Belle,
   Je m'en ai r'tourné d'abord, Belle,
   Je m'en ai r'tourné là-bas, Belle.

6 J'ai emportiqué mon ch'val,
     Belle,
   Pour te sauver la vie, Belle,
   O si j'ai plus Henry, Belle,
   C'est par t'avoir aimée, Belle.

7 S'abandonner c'est dur, Belle,
   Mais s'oublier c'est long, Belle,
   S'abandonner c'est dur, Belle,
   Mais s'oublier c'est long, Belle.

4 Said you was sick and low, Babe,
   Said you was dyin' slow, Babe,
   I hopped that long slow freight,
     Babe,
   Bound for Lou's'ana state, Babe.

5 When I got off that train, Babe,
   You couldn't call my name, Babe,
   And I turned right around, Babe,
   Then I was Texas bound, Babe.

6 My bronc' I had to sell, Babe,
   So I could get you well, Babe,
   Because between the two, Babe,
   I'd always pick on you, Babe.

7 It's not so hard to go, Babe,
   But to forget is slow, Babe,
   It's not so hard to go, Babe,
   But to forget is slow, Babe.

III

MEN AT WORK

III. 1. SOLDIERS AND SAILORS

SOLDIERS

THE FRENCHMAN'S BALL

*e*b. No. 3729. Elmer George, North Montpelier, Vt., Nov., 1939. See H. H. Flanders, *A Garland of Green Mountain Song*. Printed by permission, text rearranged.

1 I have two sons and a son-in-law,
Fighting in the wars in America,
I have two sons and a son-in-law,
Fighting in the wars in America.
But I don't know if I'll see them more
Or whether I'll visit old Ireland's shore,
　　To the rum-die-ah, fa-da-diddle-ah,
　　Whacks to the lady to the rum-die-ah.

[198]

2 My son Terry is nice and trim,
   To every leg he has one shin,
   I spied two ships a-comin' on the sea,
   "Halliloo, Bubilloo, an' I think 'tis you." (*Chorus.*)

3 "O ships, O ships, will you wait awhile,
   Till I find Terry, my own child?"
   He's mamma's pet and darling boy,
   He's the ladies t'y * and the girls' own joy. (*Chorus.*)

4 "Oh, wasn't you cunning, oh, wasn't you cute!
   You didn't git way from the Frenchman's shoot,
   'Tis not a divilish shin or leg you have at all,
   They was all knocked off at the Frenchman's ball." (*Chorus.*)

5 "O Terry, Terry, Terry, divil a bit of God in you,
   That you didn't git away from the Frenchman's shoot."
   "O mother dear, you'd ought to 've seen the fun
   When the Frenchman's ball took the legs off me." (*Chorus.*)

6 "Mother dear, you'd ought to know,
   If the boys enlist they've got to go,
   There stands old Bonypart, stalks all round,
   Fight or die or stand your ground." (*Chorus.*)

7 "My son Terry is neat and trim,
   To every leg he has one shin,
   He's mamma's pet and darling boy
   He's the ladies' t'y and the girls' own joy,
   To the rum-die-ah, fa-da-diddle-ah,
   Aye de rather rather rum-die-ah.

* "Toy."

THE TRUE PADDY'S SONG

B. No. 2353. Mason Palmer, Newberry, Mich., 1938. See Sh, 2:228.

Fast ♩ = 116

Nine years a-go I was dig-gin' up the land, With me

brogues on me feet and me sho-vel in me hand; Says I to me-self, "What a

pit-y for to see Such a tall hand-some lad-dy dig-gin' turf on the Dee!"

CHORUS

Mush-a-doo, Mush-a-doo, a-dad-dy doo-a-dum.

1 Nine years ago I was diggin' up the land,
   With me brogues on me feet and me shovel in me hand;
   Says I to meself, "What a pity for to see
   Such a tall handsome laddy diggin' turf on the Dee!"

   Chorus:
       Mushadoo,
       Mushadoo, a-daddy doo-a-dum.

2 So I laid down my shovel, shook hands with my spade,
   And it's off to the wars like a jolly young blade,
   Next the sergeant of the army he asked me to enlist,
   "Be my long-whiskered japers, put some money in my fist."

3 "Now, here's a half a crown and a half a penny more,
   You go to that corner and you git a half a score.
   "Go up to headquarters, is that what's to do?
   I don't want to be quartered, sir; neither do you!

4 "No headquarters like that, it ain't what I mean,
   You go to headquarters and they'll fit you out in green,
   You go to headquarters and they'll fit you out so rare
   That the ladies will all laugh at you coming to the fair."

5 Now the first thing they gave me it was an overcoat,
   With two sets of leathers to buckle up me throat,
   And a sword at the side and a pistol in me hand,
   Swore to kill everything before me at the word of command.

6 Now the next thing they gave me it was a gray horse
   All saddled, all bridled, all fitted for the course.
   I threw my leg over her and gave her the steel,
   And the stiff-necked devil run away through the fields.

7 Now, the next thing they give me, it was a long gun
   And under the trigger they planted me thumb,
   Placed me finger on the trigger and the thing begin to smoke,
   And it give me poor shoulder a devil of a poke.

8 Now I says to McGuire, "You may think it quite grand
   To place such a tool in any man's hands.
   No, Mister McGuire, I think I shall retire
   For the thing is running mad, can't you see her spitting fire?"

9 Now, nine years ago, thank God, I had such luck
   At the battle of the Hills and the battle of the Muck,
   Why, the smoke it was so thick and the fire it was so hot,
   Save my soul, I dare not shoot for fear of getting shot.

10 Now nine years are over, I've nothing to defend
   And I am safe back in old Ireland again.
   Why, the smoke it was so thick and the fire it was so hot,
   Save my soul, I dare not shoot for fear of getting shot.

11 Oh! it's nine years ago, and I'm glad it isn't ten;
   They've taken me back to the Old Sod again!
   Without a shilling in my pocket, just as rich as I begun!
   And this is the end of the true Paddy's Son.

TRENCH BLUES

a. No. 242. *Acc. on guitar and sung by John Bray
(Big Nig), Amelia, La., 1934. See "Careless Love," Lo.3,
p. 137, p. 218.*

"Big Nig" of Amelia, Louisiana, stood six feet and seven inches in his socks. Alan, on one of our visits, measured the spread of his mighty arms as an inch longer. When he works, "Big Nig" is the singing leader of a gang of Negroes who snake cypress out of the Louisiana swamps. "Big Nig" booms his signals to the flatboat out on the black bayou; the engineer toots his reply, and the logs come busting through the tangled swamp forest. Ten whistles means "A man dead."

On our first visit we mistakenly tipped "Big Nig" in advance of his singing, only to find out later that he had become too drunk to sing. A year or so afterwards repeated visits put on records the singing and guitar picking of this remarkable man.

The "Trench Blues," according to "Big Nig," was composed during the World War when he was a soldier in France. "They didn't give me a gun," said "Big Nig"; "all the weapons I ever had was my guitar, a shovel, and a mop."

The tune resembles "C. C. Rider" and "Careless Love" in *Negro Folk Songs As Sung by Lead Belly* (Macmillan, 1936).

—Adventures of a Ballad Hunter

Moderately fast ♩ = 126

1. When I was a-steal-in' 'cross the deep blue sea, Lawd, I's
2. My home in the trenches, liv-in' in a big dug-out, Lawd, my

wor-ry-in' with those sub-ma-rines, ___
home in the trench-es, liv-in' in a big dug-out, ___

Wor-ry-in' with those sub-ma-rines, ___ Hey, hey, hey, hey.
Home in the trenches, liv-in'in a big dug-out, ___ Hey, hey, hey, hey. ___

1 When I was a-stealin' 'cross the deep blue sea,
   Lawd, I's worryin' with those submarines,
   Worryin' with those submarines,
   Hey, hey, hey, hey.

2 My home in the trenches, livin' in a big dugout,
   Lawd, my home in the trenches, livin' in a big dugout,
   Home in the trenches, livin' in a big dugout,
   Hey, hey, hey, hey.

3 We went a-hikin' to the firing line.
   "Uncle Sammy, hear your men's a-cryin'," (2)
   Hey, hey, hey, hey.

4 Raining here, stormin' on the sea,
   "Woman I love, honey, do write to me," (2)
   Hey, hey, hey, hey.

5 The women in France hollerin', "I no compris,"
   Women in America hollerin', "Who wants me?" (2)
   Hey, hey, hey, hey.

6 We went a-hikin' to old Mount Sac hill,
   Lawd, forty thousand soldiers called out to drill, (2)
   Hey, hey, hey, hey.

7 Uncle Sam sho' don't know I'm here,
   Uncle Sam sho' don't feel my care, (2)
   Hey, hey, hey, hey.

8 I went to Belgium, blowed my bugle horn,
   Every time I blowed, motherless German gone, (2)
   Hey, hey, hey, hey.

9 We went to Berlin, went with all our will,
   Lawd, if the whites don't get him, the niggers certainly will, (2)
   Hey, hey, hey, hey.

10 Last old words I heard old Kaiser say,
   He was calling those Germans, Lawd, way long the way, (2)
   Hey, hey, hey, hey.

11 Call him in the mornin', kiss him in the night,
   Hit him in the head, make him treat American right, (2)
   Hey, hey, hey, hey.

12 We went away, leaving our happy home, (3)
   Hey, hey, hey, hey.

13 Wind a-blowin', big bell sadly tone,
   Many a soldier, Lawd, is dead and gone, (2)
   Hey, hey, hey, hey.

OLD KING COLE

No record. Tune, Bess Lomax; text, Col. Henry Breck-
enridge, New York City, 1938.

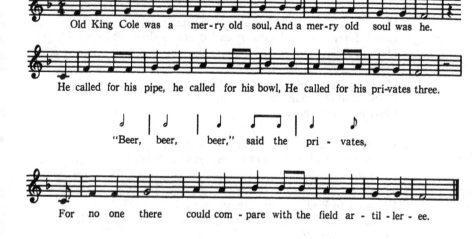

Moderately fast

Old King Cole was a mer-ry old soul, And a mer-ry old soul was he.

He called for his pipe, he called for his bowl, He called for his pri-vates three.

"Beer, beer, beer," said the pri - vates,

For no one there could com - pare with the field ar - til - ler - ee.

1 Old King Cole was a merry old soul,
  And a merry old soul was he.
  He called for his pipe, he called for his bowl,
  He called for his privates three.
  "Beer, beer, beer," said the privates,
  For no one there could compare with the field artilleree.

2 Old King Cole was a merry old soul,
  And a merry old soul was he.
  He called for his pipe, he called for his bowl,
  He called for his corporals three.
  "One-two, one-two, one," said the corporals,
  "Beer, beer, beer," said the privates,
  For no one there could compare with the field artilleree.

3 He called for his sergeants three.*
  "Forward right by squads," said the sergeants.

4 He called for his lieutenants three.
  "We want ten days leave," said the lieutenants

5 He called for his captains three.
  "We want much more pay," said the captains.

6 He called for his majors three.
  "The army's gone to hell," said the majors.

7 He called for his colonels three.
  "Nuts, nuts, nuts," said the colonels.

8 He called for his generals three.
  "We want no more war," said the generals.

* Each stanza should be expanded as the second from the first.

SAILORS

Wrap me in my tarpaulin jacket
And say a poor buffer lies low, lies low,
And six stalwart lancers shall carry me
With steps mournful, solemn, and slow.
I know I shan't get into heaven,
And I don't want to go down below-o-o-o.
Oh, ain't there some place in between them
Where this poor old buffer can go?

*   *   *

Where the laughing dolphins play,
Where the shrimps and sharks are having their larks,
Ten thousand miles away.

*   *   *

SANTY ANNO

e. No. 652. J. M. Hunt ("Sailor Dad"), Marion, Va.,
1935. See Bo, p. 129; Col, p. 84; Wha, p. 65; also
"Round the Bay of Mexico," this volume, p. 88.

Captain Richard Maitland, blue-water sailor, eighty years old but with
a body like an oak stake, says about the shanties:

"Don't you suppose we sang shanties all the time! It was only when
we hit the forties and half the ocean was coming over our side and you
didn't feel like pulling for God's sake that we used the histing shanties.
They put heart in a man, and we could all pull together better."

Moderate ♩ = 126

We're sail-ing down the riv-er from Liv-er-pool, Heave a-way, San-ty An-no;

A- round Cape Horn to Fris-co Bay, All— on the plains of Mex-i-co. —

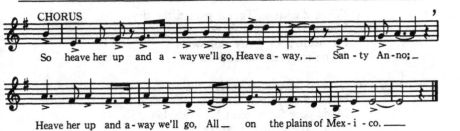

CHORUS

So heave her up and a - way we'll go, Heave a - way, — San - ty An - no; —

Heave her up and a - way we'll go, All — on the plains of Mex - i - co. —

1 We're sailing down the river from Liverpool,
   Heave away, Santy Anno;
   Around Cape Horn to Frisco Bay,
   All on the plains of Mexico.

   Chorus:
       So heave her up and away we'll go,
       Heave away, Santy Anno;
       Heave her up and away we'll go,
       All on the plains of Mexico.

2 She's a fast clipper ship and a bully good crew,
   Heave away, Santy Anno;
   A down-East Yankee for her captain, too,
   All on the plains of Mexico.

3 There's plenty gold, so I've been told,
   Heave away, Santy Anno;
   There's plenty gold, so I've been told,
   Way out West to Californio.

4 Back in the days of Forty-nine,
   Heave away, Santy Anno;
   Those are the days of the good old times,
   All on the plains of Mexico.

5 When Zacharias Taylor gained the day,
   Heave away, Santy Anno;
   He made poor Santy run away,
   All on the plains of Mexico.

6 General Scott and Taylor, too,
   Heave away, Santy Anno;
   Made poor Santy meet his Waterloo,
   All on the plains of Mexico.

7 When I leave the ship, I will settle down,
   Heave away, Santy Anno,
   And marry a girl named Sally Brown,
   All on the plains of Mexico.

8 Santy Anno was a good old man,
   Heave away, Santy Anno;
   Till he got into war with your Uncle Sam,
   All on the plains of Mexico.

HAUL AWAY, MY ROSY

Bb. No. 652. J. M. Hunt ("Sailor Dad"), Marion,
Va., 1935. See Col, p. 41; Wha, p. 85.

"This song was a song we used in hoisting the sails. The chorus comes on the last word of the verse to give the pull. It's usually one pull, but, supposing the mate or the second mate who's officer of the watch turns out wrong side to, he may think the work is going too slow, he'll let a yell out of him, 'Double up! Double up on that song! I ain't got all night to wait!' Then it means that you take a pull on the first part of the shanty and the second part also." —CAPTAIN DICK MAITLAND.

Moderate ♩ = 108

You talk a-bout your har-bor girls A-round the corn-er Sal-ly.

1 You talk about your harbor girls
Around the corner Sally.

Chorus:
   Way, haul away,
   Haul away, my Rosy;
   Way, haul away,
   Haul away, my Johnsy-o.

2 They couldn't come to gee
With the girls from Ruble Alley.

3 I once had a French girl,
But she was all a-posy.

4 Now, I've got an English girl,
I treat her like a lady.

5 When we sailed into Glasgow,
I met a bonny lassie;

6 She was handsome, young, and fair,
And sweet as 'lasses candy.

7 Oh, once I was in Ireland
Digging turf and praties,

8 Now, I'm in a Yankee ship,
A-hauling sheets and braces.

9 Oh, once I had an Irish girl
And she was fat and lazy;

10 And next I got a German girl
And she was fat and grazy,

11 And now I've got a Yankee girl
And she damn near drives me crazy.

12 Then we sailed away from Liverpool,
Bound for Rio Janerio;

13 We loaded cargo there, my boys,
And we took it mighty easy.

14 Now, we're homeward bound again
And we're feeling mighty easy.

[209]

THE LOW-DOWN, LONESOME LOW

A. No. 2506. Acc. on guitar and sung by Blaine Stubblefield, Washington, D.C., 1939. See "The Golden Vanity,"
Child No. 286; Sh, 1:282; Ga.2, p. 214; Col, p. 154; Be,
p 97.

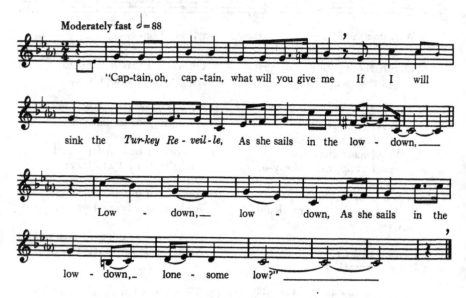

Moderately fast ♩=88

"Cap-tain, oh, cap-tain, what will you give me If I will sink the *Tur-key Re - veil - le,* As she sails in the low - down,____ Low - down,__ low - down, As she sails in the low - down,__ lone - some low?"

1 "Captain, oh, captain, what will you give me
   If I will sink the *Turkey Reveille*,
   As she sails in the low-down,
   Low-down, low-down,
   As she sails in the low-down, lonesome low?"

2 "Gold and silver, shining so bright
   And my fairest daughter shall wed you tonight,
   If you sink her in the low-down,
   Low-down, low-down,
   If you sink her in the low-down, lonesome low."

[210]

3 Then he bared his breast and he swam on the sea
Till he came along by the *Turkey Reveille*
As she sailed in the low-down,
Low-down, low-down,
As she sailed in the low-down, lonesome low.

4 Some with their cards and some with their dice,
And some were taking their best friend's advice,
As she rowed in the low-down,
Low-down, low-down,
As she rowed in the low-down, lonesome low.

5 Then he bared his breast and he swam in the tide,
And he bored ten holes in the old ship's side,
And she sank in the low-down,
Low-down, low-down,
And she sank in the low-down, lonesome low.

6 Some with their hats and some with their caps
Were trying to stop them salt-water gaps,
As she sailed in the low-down,
Low-down, low-down,
As she sailed in the low-down, lonesome low.

7 Then he bared his breast and he swam in the tide
Until he come along by his own ship's side,
As she rolled in the low-down,
Low-down, low-down,
As she rolled in the low-down, lonesome low.

8 "Captain, oh, captain, take me on board,
For if you don't you have forfeited your word,
As you sail in the low-down,
Low-down, low-down,
As you sail in the low-down, lonesome low."

9 "Sailor boy, sailor boy, don't appeal to me,
For you drowned fifty souls when you sank the *Reveille*,
As she sailed in the low-down,
Low-down, low-down,
As she sailed in the low-down, lonesome low."

10 "If it wasn't for the love that I have for your men,
   I would serve you the same as I've served them,
   As you sail in the low-down,
   Low-down, low-down,
   As you sail in the low-down, lonesome low."

11 Then he hoisted his sails, and away sailed he,
   And he left the poor sailor boy to drown in the sea,
   To drown in the low-down,
   Low-down, low-down,
   To drown in the low-down, lonesome low.

12 So he bared his breast and down swam he,
   He swam till he came to the bottom of the sea,
   And he drowned in the low-down,
   Low-down, low-down,
   And he drowned in the low-down, lonesome low.

THE HIGH BARBAREE

No record. Text sent in by Capt. A. E. Dingle, Cove
Cottage, West Bermuda. Tune from Stanton Henry King's
Book of Chanties, p. 25 (Oliver Ditson Co., N. Y., 1918)
See Wha, p. 78.

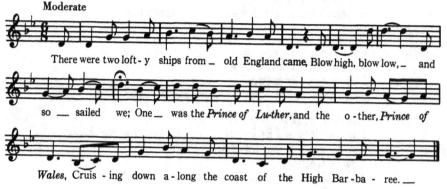

1 There were two lofty ships from old England came,
 Blow high, blow low, and so sailed we;
 One was the *Prince of Luther;* and the other, *Prince of Wales,*
 Cruising down along the coast of the High Barbaree.

2 "Aloft there, aloft!" our jolly boatswain cries,
 Blow high, blow low, and so sailed we;
 "Look ahead, look astern, look aweather and alee,
 Look along down the coast of the High Barbaree."

3 "There's naught upon the stern, there's naught upon the lee,"
 Blow high, blow low, and so sailed we;
 "But there's a lofty ship to windward, and she's sailing fast and free.
 Sailing down along the coast of the High Barbaree."

4 "Oh, hail her, oh, hail her!" our gallant captain cried,
 Blow high, blow low, and so sailed we.
 "Are you a man-o'-war or a privateer," said he,
 "Cruising down along the coast of the High Barbaree?"

5 "Oh, I am not a man-o'-war nor privateer," said he,
 Blow high, blow low, and so sailed we;
 "But I'm a salt-sea pirate a-looking for me fee,
 Cruising down along the coast of the High Barbaree."

6 Oh, 'twas broadside to broadside a long time we lay,
 Blow high, blow low, and so sailed we;
 Until the *Prince of Luther* shot the pirate's masts away,
 Cruising down along the coast of the High Barbaree.

7 "Oh, quarter, oh, quarter," those pirates then did cry,
 Blow high, blow low, and so sailed we;
 But the quarter that we gave them—we sunk them in the sea,
 Cruising down along the coast of the High Barbaree.

GREENLAND WHALE FISHERY

d to *e*. No. 2325. Capt. Asel Trueblood, St. Ignace,
Mich., 1938. See Col, p. 151; Wha, p. 69; Be, 104.

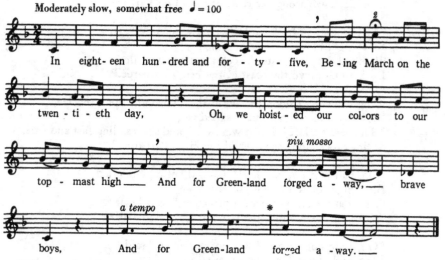

Moderately slow, somewhat free *d* = 100

In eight-een hun-dred and for-ty-five, Be-ing March on the

twen-ti-eth day, Oh, we hoist-ed our col-ors to our

top-mast high___ And for Green-land forged a-way,___ brave

piu mosso

a tempo *

boys, And for Green-land forged a-way.___

* The singer drops into speaking voice on the last word of the last stanza.

1 In eighteen hundred and forty-five,
   Being March on the twentieth day,
   Oh, we hoisted our colors to our topmast high
   And for Greenland forged away, brave boys,
   And for Greenland forged away.

2 When we struck that Greenland shore
   With our gallant ship in full fold,
   We wished ourselves back safe at home again
   With our friends all on the shore, brave boys,
   With our friends along the shore.

3 Our mate he stood on the forecastle yard
   With a spyglass in his hand,
   "There's a whale, there's a whale, there's a whale!" cried he,
   "And she blows at every span, brave boys,
   And she blows at every span."

[214]

4 Oh, when this whale we did harpoon
   She made one slap with her tail,
   She capsized our boat, we lost five of our crew,
   Neither did we catch that whale, brave boys,
   Neither did we catch that whale.

5 "Sad news, sad news," to our captain we cried,
   Which grieved his heart in full store,*
   But the losing of five of his jolly, jolly crew,
   Oh, it grieved him ten times more, brave boys,
   Oh, that grieved him ten times more.

6 "Hist your anchors then, brave boys," said he.
   "Let us leave this cold countery
   Where the storm and the snow and the whalefish does blow,
   And daylight's seldom seen, brave boys,
   And daylight's seldom seen."

* "In full sore,"

THE BEAVER ISLAND BOYS

d. No. 2274. Tune, Dominick Gallegher: text, A.A.F.S. No. 2273. Johnny Green, Beaver Island, Mich., Sept., 1938. See Ri, p. 159.

"It was in '74 that this song was composed by a man by the name of Daniel Malloy. He was an old whale fisherman. He spent two years among the Eskimos up in the North Pole when he was whale fishing.

"Three men went out of this harbor in a small boat to go to Traverse City for supplies, and they left there in a gale of wind. They only had a twenty-four-foot boat, and she foundered and they were all lost.

"That was in '73, and I was born in '67. The way I remember, my father left home with those boys that was drownded, and when he got to Traverse City and was ready to come back, old Captain Roddy, who had a little sailing vessel there, coaxed him to stay over and come home with him next day when it would be comfortable. He knew it wasn't fit for them to go out in that open boat, that small boat, understand? It was blowin' a gale of wind, it was, blowin' the tops right off the seas.

"My father was goin' right down in the boat, and Roddy said, 'Dominick, you aren't crazy, are you, to go in that boat today?' 'Well,' he said, 'I'll tell you: my wife is sick, and I want to get home.' 'Well,' he said, 'it's better

for your wife to be without you for two or three days than to be without you forever.' And my uncle Roddy went down into the boat, and he took my father by the shoulder an' he kept him from goin'.

"We heard the next morning that the boat was lost. Well, my mother knew that my father was in the boat, you see, because he had left the harbor and went to Traverse City with them, and she didn't know of this Roddy bein' in Traverse City. And when the news came and the report was that all hands was lost, I remember runnin' and hangin' around mother. I couldn't realize what they were all cryin' about. I had six sisters and they were all home and they were all cryin', too. That night they had a wake and all just as though he was there, and all the next day the neighbors came around.

"Well, when this Captain Roddy came home the next day in his vessel and when they come to St. James, the harbor, they heard there that we had held a wake over father that night. My father and this Captain Roddy was great friends, and some of 'em got a jug of whisky and they started home rejoicing that he didn't come in the boat that was lost. When my father come home he started to dance—he was always for singin' and dancin' when he had drinks. (He never drank much except occasionally.) I remember he had some toys for me, the first toys I ever had in my life, a little cast-iron shovel and a little pail, and I left the old folks in the house and went out to dig sand with my little shovel and my little pail. . . . But this is the way old Dan Malloy's song of it goes."

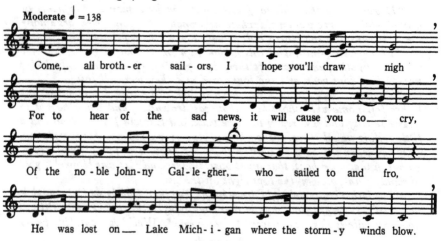

Moderate ♩ = 138

Come,— all broth-er sail-ors, I hope you'll draw nigh

For to hear of the sad news, it will cause you to—— cry,

Of the no-ble John-ny Gal-le-gher,— who— sailed to and fro,

He was lost on— Lake Mich-i-gan where the storm-y winds blow.

1 Come, all brother sailors, I hope you'll draw nigh
    For to hear of the sad news, it will cause you to cry,
    Of the noble Johnny Gallegher, who sailed to and fro,
    He was lost on Lake Michigan where the stormy winds blow.

2 "Oh, Johnny, my dear son, in the dead of the night
    I woke from a dream which gave me a fright,
    And to Traverse City I beseech you not to go,
    For you'll never cross Lake Michigan where the stormy winds blow.

3 "Oh, mother, dear mother, those dreams are not true,
    I will shortly return and prove it to you,
    For the Lord will protect me wherever I go
    And I'll cross o'er Lake Michigan where the stormy winds blow."

4 It was in October in '73,
    We left Beaver harbor and had a calm sea,
    Bound away, Traverse City was our destination to go,
    We were crossing Lake Michigan where the stormy winds blow.

5 We left Traverse City at nine the next day
    And down to Elk Rapids we then bore away;
    We took in our stores and to sea we did go,
    For to cross o'er Lake Michigan where the stormy winds blow.

6 At nine that same night a light we did spy
    That is Beaver Island, we are drawing nigh,
    We carried all sails, the *Lookout,* she did go,
    We were crossing Lake Michigan where the stormy winds blow.

7 Oh, Johnny got up and he spoke to his crew,
    He says, "Now, brave boys, be steady and true,
    Stand by for your halliards, let your main halliards go,
    There's a squall on Lake Michigan where the stormy winds blow."

8 The *Lookout* she's a-running before a hard gale,
    Upset went her rudder and overboard went her sail;
    The billows were foaming like mountains of snow,
    We shall ne'er cross Lake Michigan where the stormy winds blow.

9 Siz own brother Johnny, "It grieves my heart sore
  To think we will never return to the shore;
  God help our poor parents, their tears down will flow;
  For we'll sleep in Lake Michigan where the stormy winds blow."

DARK–EYED CANALLER
(Dark-Eyed Sailor)
e. No. 1007. Capt. P. R. Nye, Akron, Ohio, 1937. See
Cox, p. 319; Ma, p. 172; Ga.2, p. 160; Gr, p. 58.

*"My sister furnished all except the first stanza to this song. I sent to
England for the first stanza and received it with a statement asking six hundred dollars for the remainder of the song. Since I already had plenty of
stanzas, and didn't have the six hundred dollars, I just let the English keep
the rest of their song. This song was known from one end of the Canal to
the other, from Cleveland through Akron down to the Ohio River."*

—Captain Nye.

It was a come-ly young la-dy fair, Was walking out to take the air.
She met a ca-nal-ler up-on the way, So I paid at-ten-tion,
So I paid at-ten-tion, To hear what they did say.

1 It was a comely young lady fair,
  Was walking out to take the air.
  She met a canaller upon the way,
  So I paid attention, so I paid attention,
  To hear what they did say.

2 "Fair maid," said he, "while you roam alone—
  The night is coming and the day's far gone."

[218]

She drew a dagger, and then did cry,
"For my dark-eyed canaller, for my dark-eyed canaller,
Though may he live or die.

3 "My every hope is based on him;
True love will wait, true love will win."
She said, while tears from her eyes did fall,
" 'Tis my dark-eyed canaller, 'tis my dark-eyed canaller,
A-proving my downfall.

4 "His coal-black eyes and curly hair,
His flattering tongue my heart ensnared;
Genteel was he, no rake like you,
To advise a maiden, to advise a maiden
To slight this jacket blue.

5 "It is six long years since he left our boat,
A gold ring he took and gently broke;
He left this token—here's half, you see,
And the other he's keeping, and the other he's keeping
To remind him oft of me."

6 Cried William, "Drive him from off your mind,
Many as good a canaller as him you'll find;
Love turned aside and cold did grow,
Like a winter's morning, like a winter's morning
When the hills are clad with snow."

7 When William did this ring unfold,
She seemed too struck with joy and woe;
"You're welcome, William, I've land and gold
For my dark-eyed canaller, for my dark-eyed canaller,
So manly, true, and bold."

8 Come, girls—yes, listen, oh, come and see,
And a warning take, oh, take from me.
Always be true while your love's away,
For a cloudy morning, for a cloudy morning,
Often brings a pleasant day.

[219]

THE *BIGLER*

A to *B♭*. No. 2323,4. Tune and part of text from Capt. Asel Trueblood, St. Ignace, Mich., 1939. Remainder of text from R. F. Hasbrook, Bessemer, Mich. See Col, p. 200; Ri, p. 168.

"*I learned this song a good fifty years ago. I was twenty-three at the time. I've walked the old Bigler's decks many times though I never sailed on her. She was supposed to be the slowest vessel in the fleet, and of course they had winds and all that and she'd bile along like everything but the other vessels would beat her. They stopped many places on the way down, and a new verse was composed about every place they stopped in and every place they'd pass. And when they got down in Lake Erie, before they got to Buffalo, they met the fleet coming back.*

"*I knew this feller that composed this song about the Bigler, but I forgot his name. It was a kind of a joky song like, because they got beat. He said they'd 'a' beat the fleet if the fleet had 'a' hove to. The places they stopped in were the whorehouses on the way down, and they'd get in there drinkin' beer and singin' this song, and it bought 'em a lot of free beers.*"

—CAPTAIN ASEL TRUEBLOOD.

"*The best known song that came out of the lumber trade on the lakes is the well-known 'Timber-Drover Bigler'. . . . The schooner Bigler, which was evidently carrying a cargo of grain on the trip narrated in the song, was a blunt-nosed, clumsy canaller that was slow and hard to steer. . . . The 'juberju' mentioned in the chorus has been variously described as the jib boom, the raffee yard, and the crossfire, upon which the sailors at times climbed to ride the halliard down to the deck. . . .*"

—IVAN H. WALTON, *University of Michigan.*

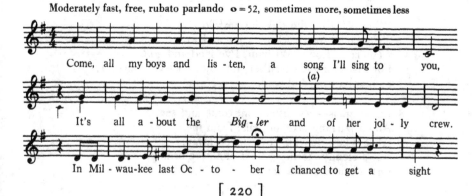

Moderately fast, free, rubato parlando o = 52, sometimes more, sometimes less

Come, all my boys and lis - ten, a song I'll sing to you,

(a)

It's all a - bout the *Big - ler* and of her jol - ly crew.

In Mil - wau-kee last Oc - to - ber I chanced to get a sight

Men at Work

In the schoon-er called the *Big-ler* be - long-ing to De - troit.

CHORUS

Watch her, catch her, jump up in her ju - ber - ju,

Give her sheet and let her go, we're the lads can pull her through.

Oh, don't you hear us howl-ing, oh, the wind is blow-ing free,

On our down trip to Buf-fa - lo from Mil - wau - kee.

(a) *In stanza 2, insert here the following measure:*

Big - ler in (to)

* The singer drops into speaking voice on the last three words of the last stanza.

1 Come, all my boys and listen, a song I'll sing to you,
It's all about the *Bigler* and of her jolly crew.
In Milwaukee last October I chanced to get a sight
In the schooner called the *Bigler* belonging to Detroit.

Chorus:
　　Watch her, catch her, jump up in her juberju,
　　Give her sheet and let her go, we're the lads can pull her through.
　　Oh, don't you hear us howling, oh, the wind is blowing free,
　　On our down trip to Buffalo from Milwaukee.

2 It was on one Sunday morning just at the hour of ten,
  When the tug *Nickle Roberts* towed the schooner *Bigler* into Lake Michigan,
  Oh, there we made our canvas, in the middle of the fleet,
  Oh, the wind hauled to the south'ard, boys, and we had to give her sheet.
  (*Chorus.*)

3 The wind come down from the south-southeast, it blowed both stiff and strong!
  You had orter seen that little schooner *Bigler* as she plowed Lake Michigan.
  Oh, far beyond her foaming bows the fiery waves to fling
  With every stitch of canvas and her course was wing and wing. (*Chorus.*)

4 We made Skilagalee and Wabbleshanks, the entrance to the straits,
  And might have passed the whole fleet there if they'd hove to and wait;
  But we drove them all before us the nicest you ever saw
  Clear out into Lake Huron through the Straits of Mackinac.

5 First Forty-Mile Point and Presque Isle Light, and then we boomed away,
  The wind being fresh and fair, for the Isle of Thunder Bay.
  The wind it shifted to a close haul, all on her sta'b'rd tack,
  With a good lookout ahead we made for Point aux Barques.

6 We made the light and kept in sight of Michigan's east shore,
  A-booming for the river as we'd often done before.
  And when abreast Port Huron Light, our small anchor we let go;
  The tug *Kate Moffet* came along and took the *Bigler* in tow.

7 The *Moffet* took six schooners in tow, and all of us fore-and-aft,
  She took us down to Lake St. Clair and stuck us on the Flats,
  She parted the *Hunter's* towline in trying to give relief,
  And stem to stern went the *Bigler* smash in the *Mapleleaf.*

8 Then she towed us through and left us outside the river light,
  Lake Erie for us to wander and the blustering winds to fight.
  The wind was from the sou'west, and we paddled our own canoe;
  Her jib boom pointed the Dummy, she's hell-bent for Buffalo.

III. 2. LUMBERJACKS AND TEAMSTERS

"And here's good luck to the shanty boys
That makes the wild woods ring,
For they cut the pine in the wintertime
And drive it in the spring."

*   *   *

"All names I will not mention, as you may understand,
There were twenty-five or thirty, all good and noble men,
All working with good courage while scattered to and fro,
*And it was their delight, coming home at night, to see the landings grow.**

*   *   *

It was early in the season in the spring of '63,
A preacher of the gospel one morning came to me.
Said he, "My jolly fellow, how would you like to go
To spend one winter pleasantly in Michigan-i-o?"

When we arrived in Saginaw, in Michigan-i-o,
We started for the camp, but the roads we did not know,
The dogs might laugh that our beds were on the snow,
In the cold and frosty morning we shivered with the cold,
God grant there is no worser hell than Michigan-i-o.

* Eckstorm and Smyth, *Minstrelsy of Maine.*

THE LITTLE BROWN BULLS

e♭. No. 2265. Carl Lathrop, Mt. Pleasant, Mich., 1939.
Through the courtesy of Dr. E. C. Beck, Central State
Teachers College, Mt. Pleasant, Mich. Dr. Beck has an
unsurpassed collection of lumberjack songs. See Ri, p. 65;
Go, p. 56.

*"When you get to the last of the song, you speak the words so that every-
one will know the song is ended, at least I suppose that's why you do it.
Anyhow, whether that is why or not, that's what all the old-time woods
singers I ever heard always did."*

—BILL McBRIDE, *Mt. Pleasant, Michigan.*

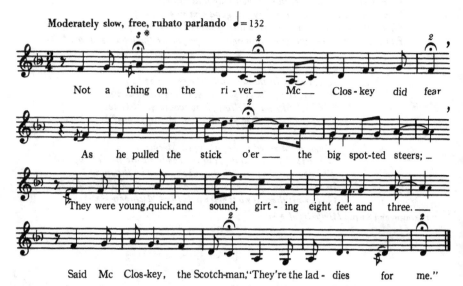

Moderately slow, free, rubato parlando ♩=132

Not a thing on the ri-ver— Mc— Clos-key did fear

As he pulled the stick o'er — the big spot-ted steers; —

They were young, quick, and sound, girt-ing eight feet and three. —

Said Mc Clos-key, the Scotch-man, "They're the lad-dies for me."

*In this and similar songs of "come-all-ye" character, extended tones and extended or inserted rests
vary widely from stanza to stanza, both in length and in position.

1 Not a thing on the river McCloskey did fear
  As he pulled the stick o'er the big spotted steers;
  They were young, quick and sound, girting eight feet and three.
  Said McCloskey, the Scotchman, "They're the laddies for me."

2 Bold Gordon, the Yankee, of skidding was full,
   As he said, "Wo-ho" to his little brown bulls,
   Short-legged and shaggy, girting six feet and nine.
   Said McCloskey, the Scotchman, "Too light for our pine."

3 'Twas three to the thousand and our contract did call,
   The skidding was good for the timber was tall.
   McCloskey he swore that he'd make the day full
   And he'd skid two to one of the little brown bulls.

4 "Oh, no!" said Bold Gordon. "That you cannot do,
   Although we all know you're the pets of the crew;
   But mark you, my boy, you will have your hands full
   If you skid one more log than my little brown bulls."

5 The day was appointed and soon it drawed nigh
   For twenty-five dollars their fortunes to try.
   Each eager and anxious that morning was found
   As the scalers and judges appeared on the ground.

6 With a whoop and a yell came McCloskey to view,
   With his spotted steers, the pets of the crew,
   Both chewing their cuds, "Oh, boys, keep your jaws full,
   For you easily can beat them, the little brown bulls."

7 Then up stepped Bold Gordon, with his pipe in his jaw,
   With his little brown bulls with their cuds in their mouths,
   And little did we think when we see them come down
   That a hundred and forty they could jerk around.

8 Then up spoke McCloskey, "Come strip to the skin,
   For I'll dig you a hole and I'll tumble you in,
   I will learn a damn Yankee to face the bold Scot
   I'll cook you a dose and you'll get it red-hot."

9 Said Gordon to Stebbin, with blood in his eye,
   "Today we must conquer McCloskey or die."
   Then up spoke old Kennebec, "Oh, boys, never fear,
   For you never will be beaten by the big spotted steers."

10 The sun had gone down, when the foreman did say,
"Turn out, boys, turn out, you've enough for the day,
We've scaled them and counted them, each man to his team
And it's well do we know now which one tips the beam."

11 After supper was over, McCloskey appeared,
With a belt ready-made for his big spotted steers,
To form it he'd torn up his best Mackinaw
For he swore he'd conduct it according to law.

12 Then up spoke the scaler, "Hold on you, awhile,
For your big spotted steers are behind just one mile.
You've skidded one hundred and ten and no more
And the bulls have you beaten by ten and a score."

13 The shanty did ring and McCloskey did swear
As he tore up by handfuls his long yellow hair;
Says he to Bold Gordon, "My colors I pull,
So, here, take the belt for your little brown bulls."

14 Here's health to Bold Gordon and Kennebec John;
The biggest day's work on the river they've done.
So fill up your glasses, boys, fill them up full
We will drink to the health of the little brown bulls.

MOOSEHEAD LAKE

B. No. 3714. Elmer George, North Montpelier, Vt., 1939. Printed by permission of Helen Hartness Flanders. See Cr, p. 265; Gra, p. 60.

"I learned this song from a feller by the name of Brant Breaux that I lumbered on Sterling Mountain with. I think I got the whole of it, or most of it, from him. I don't know as I've heard any one else sing it."

Men at Work

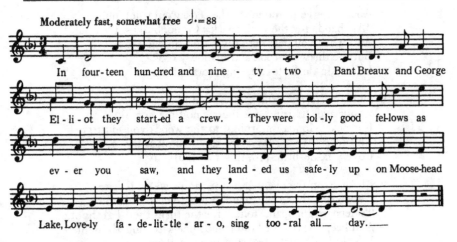

Moderately fast, somewhat free ♩ = 88

In four-teen hun-dred and nine-ty-two Bant Breaux and George El-li-ot they start-ed a crew. They were jol-ly good fel-lows as ev-er you saw, and they land-ed us safe-ly up-on Moose-head Lake, Love-ly fa-de-lit-tle-ar-o, sing too-ral all__ day.__

1 In fourteen hundred and ninety-two
Bant Breaux and George Elliot they started a crew.
They were jolly good fellows as ever you saw,
And they landed us safely upon Moosehead Lake,
Lovely fa-de-little-aro, sing tooral all day.

2 It's upon the Northwest Carry we met with the boss,
And then we got on a spree,
We built him a storehouse and likewise a camp,
Lost one of our bold woodsmen all on that wild tramp,
Lovely fa-de-little-aro, sing tooral all day.

3 He hired a man from Bangor, Maine,
To swamp in our crew, Bill Williams by name,
And when he got there, "I'm a chopper," said he,
'Bout the best he could do was to lodge every tree.
Lovely fa-de-little-aro, sing tooral all day.

4 About five in the morning the cook would sing out,
"Come, bullies, come, bullies, come, bullies, turn out."
Oh, some would not mind him and back they would lay.
Then it's "Jesus H. Christ, will you lay there all day!"
Lovely fa-de-little-aro, sing tooral all day.

[227]

5 About twelve in the morn the cook would sing out,
  "All hands for the cook shack. Come, bullies, turn out."
  And when you get there divil a bit do you see
  But the dirty old cook and his lousy cookie.
  Lovely fa-de-little-aro, sing tooral all day.

6 Sunday afternoon the boss, he would say,
  "Your axes to grind, for there's no time to play,
  For next Monday morning, to the woods you must go,
  And forty-five spruce every day you must throw."
  Lovely fa-de-little-aro, sing tooral all day.

7 About six in the evening to the camps we'd all steer,
  "Sideboard the grindstone," was all you could hear,
  "Sideboard the grindstone," for the turns they'd all fight,
  And keep the damned old grindstone a-furling all night."
  Lovely fa-de-little-aro, sing tooral all day.

JOHNNY STILES, OR THE WILD MUSTARD RIVER

d´. No. 2353. Archie Stice, Newberry, Mich., 1938. See
Ga.2, p. 276.

*"They asked me if I was cold when they pulled me out of the ice in the
river. 'Well,' I said, 'I ain't a damn bit sweaty.'"*

*　　*　　*

*"See that deep hollow place between his eyes? Well, that was made
when a tree fell and pinned his head against a stump. The doctor gave him
one and a half hours to live, but you can't kill a lumberjack."*

*　　*　　*

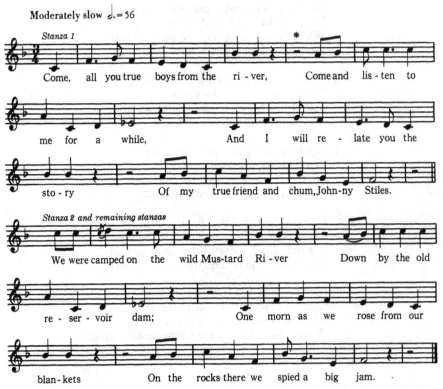

Moderately slow ♩. = 56

Stanza 1

Come, all you true boys from the ri - ver, Come and lis - ten to me for a while, And I will re - late you the sto - ry Of my true friend and chum, John-ny Stiles.

Stanza 2 and remaining stanzas

We were camped on the wild Mus-tard Ri - ver Down by the old re - ser - voir dam; One morn as we rose from our blan-kets On the rocks there we spied a big jam.

* Throughout all stanzas, half rests either are shortened by one beat or—more often—are omitted entirely.

1 Come, all you true boys from the river,
Come and listen to me for a while,
And I will relate you the story
Of my true friend and chum, Johnny Stiles.

2 We were camped on the wild Mustard River
Down by the old reservoir dam;
One morn as we rose from our blankets
On the rocks there we spied a big jam.

3 As soon as we'd eaten our breakfast,
  We pulled for the head of the jam,
  While two of our boys took the pole trail,
  For to flood from the reservoir dam.

4 The water came rushing and howling;
  With peaveys and pike poles we tried,
  Till at last we gave space in the middle
  And right quickly from there she did fly.

5 While a-riding her into dead water
  His foot it got caught in the jam;
  He never once squealed till in under,
  For he always had plenty of sand.

6 Five hours we worked at hard labor
  Till the sweat from my brow it did pour;
  We dragged his dead body from in under,
  But it didn't look like Johnny any more.

7 He was scratched from his heels to his middle
  And his head was cut off in the jam;
  We buried him down by the river
  Where the larks and the whippoorwills sang.

Men at Work

I CAME TO THIS COUNTRY IN 1865

B. No. 1548. Tune and first four stanzas from Jimmy Morris, Hazard, Ky.; stanza 6 from Shoemaker's *Mountain Minstrelsy of Pennsylvania*. See Ri, p. 132; Cox, p. 404; Ga.2, p. 407.

Eighteen miles of rocky road,
Sixteen miles of sand;
If I ever travel this road again,
I'll be a married man.

In pioneer days the teamster combined all the functions nowadays fulfilled by the fireman, the engineer, the roundhouse crew, the conductor, the express agent, the baggagemaster, and the door-to-door deliveryman. His was a proud profession and a responsible post. The man who could work a team of horses or a yoke of oxen over a wilderness road without injuring them had to have all the qualities of sensitive craftsmanship of the modern air pilot. As the song indicates, however, he had a little more leeway in his moments of relaxation.

One of the sturdiest indigenous folk songs, this ballad is said to have originated in the Green Mountains of Vermont. We have noted its occurrence in Pennsylvania, eastern Kentucky, New York, and Michigan.

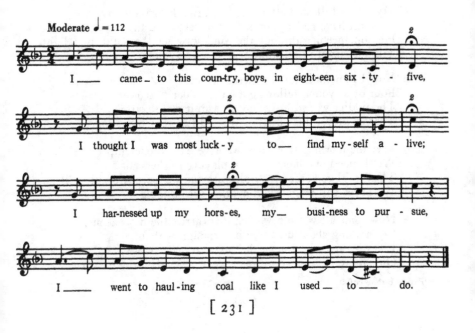

Moderate ♩ = 112

I —— came to this coun-try, boys, in eight-een six - ty - five,
I thought I was most luck - y to —— find my - self a - live;
I har-nessed up my hors-es, my —— busi-ness to pur - sue,
I —— went to haul -ing coal like I used —— to —— do.

[231]

1 I came to this country, boys, in eighteen sixty-five,
    I thought I was most lucky to find myself alive;
    I harnessed up my horses, my business to pursue,
    I went to hauling coal like I used to do.

2 The alehouse doors was open, boys, the liquor running free,
    As soon as one glass emptied, another filled for me;
    Instead of hauling six loads, I did not haul but four,
    I got so darned drunk, boys, that I couldn't hold no more.

3 I finished up my supper and went out to the barn,
    I saddled up the old Gray, not meanin' any harm,
    I rode to the gate and passed the flour mill,
    I scarcely knew a thing till I come to Watson's Hill

4 I met an old acquaintance, I need not tell his name;
    I asked him where he was going, and he questioned me the same.
    We tittled and we tattled, and at last we did agree,
    And he told me that night where the party was to be.

5 My father followed after me, I've often heard him say,
    He must have had a pilot or he'd never found the way;
    He came peeping through the windows where he could spy a light,
    Till his hair grew all white with the frosty dews of night.

6 Now I remember the last circumstance,
    Four of us young fellows got on the floor to dance,
    The fiddler was so jolly and his arm it was so strong,
    That he played the bowls of Ireland full four hours long.

7 I see the morning star, boys, we have danced enough,
    We'll spend one hour more in playing Kasher-cuff.*
    Then we'll go home to our pleasure and we'll whistle and we'll sing,
    We never will be guilty of another such a thing.

8 Now come all you old women that carries the news about,
    Say nothing about us, we're bad enough without,
    Likewise you old women that likes to make a fuss,
    Oh, you're just as bad as we are, perhaps a damn sight worse.

* "Paying cash to cuff."

[232]

OX–DRIVING SONG

e♭. No. 2648. Herman R. Weaver, Merryville, La.,
1939. See Be, p. 300.

The contrast between this quietly bloodthirsty song and the others in
this section typifies the contrast between Northern and Southern folk music
as a whole. It has a quality of dark brooding imagination that can be found
nowhere in the candidly cheerful or blatantly doleful songs of the Northern
pioneer. Mr. Herman Weaver of Merryville, Louisiana, says:

*"I am enclosing parts of the Ox-Driving Song as remembered by me,
but it is still very incomplete. My sister thinks the town of Saludio is in
Missouri or Kentucky, probably where it originated [the song]. My father
knew it, I think, when he came to Texas in 1855."*

Fast ♩ = 112

STANZA: I pop my whip, I bring the blood, I
CHORUS: To my rol, to rol, to my ri - de - o, To my

make my lead-ers take the mud, We grab the wheels and
rol, to rol, to my ri - de - o, To my ri - de - o, To my

turn them round, One long, long pull, we're on hard ground.
ru - de - o, To my rol, to my rol, to my ri - de - o.

    1 I pop my whip, I bring the blood,
      I make my leaders take the mud,
      We grab the wheels and turn them round,
      One long, long pull, we're on hard ground.

    2 On the fourteenth day of October-o,
      I hitched my team in order-o,
      To drive the hills of Salud-i-o,
      To my rol, to my rol, to my rideo.

[233]

Chorus:

To my rol, to rol, to my rideo,
To my rol, to rol, to my rideo,
To my rideo, to my rudeo,
To my rol, to my rol, to my rideo.

3 When I got there the hills were steep,
'Twould make any tender-hearted person weep
To hear me cuss and pop my whip,
To see my oxen pull and slip.

4 When I get home I'll have revenge,
I'll land my family among my friends,
I'll bid adieu to the whip and line
And drive no more in the wintertime.

YO SOY DE LA TIERRA
g. No. 7. Refugio Castillo, Cotulla, Texas, Feb., 1934.

The song of a *carretera,* or ox-driver, from northern Mexico. The sense of it seems to be: "I'm from a far country where you can't see the sunrise. Little girl, pray God that I don't die [on the road]. I'm leaving now, God knows if I'll get back."

Moderate ♩=69

Yo soy_ de la tier-ra,___ y de don-de por a-llá, Don-de por a-

llá___ Que ni el sol se mir' al sa-lir.___ Jo-ven-ci-ta pi-

da-le à Di-os Que no me vay(a) á mor-ir Ya me

voy á na - ve - gar,_____ Ya _____ me voy á na - ve -

(falsetto)

gar, Sa - be Di - os si__ vol - ve - ré?_____ (hm).

Yo soy de la tierra,
Y de donde por allá,
Donde por allá,
Que ni el sol se mir' al salir.
Jovencita, pidale á Dios
Que no me vaya á morir
Ya me voy á navegar,
Ya me voy á navegar,
Sabe Dios si volveré.

III.   3. COWBOY SONGS

"Every time you build a fence," said the old, grizzled cowpuncher, *"you cut a cowboy's throat, for how can a cowboy sing when his life is passing away?"*

*   *   *

In 1907 Andy Adams, the author of the best story of the cattle trail ever written, said:

"There is such a thing as cowboy music. It is a hybrid between the weirdness of an Indian cry and the croon of the black mammy. It expresses the open, the prairie, the immutable desert."

*   *   *

I'll tell St. Peter that I know
A cowboy's soul ain't white as snow,
But in that far-off cattle land
He sometimes acted like a man.

*   *   *

1 Oh, slow up, dogies, quit your roving round,
You have wandered and tramped all over the ground;
Oh, graze along, dogies, and feed kinda slow,
And don't forever be on the go—
Oh, move slow, dogies, move slow.

2 I have circle-herded, trail-herded, night-herded, too,
But to keep you together, that's what I can't do;
My horse is leg-weary and I'm awful tired,
But if I let you get away I'm sure to get fired—
Bunch up, little dogies, bunch up.

3 Oh, say, little dogies, when you goin' to lay down
And quit this forever siftin' around?
My limbs are weary, my seat is sore;
Oh, lay down, dogies, like you've laid before—
Lay down, little dogies, lay down.

4 Oh, lay still, dogies, since you have laid down,
Stretch away out on the big open ground;
Snore loud, little dogies, and drown the wild sound
That will all go away when the day rolls round—
Lay still, little dogies, lay still.*

* *Cowboy Songs and Other Frontier Ballads,* pp. 60–61 (revised and enlarged ed., New York, Macmillan, 1938).

GIT ALONG, LITTLE DOGIES*

The old blind man shuffled along beside me, clasping his guitar as I guided him over the rough places in our path. We were headed for the trees that fringed the West Fork of the Trinity River near Forth Worth, Texas. Often I stumbled, for I was carrying a heavy Edison recording machine. They built them strong in 1908.

Out on a busy corner near the cattle pens of the Stockyards I had found my companion that morning twanging his guitar while he sang doleful ditties and listened for the ring of quarters in his tin cup.

"I don't know any cowboy songs," he had explained to me. "But lead me home to lunch. My wife can sing you a bookful."

We found her out behind a covered truck, a forerunner of the trailer, seated in front of a gayly colored tent. She wore a gypsy costume, richly brocaded, and she had used paint and powder with skillful discretion on a face naturally comely. While I chatted with her, the old man disappeared into the tent. In a few minutes, out he came. Gone were the round, humped shoulders, the white hair, the shambling gait, the tottering figure. Before me stood a handsome, dark-eyed man, alert and athletic. He made no explanation. He was a perfect faker.

"My wife shakes down the saps who like to hold her hand while she reads their fortunes in the stars. All the self-righteous fools go away from

* See *Cowboy Songs and Other Frontier Ballads,* pp. 4–7 (Macmillan, 1938).

[237]

my tin cup happy, marking down one more good deed on their passports to heaven. We aim to please our customers, and I think we do." Thus the faker rambled on while a smiling Negro man served delicious food and a bottle of wine.

Later on through the long Texas afternoon, amid the cheerful talk, the faker lady, in a voice untamed and natural and free as a bird's, would sing us songs of the road. She and her family for generations back had lived as gypsies.

"This lady," said the faker, "who has joined her fortunes with mine, and passes as my wife, travels with me now from Miami, Florida, to San Diego, California. We belong to that fringe of human society who take life the easiest way. We toil not, neither do we spin, yet none of Sharon's daughters was clad as she or slept more sweetly." Raising a tent flap he showed me rich purple hangings, thick Persian rugs, a divan spread with soft silken covers, amazing magnificence. "With our burros, Abednego and Sennacherib, to pull our covered wagon, we travel as we like. Our rackets roll in the money." He lay flat on his back on the mesquite grass, puffing a cigar, as he gazed at the white patches of clouds that swept across the rich azure of a Texas sky.

I glanced curiously at Abednego and Sennacherib as they munched their alfalfa. They seemed as old as the pyramids and as solemn as a pair of Aztec idols—which they, indeed, resembled. They seemed to talk to each other with their ears. Fastened loosely to the great bony heads, these absurdly long appendages moved constantly in a fashion that astonished and fascinated me. And here close by sat this pearl of a woman, dressed like a princess, strumming her guitar and singing the songs of gypsy life.

She despised the clumsy horn fastened to my recording machine, and I caught few of the tunes. I remember that she sang me the first blues that I had ever heard, moving me almost to tears; and a pathetic ballad of a factory girl, who got splinters in her toes. Many and many another she sang that, unhappily, are gone with the Texas wind.

Finally came the tune of

> *Whoopee-ti-yi-yo, git along, little dogies,*
> *It's your misfortune and none of my own.*

I had never before heard it.

"To me," she said, "that's the loveliest of all cowboy songs. Like others, its rhythm comes from the movement of a horse. It is not the roisterous, hell-for-leather, wild gallop of 'The Old Chisholm Trail,' nor the slow easy canter of 'Goodby Old Paint.' You mustn't frighten the dogies. They get nervous in crowds. Lope around them gently in the darkness as you sing about punching them along to their new home in Wyoming. They'll sleep the night through and never have a bad dream."

This is the story of the first recording of this now famous cowboy tune. The gypsy woman's song has been sung over the air thousands of times, and we wonder whether she chuckled somewhere in a gypsy tent when Billy Hill's almost notorious "The Last Roundup" was on the air every day and night.

In the meantime we have recorded two tunes which show that "Whoopee-ti-yi-yo" has wandered as far afield and disguised itself as subtly as any gypsy.

—Adventures of a Ballad Hunter

AS I WENT A-WALKING ONE FINE SUMMER'S EVENING

f. No. 2444. Mose Bellaire, Sec. 12, Baraga, Mich., 1938. Learned in the Canadian lumber woods twenty or more years ago. Also recorded in Vermont from a Yankee basketmaker, Jonathan Moses (No. 3703B2). See Lo.1, pp. 4 ff.

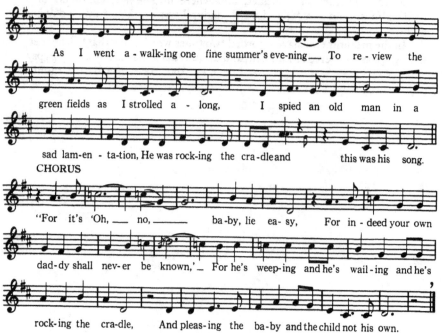

1   As I went a-walking one fine summer's evening,
    To review the green fields as I strolled along,
    I spied an old man in a sad lamentation,
    He was rocking the cradle and this was his song.

Chorus:
        "For it's 'Oh, no, baby, lie easy,
        For indeed your own daddy shall never be known,'

For he's weeping and he's wailing and he's rocking the cradle,
And pleasing the baby and the child not his own.

2 "When I first fell in love with your innocent mother,
Like an old fool that was left with a wife,
But through all mistakes and through my misfortunes,
For I'm born to be plagued in the days of my life.

3 "When evening comes on she's off to some party,
She will leave me to sing and to rock all alone;
But the innocent baby she'll call me her daddy,
But it's little she knows I'm never so.

4 "Now come all you young men if you want to get married,
I pray you take warning and leave women alone,
For by the Lord Harry, if you ever get married,
You'll be rocking the cradle and the child not your own."

THE SPORTING COWBOY

*d*b. Paramount 3006B. Acc. on guitar and sung by
Watts and Wilson. See Cox, p. 12; Lo.1, p. 254.

Moderately fast ♩ = 112

When I was a cow-boy I learned to throw the line, —
I learned to pock-et mon-ey and not to dress so fine,
Went out on — the prai-rie, to learn to rob — and steal,
When I robbed a cow-boy, how hap-py did I feel.

1 When I was a cowboy I learned to throw the line,
  I learned to pocket money and not to dress so fine,
  Went out on the prairie, to learn to rob and steal,
  When I robbed a cowboy, how happy did I feel!

2 For working I'm not able and beggin' is too low,
  Stealin' is so dreadful, to jail I must go;
  Yonder comes the jailer, his jury to come today,
  Who knows that I am guilty, I'm bound to go that way.

3 I saw the jailer coming, about eleven o'clock,
  Hands full of jail keys, them doors to unlock.
  "Cheer up, cheer up, you prisoner," I heard the jury say—
  I'm bound to Dallas County for ten long years to stay.

4 I wore my broad and summeralls, my hoss and saddle was fine,
  When I spied those pretty girls, you bet I called them mine,
  Spotted 'em all for beauty, oh, Lord, it was in vain,
  I'm bound to Dallas County to wear the ball and chain.

5 Saw my darling coming, ten dollars in her hand.
  "Give it to the cowboy, 'tis all that I command,
  Give it to the cowboy, remember olden times,
  So he won't forget his darling he's left so far behind."

RUN ALONG, YOU LITTLE DOGIES

B. No. 1849. Francis Sullivan, architect, Washington,
D.C., 1938.

Frank M. Sullivan, architect of Washington, D.C., learned this version of "Git Along, Little Dogies," on an Idaho dude ranch in 1910. The tune is closely related to and probably derived from the ballad, "As I Went a-Walkin' One Fine Summer's Evening," printed above. Mr. Sullivan told us that the cowboys in Idaho used the song as a cattle lullaby.

Men at Work

Slow, somewhat free ♩ = 108

Stanza 1 only

1. As I looked out of my win-dow, I saw a

Stanzas 2,3,4

2. When spring comes a-long, we round up the do-gies, We stick on their

Stanzas 1,2,3,4

1. cow-boy come rid-ing a-long, His hat was shoved back and his
2. brands and we bob off their tails, *etc.*

spurs kept a-jingl-ing, And as he drew near he was sing-ing this song.

CHORUS

Hush-ie ci-o-la, lit-tle ba-by, lie ea-sy,

Who's your real fa-ther may nev-er be known,

Oh, it's weep-ing, wail-ing, rock-ing the cra-dle

And tend-ing a ba-by that's none of your own.

1 As I looked out of my window,
   I saw a cowboy come riding along,
   His hat was shoved back and his spurs kept a-jingling,
   And as he drew near he was singing this song.

Chorus 1:
>   Hush-ie ciola, little baby, lie easy,
>   Who's your real father may never be known,
>   Oh, it's weeping, wailing, rocking the cradle
>   And tending a baby that's none of your own.

2 When spring comes along, we round up the dogies,
  We stick on their brands and we bob off their tails,
  Pick out the strays, then the herd is inspected
  And then the next day we go on the trail.

Chorus 2:
>   Singing hoop—pi-o-hoop! run along, you little dogies,
>   For Montana will be your new home,
>   Oh, it's whooping, swearing, driving the dogies,
>   It's our misfortune we ever did roam.

3 Oh, it's worst in the night just after a roundup
  When dogies are grazing from the herd all around,
  You have no idea of the trouble they give us,
  To the boys who are holding them on the bed ground.

4 Oh, some think we go on the trail for pleasure
  But I can tell them that they are dead wrong,
  If I ever got any fun out of trailing,
  I'd have no reason for singing my song.

Tom Hight and I spent two happy days together in an Oklahoma City hotel. Tom was made happier, as I am sure I was, by the added presence of two quart bottles of rye which he consulted frequently between songs. Tom knew more cowboy melodies than any other person I have ever found.

"Ever since I was a boy," said Tom, "I have been a singing fool. I could sing down any man in our cow camp in the Panhandle. When the fellers backed me against the neighboring camp, I won. They challenged the whole damn Panhandle. The champeens of each camp met at a central point and we lifted up our heads like a pack of coyotes, only we lifted 'em one at a time. The rules was that each man was to sing in turn, one after the other, round and round. The man that sung the last song, he won the prize. It took us mighty near all night to get sung out. The other fellows couldn't sing no more, because they didn't know no more songs. But I was ready with the last one and had more roped and ready. Of course you couldn't use no books and no writing. I was mighty proud of being the champeen singer of the Texas Panhandle. My cowboy friends gave me a pair of silver-mounted spurs for a prize with my name engraved on them."

—Adventures of a Ballad Hunter

TEXAS RANGERS

d′, f′♯. No. 1561. Tune and first stanza, Pauline Farris, Gladys Wilder, Dora Lewis, and Reda West, Liberty, Ky., 1937. Other stanzas, Lo.2, p. 359. See Cox, p. 362; Fl.2, p. 226; Be, p. 336.

He leaves unplowed his furrow, he leaves his books unread
For a life of tented freedom, by the lure of danger led.
No more he'll go a-ranging, the savage to affright;
He has heard his last war-whoop and fought his last fight.

Moderately fast ♩ = 100

SECOND SINGER

FIRST SINGER
Come all you Tex-as Ran-gers, wher-ev-er you may be,

A sto-ry I will tell you which hap-pened un-to me.

My name is noth-ing ex - try, the truth to you I'll tell, —

I am a Tex-as Ran-ger, so, la-dies, fare you well.

* The above notation is a transcription of the two parts heard on the record.

[245]

1 Come all you Texas Rangers, wherever you may be,
A story I will tell you which happened unto me.
My name is nothing extry, the truth to you I'll tell,
I am a Texas Ranger, so, ladies, fare you well.

2 It was at the age of sixteen that I joined the jolly band,
We marched from San Antonio down to the Rio Grande.
Our captain he informed us, perhaps he thought it right,
"Before we reach the station, boys, you'll surely have to fight."

3 And when the bugle sounded our captain gave command,
"To arms, to arms," he shouted, "and by your horses stand."
I saw the smoke ascending, it seemed to reach the sky;
The first thought that struck me, my time had come to die.

4 I saw the Indians coming, I heard them give the yell;
My feelings at that moment, no tongue can ever tell.
I saw the glittering lances, their arrows round me flew,
And all my strength it left me, and all my courage too.

5 We fought full nine hours before the strife was o'er,
The like of dead and wounded I never saw before.
And when the sun was rising and the Indians they had fled,
We loaded up our rifles and counted up our dead.

6 And all of us were wounded, our noble captain slain,
And the sun was shining sadly across the bloody plain.
Sixteen as brave Rangers as ever roamed the West
Were buried by their comrades with arrows in their breast.

7 'Twas then I thought of Mother, who to me in tears did say,
"To you they are all strangers, with me you had better stay."
I thought that she was childish, the best she did not know;
My mind was fixed on ranging, and I was bound to go.

8 Perhaps you have a mother, likewise a sister too,
And maybe so a sweetheart to weep and mourn for you;
If that be your situation, although you'd like to roam,
I'd advise you by experience, you had better stay at home.

9 I have seen the fruits of rambling, I know its hardships well;
   I have crossed the Rocky Mountains, rode down the streets of hell;
   I have been in the great Southwest where the wild Apaches roam,
   And I tell you from experience you had better stay at home.

DIAMOND JOE *

d. No. 537. J. B. Dillingham, Austin, Texas, 1935. See Lo.1, p. 65; Od.2, p. 130.

"Diamond Joe was a Texas cattleman, the story goes, so rich that he was said to wear diamonds for his vest buttons. I learned this song years ago," says J. B. Dillingham, for fifty years a conductor on Houston and Texas Central trains running out of Austin.

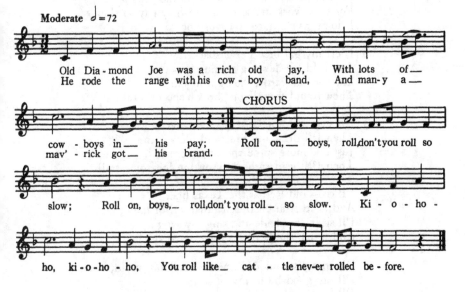

Moderate ♩ = 72

Old Dia-mond Joe was a rich old jay, With lots of—
He rode the range with his cow-boy band, And man-y a—

CHORUS

cow-boys in— his pay; Roll on,— boys, roll, don't you roll so
mav'-rick got— his brand.

slow; Roll on, boys,— roll, don't you roll— so slow. Ki-o-ho-

ho, ki-o-ho-ho, You roll like— cat-tle nev-er rolled be-fore.

1 Old Diamond Joe was a rich old jay,
  With lots of cowboys in his pay;
  He rode the range with his cowboy band,
  And many a mav'rick got his brand.

* *Cowboy Songs and Other Frontier Ballads,* pp. 65–66 (New York: Macmillan, 1938)

Chorus:
> Roll on, boys, roll, don't you roll so slow;
> Roll on, boys, roll, don't you roll so slow.
> Ki-o-ho-ho, ki-o-ho-ho,
> You roll like cattle never rolled before.

2   I am a pore cowboy, I've got no home,
    I'm here today and tomorrow I'm gone;
    I've got no folks, I'm forced to roam,
    Where I hang my hat is home, sweet home.

3   If I was as rich as Diamond Joe,
    I'd work today and I'd work no mo';
    For they work me so hard and they pay so slow *
    I don't give a durn if I work or no.

4   I left my gal in a Texas shack,
    And told her I was a-coming back;
    But I lost at cards, then got in jail,
    Then found myself on the Chisholm Trail.

5   I'll stay with the herd till they reach the end,
    Then I'll draw my time and blow it in;
    Just one more spree and one more jail,
    Then I'll head right back on the lonesome trail.

6   I'll cross old Red at the Texas line,
    And head straight back to that gal of mine;
    I'll sit in the shade and sing my song,
    And watch the herds as they move along.

7   When my summons come to leave this world,
    I'll say good-by to my little girl;
    I'll fold my hands when I have to go,
    And say farewell to Diamond Joe.

[248]

IF HE'D BE A BUCKAROO

F. No. 1635. Acc. on guitar and sung by Blaine Stubblefield, Washington, D.C., 1938.

Moderately fast ♩ = 92

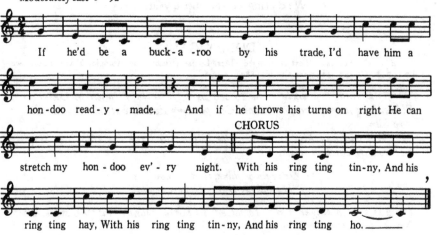

If he'd be a buck-a-roo by his trade, I'd have him a hon-doo read-y - made, And if he throws his turns on right He can stretch my hon - doo ev' - ry night. With his ring ting tin-ny, And his ring ting hay, With his ring ting tin-ny, And his ring ting ho.

1 If he'd be a buckaroo by his trade
I'd have him a hondoo ready-made,
And if he throws his turns on right
He can stretch my hondoo every night.

Chorus:
> With his ring ting tinny,
> And his ring ting hay,
> With his ring ting tinny,
> And his ring ting ho.

2 If he'd be a preacher by his trade,
I'd have him a pulpit ready-made,
And I'd hold fast to his snubbing post
While he goes at me with his Holy Ghost.

3 If he'd be a sheepherder by his trade,
I'd have him corrals all ready-made,
And when he goes to separate
Then he can use my dodging gate.

[249]

4 If he'd be a sailor by his trade
   I'd have him a ship all ready-made;
   With him to row and me to steer
   We'd bring a cargo once a year.

DONEY GAL

d to *c*. No. 542. Text rearranged. Mrs. Louise Henson, San Antonio, Texas, 1937. See Lo.1, p. 8; Od.2, p. 129. See also No. 887.

"One time my uncle came to see us folks on our ranch in Oklahoma. When he got ready to go the rain was pouring down; but the weather didn't stop him.

"We watched him ride over the hill headed for the roundup, singing his favorite cowboy song

"It's rain or shine, sleet or snow,
Me and my Doney Gal are bound to go.

He was a good singer, too. He called his horse 'Doney Gal,' his sweetheart. None of us ever saw him again."

—Mrs. Louise Henson, *San Antonio, Texas.*

Slow ♩.= 42

* The Introduction does not appear on the record used for transcription of the main part of this song. It has been inserted as transcribed by Edward N. Waters from another recording, for use in *Cowboy Songs* by John A. and Alan Lomax.

Men at Work

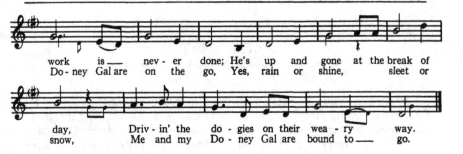

work   is ___   nev - er   done; He's   up   and   gone   at the break of
Do - ney Gal are   on   the   go,   Yes,   rain   or   shine,   sleet or

day,   Driv - in' the   do - gies on their wea - ry   way.
snow,   Me   and my   Do - ney Gal are   bound to ___   go.

Introductory:

   1 We're alone, Doney Gal, in the wind and hail,
     Got to drive these dogies down the trail.

Stanzas:

   1 We'll ride the range from sun to sun,
     For a cowboy's work is never done;
     He's up and gone at the break of day,
     Drivin' the dogies on their weary way.

   2 It's rain or shine, sleet or snow,
     Me and my Doney Gal are on the go,
     Yes, rain or shine, sleet or snow,
     Me and my Doney Gal are bound to go.

   3 A cowboy's life is a weary thing,
     For it's rope and brand and ride and sing;
     Yes, day or night in the rain or hail,
     He'll stay with his dogies out on the trail.

   4 Rain or shine, sleet or snow,
     Me and my Doney Gal are on the go;
     We travel down that lonesome trail
     Where a man and his horse seldom ever fail.

   5 We whoop at the sun and yell through the hail,
     But we drive the poor dogies down the trail;
     And we'll laugh at the storms, the sleet and snow,
     When we reach the little town of San Antonio.

PETER GRAY

e. No. 2505. Frank A. Melton, Univ. of Oklahoma, Norman, Okla., 1939.

Professor Frank A. Melton of the University of Oklahoma says his father sang "Peter Gray" to him thirty years ago in Kansas, sang it soberly as a straightforward, factual account. The editors of the Harris Collection of American Poetry and Plays add, " 'Peter Gray' (1858) seems to have been, like 'Springfield Mountain,' an American ballad which proved irresistibly comic once it got on the stage." Oral transmission has brought various changes both in the words and in the music.

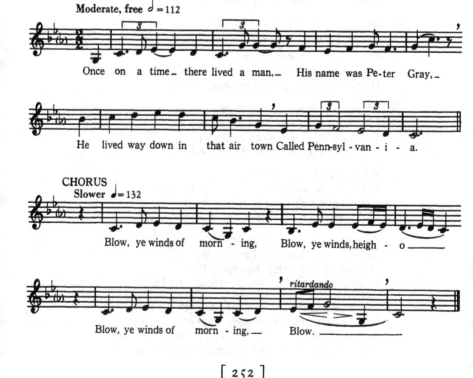

Once on a time＿ there lived a man,＿ His name was Pe-ter Gray,＿

He lived way down in that air town Called Penn-syl-van-i-a.

CHORUS
Slower ♩ = 132

Blow, ye winds of morn - ing, Blow, ye winds, heigh - o ＿＿＿

ritardando

Blow, ye winds of morn - ing, — Blow. ＿＿＿＿

1 Once on a time there lived a man,
His name was Peter Gray,
He lived way down in that air town
Called Pennsylvan-i-a.

Chorus:
Blow, ye winds of morning,
Blow, ye winds, heigho,
Blow, ye winds of morning,
Blow.

2 Now Peter fell in love all with
A nice young girl;
The first three letters of her name
Were Lucy Annie Pearl.

3 Just as they were gwine to wed
Her father did say no,
And quin-ci-cont-ly she was sent
Beyond the Ohio.

4 When Peter heard his love was lost,
He knew not what to say,
He'd half a mind to jump into
The Susquehan-i-a.

5 Now Peter went away out West
To seek his for-ti-an,
But he was caught and scal-pi-ed
By blood-i In-di-ans.

6 When Lucy heard of this bad news
About poor Peter Gray,
She wep' and wep' and wep'-i-ed
Her dear sweet life away.

III. 4. RAILROADERS AND HOBOS

> I don't like no railroad man,
> Railroad man will kill you if he can,
> I don't like no railroad man.
>
> I don't like no railroad fool,
> Railroad fool's got a head like a mule,
> I don't like no railroad fool.

THE WRECK ON THE SOMERSET ROAD

c. No. 1532. Justis Begley, Hazard, Ky., 1937. Compare with "The Wreck of the Old '97."

> Soon one mornin', was mistin' rain,
> Round the curve come a passenger train,
> Just as he struck Reno Hill,
> Blowed his whistle an awful squill,
> Womens and chilluns come screamin' an' cryin',
> Big Joe Carmichael comin' down the line.

The two smart song writers who picked up "Casey Jones" from Mississippi Negroes and smoothed it up for vaudeville got all the credit and the money, too; but the folk song that made the headlines was "The Wreck on the Old '97." Vernon Dalhart put it on Victor records, and they sold a million copies in the late nineteen-twenties. By 1933 a suit against Victor was filed by one David G. George of Atlanta, Georgia, who insisted that he had composed the song in 1903 immediately after the wreck occurred. Robert Gordon gathered evidence to show that the song was made up not by David George, but by several men, yet the court upheld the plaintiff. The case is still being appealed.

It was never claimed, of course, that the tune was original, for "The Wreck of the Old '97" was sung to the doleful old air, "The Ship That Never Returned." That this tune had been similarly used before and for more or less the same purpose is indicated in the following ballad, possibly an older song and the foster parent of the "Old '97," which hints darkly of dark doings on the "old, old Somerset Road."

[254]

Men at Work

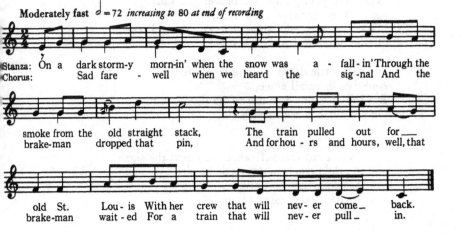

Moderately fast ♩=72 *increasing to 80 at end of recording*

Stanza: On a dark storm-y morn-in' when the snow was a - fall-in' Through the
Chorus: Sad fare - well when we heard the sig -nal And the

smoke from the old straight stack, The train pulled out for___
brake-man dropped that pin, And for hou - rs and hours, well, that

old St. Lou - is With her crew that will nev - er come___ back.
brake-man wait - ed For a train that will nev - er pull___ in.

1 On a dark stormy mornin' when the snow was a-fallin'
Through the smoke from the old, straight stack,
The train pulled out for old St. Louis
With her crew that will never come back.

Chorus:
Sad farewell when we heard the signal
And the brakeman dropped that pin,
And for hours and hours, well, that brakeman waited
For a train that will never pull in.

2 "Just one more trip," said the sleepy brakeman
As he tumbled out of his bed,
"For tomorrow night the panthers are coming
For to paint old Somerset red."

3 "Just one more trip," said the sleepy conductor
As he kissed his lovin' wife,
"For we've stole enough of money from the railroad company
To last us all through life."

[255]

4 Well, five young men had broken the railing
   And robbed them of their load,
   'Twas the worst old wreck that we ever did see
   On the old, old Somerset Road.

5 We will settle down in some lonely forest
   And live there all alone,
   But the last man found was the dead conductor
   On the old, old Somerset Road.

Alternate Chorus:
   Was a sad farewell when we heard the signal
   As the brakeman dropped the pin,
   He come out and give us the signal
   As he backed the old train in.

THE WHITE HOUSE BLUES

B. No. 1523. Acc. on guitar and sung by Maynard Britton, Clay County, Ky., 1937. For a variant, see "Cannonball Blues," by the Carter Family, Perfect No. 7055.

When McKinley was dead and Roosevelt in the White House drinking from the silver cup, the people thought the matter over slowly and made up a song to mourn McKinley's death. When the song was done, it did not speak of the crowds at his bier, the flags at half-mast or of thunderous salutes to symbolize their sorrow, but, instead, put the Cannonball Express on the road from Buffalo to Washington, tearing down through Maine, screaming out the sad news to America with its shrill whistle, snorting its sympathy in its steam valves.

Moderately fast ♩ = 84

foot-tapping

Roo - se - velt's in the White House, do - ing his best,

Mc Kin - ley in the grave-yard, tak - ing his rest,

[256]

Men at Work

CHORUS
Stanzas 1,3,7,8

He's   gone   a   long   old   time.

CHORUS
Stanzas 2,4,5,6

From   Buf-fa-lo   to   Wash-ing - ton.

1 Roosevelt's in the White House, doing the best,
   McKinley in the graveyard, taking his rest,
   He's gone a long old time.

2 "Look a-here, little children, now don't you fret,
   You'll draw a pension at your papa's death."
   From Buffalo to Washington.

3 He said, "There's one thing that's grieved my mind,
   That is to die and leave my poor wife behind.
   I'm gone a long old time."

4 "Look a-here, you rascal, and see what you've done,
   You've shot my husband and I've got no gun."
   From Buffalo to Washington.

5 He jumped on his horse, and he tore down through Maine,
   Says to that horse, "You've got to outrun that train,
   From Buffalo to Washington."

6 Standing at the station, lookin' at the time,
   Number Five runnin' by at half past nine,
   From Buffalo to Washington.

7 Yonder comes the train running down the line,
   Blowing at every station, McKinley is dying,
   Hard times, hard times.

[257]

8 Roosevelt's in the White House, drinkin' out of a silver cup,
McKinley's in the graveyard, never waked up,.
He's gone a long old time.

JOHN HENRY

A^b. No. 2668. Arthur Bell, Cummins State Farm, Pine Bluff, Ark., 1939. See Guy B. Johnson, *John Henry*; Louis W. Chappell, *John Henry*.

Any general collection of American folk songs that does not include the ballad of John Henry, the Negro steel-drivin' man, would not seem to us in any wise complete. This almost epic ballad of the industrial revolution with its lights and shadows from the tunnel workings of the West Virginia hills, its burly and laughing defiance of the earth and the machine and of death, is probably America's greatest single piece of folk lore. Although, therefore, the earlier volume of *American Ballads and Folk Songs* contains a long composite version, we print here nine stanzas and a tune recorded near Pine Bluff, Arkansas. It is a western version in which John Henry is pictured as the Louisiana section-gang worker. We have found no exact parallel to this stirring air among the thirty or forty versions in the Library of Congress Folk Song Archive.

* * *

"*I can tell you all about double-jinted people. You couldn't let them be prize fighters because any double-jinted man could knock you out. A double-jinted man, he's got two jints to your one, he's always fat and stout and everything, and he can just tear you up just like that, you understand.*

"*I knowed old man Eph Brown, which my father showed him to me when I was a little small boy. We was down in the gin house where they was ginning cotton into bales that weighed 550 and 575 pound. Well, it take four or five men to put a bale on a wagon, but old man Eph Brown just go there and, 'cause he was double-jinted, just picks up the bale of cotton, chunk it in the wagon, git in the wagon and go ahead on home.*

"*Nowadays mighty few men you find 'll be double-jinted. Once I was a boy, I was about sixteen years old and we was carryin' corn to the mill down South. I'd always been a good knocker. I could knock with my fists, and I run up on a boy, he was double-jinted. Boys round in them times, you know, was always round talking 'bout one another's knocking, and all the boys*

[258]

told him, 'You know old Lead Belly is a good knocker.' I could run and knock. I always tried to be the winner. We wouldn't hit the side of the head, we would always hit on the breast and in the short ribs and along the arms. I used to jive 'em by hittin' 'em in the grind, slap 'em with the back of my hand that way, causin' 'em to bow. Then I'd meet 'em with a blow in the breast when they'd bow.

"I went up to this fellow, and he looked awful funny, he was bracin' for a knock. He said, 'Look here, Lead Belly, don't you want to knock?' I said, 'No, I'm out here grindin' corn today; I don't want to knock.' He says, 'Oh, yes, you gotta knock me.' I says, 'Oh, no, I ain't gonna knock.'

"I kept lookin' at him and he looked so fat and his arms so big, I says, 'What is you anyhow? You double-jinted?' He say, 'Yeah.' I say, 'Christ, man, you think I'm goin' knock you? I'm single-jinted; I don't knock with no double-jinted man.' If he want to knock with me, I'm gonna knock with a piece of stovewood or something; I ain't gonna knock with no double-jinted man."

"John Henry was a double-jinted man too. When he was a little boy, he weighed twenty pounds, a newborn baby, and his limbs was just as fat and stout—I had a picture of him; I know. I kept that picture a long time; I believe it's down at the house now. He was layin' up there so fat and stout. Even when he was a little baby he wanted to be a railroad man. He was a steel driver, the best there ever was in the world. He was double-jinted and he was a man with it. Always don't forget about John Henry that he was a double-jinted man, had two jints to your one.

"Had a little wife named sweet Polly Ann, and John Henry got low sick and he had malaria fever. And he was in the bed, doctor comin', an' before Polly Ann would let the steel driving go she went out and drove steel just like John Henry did. So every day she went out and drove steel till John Henry got better so he could go back on the job."   —Lead Belly

1   *John Henry's mother had a little baby,*
     She was holding him in her hand,
     If she be lucky and raise this child,
     She'll have another steel-driving man.

2   *John Henry's mother told him,*
     Says, "Son, you're doing awful fine,
     You go ahead 'long, do the best you can,
     That's the way yo' daddy died."

[259]

3 *John Henry was a little boy,*
And he was on his way to school,
Looked at the teacher and these words he said,
"I want to learn how to hammer, too."

Moderate ♩ =120 *increasing to* 144 *at end of recording*

Well, ev'-ry— Mon-day— morn-in'— When the blue-birds begin to sing,— You can hear those— ham-mers a mile or—
mo', You can hear John Hen-ry's ham-mer ring, Oh,
Lawd-y, Hear John Hen-ry's ham-mer ring.

1 Well, every Monday mornin'
   When the bluebirds begin to sing,
   You can hear those hammers a mile or mo',
   You can hear John Henry's hammer ring, oh, Lawdy,
   Hear John Henry's hammer ring.

2 John Henry told his old lady,
   "Will you fix my supper soon?
   Got ninety miles o' track I've got to line,
   Got to line it by the light of the moon, oh, Lawdy,
   Line it by the light o' the moon."

3 John Henry had a little baby,
   He could hold him out in his hand;
   But the last word I heard that po' child say,
   "My dad is a steel-drivin' man, oh, Lawdy,
   Daddy is a steel-drivin' man."

[260]

4 John Henry told his old capt'in,
   Said, "A man ain't nothin' but a man,
   Before I let yo' steel gang down
   I will die with the hammer in my hand, oh, Lawdy,
   Die with the hammer in my hand."

5 John Henry told his capt'in,
   "Next time you go to town
   A-jes' bring me back a ten-pound maul
   Fer to beat yo' steel-drivin' down, oh, Lawdy,
   Beat yo' steel-drivin' down."

6 John Henry had a old lady,
   An' her name was Polly Ann.
   John Henry tuck sick an' he had to go to bed;
   Pauline drove steel like a man, oh, Lawdy,
   P'line drove steel like a man.

7 John Henry had a old lady,
   An' the dress she wo' was red;
   Well, she started up the track an' she never looked back,
   "Gwine where my man fell dead, oh, Lawdy,
   Where my man fell dead."

8 Well, they taken John Henry to Wash'n'ton,
   An' they bury him in the san',
   There's people from the East an' there's people from the West
   Come to see such a steel-drivin' man, oh, Lawdy,
   See such a steel-drivin' man.

9 Well, some say he's fum England,
   Well, an' some say he's fum Spain,
   But I say he's nothin' but a Lou's'ana man,
   Jes' the leader of a steel-drivin' gang, oh, Lawdy,
   Leader of a steel-drivin' gang.

SIS JOE

ƒ. No. 2654. Henry Truvillion, Newton, Texas, 1939. See Od.2, p. 262; Lo.2, pp. 14–17; Whi, p. 263; also Hu, pp. 316 ff.

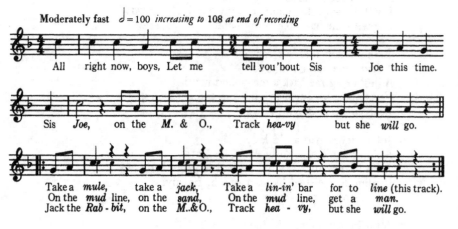

Moderately fast ♩ = 100 *increasing to* 108 *at end of recording*

All right now, boys, Let me tell you 'bout Sis Joe this time.

Sis Joe, on the M. & O., Track *hea-vy* but she *will* go.

Take a *mule,* take a *jack,* Take a *lin-in'* bar for to *line* (this track).
On the *mud* line, on the *sand,* On the *mud* line, get a *man.*
Jack the *Rab-bit,* on the *M..&O.,* Track *hea - vy,* but she *will* go.

Track Lining Holler

"*When steel gets tight with the sun shinin' right warm on it, the track buck and it looks just something like an old slavery-time fence row, in and out. Well, this day the sun was shinin', the track was buckin', and I was walkin' an' talkin'. The passenger train's due now, and I got to git out down there and line that track up straight. It's just like a knittin' needle before the passenger train gets there. I holler and call six of my best men by name. Chances are I'll call Hank Stevens, Sonny Watkin, Sam Justis, Jim Williams, to get their linin' bars and go down there. I have to tell 'em where to get it.*"

FOREMAN

Go get the third johnny head and touch it north,
So the track runnin' east and west;
Touch it north!

SINGING LEADER

All right now, boys,
Let me tell you 'bout Sis Joe this time.

[262]

Men at Work

LEADER AND GANG

Sis *Joe*, on the *M. & O.*,*
Track *heavy*, but she *will* go.

Take a *mule*, take a *jack*,
Take a *linin'* bar for to *line* this track.

On the *mud* line, on the *sand*,
On the *mud* line, get a *man*.

Jack the *Rabbit*, on the *M. & O.*,
Track *heavy*, but she *will* go.

FOREMAN

Run on down yonder to the third johnny head and touch it easy,
Quick, make haste, I hear the train comin'.

SINGING LEADER

All right now, boys,
Let me tell you what I had for breakfast now.

LEADER AND GANG

Little *rice*, little *bean*,
No *meat* to be *seen*.

Hard *work* ain' *easy*,
Dry *bread* ain' *greasy*.

Oh, *Joe*, Joe *Lily* Butt,
Oh, *Joe*, caincha *pick* it up?

FOREMAN

Now, wait a minute, you stop right there,
Now, put your guns on your shoulders,
And come walkin' back.
Go on to the next one and touch it just a fraction,
To the next one now and just barely move it.
I want you to just barely touch it,
Touch it just a little bit,
Just something another like a fraction.

SINGING LEADER

All right now, boys,
Let me tell you 'bout tampin' ties this time.

* The men heave on their lining bars on the beats indicated by the italicized words.

LEADER AND GANG
Have to *tamp* 'em up *solid*,
Have to *tamp* 'em kinda *slow*.

Jack the *Rabbit*, Jack the *Bear*,
Caincha *move* it, just a *hair*?

Sis *Joe*, don't you *hear* me now?
Sis *Joe*, don't you *hear* me now?

FOREMAN
Now, you'll have to put your guns on your shoulders an' come by me,
An' come in a hurry,
Come trottin',
Come laughin',
Come like you gonna get paid for it,
Get a move on you,
An' go by the water tank and get you some water.
Git your linin' bars an' git your backbreakin' holts,
Throw it north.

LEADER AND GANG
Yea——
In the *mornin'* when you *rise*,
Pick and *shevil* by your *side*.

In the *mornin'* when you *rise*,
Got a *pain* in your *side*.

FOREMAN
Now, boys, put yo' guns on yo' shoulders an' get back in the shade.

OH, ROLL ON, BABE

a. No. 1589. Acc. on banjo and sung by James Mullins, Florress, Ky., 1937. See Od.2, pp. 102 ff.; Sh, 2:42; Lo.2, p. 20; *PTFLS*, No. 5, p. 168.

In eastern Kentucky, this song is said to have been made up when the L. & N. Railroad was pushed through the mountains, and local opinion is divided as to whether the "composin'" was done by whites, Negroes, or both. Mention of John Henry in many versions and its close textual and melodic connection with other Negro work songs, however, indicates its origin is probably Negro, although it has now become a standard part of the repertory of Southern banjo pickers and is sung, so far as we know, exclusively by them.

The following stanzas that occur in other versions indicate its work-song origin more clearly than does the banjo version printed here in full.

> *I looked at the sun and the sun looked red,*
> *I looked at my partner and he was almost dead.*
>
> *This old hammer killed John Henry,*
> *But it can't kill me, buddy, it can't kill me.*

Moderate, somewhat free ♩ = 160

CHORUS: Oh, roll on, babe, don't roll so slow
STANZA: I dremp last night poor Lu-lu were dead

When the sun goes down, you'll roll no more.
And her a-pern strings tied a-round my head.

Chorus:
> Oh, roll on, babe, don't roll so slow,
> When the sun goes down, you'll roll no more.

1 I dremp last night poor Lulu were dead
And her apern strings tied around my head.

> Oh, roll on, babe, and make your time,
> My wheel's broke down, and I can't make mine.

2 I asked that girl to be my bride;
She said she would before she died.

> Oh, roll on, babe, and do your best,
> When the sun goes down, sit down and rest.

3 I looked at the east, and I looked at the west,
I looked at the girl that I love best.

> Oh, roll on, babe, don't roll so slow,
> When the sun goes down, you'll roll no more.

4 I ain't got no money, but I will have some
  A-Saturday night when the pay train comes.

    Oh, roll on, babe, don't roll so slow,
    When the pay train comes, you will roll no more.

5 I love nobody, nobody loves me,
  I'm a-lonely and single, spend my money free.

    Oh, roll on, babe, and make your time,
    For I am sick, and I can't make mine.

6 I looked at the train as she blew by,
  I thought of home, set down and cried.

    Oh, roll on, babe, don't roll so slow,
    When the sun goes down, you'll roll no more.

7 I looked at the sun and the sun looked high,
  I looked at my love and she looked shy.

    Oh, roll on, babe, and do your best,
    When the sun goes down, sit down and rest.

8 That same old train that runs the track,
  That same old train will bring me back.

    Oh, roll on, babe, don't roll so slow,
    When the sun goes down, you'll roll no more.

*   *   *

I met a man the other day I never met before,
He asked me if I wanted a job a-shoveling iron ore.
I asked him what the wages were.
He said, "Ten cents a ton."
I said, "Old fellow, go chase yourself, I'd rather be a bum."

*   *   *

Works awhile and makes a pay day,
Rides de cushion or de beam;
Boys, de itchin' done got me,
Home ain't nothin' but a dream.

AS I WENT OUT FOR A RAMBLE

d'b. No. 1542. Hazel Hudson, Hazard, Ky., 1937.

Moderate ♩.=76

As I went out for a ram-ble, It's I stopped in a lit-tle town,

It's I fell in love with a pret-ty lit-tle girl— And her eyes they were— dark— brown.

1 As I went out for a ramble,
  It's I stopped in a little town,
  It's I fell in love with a pretty little girl
  And her eyes they were dark brown.

2 This girl I love so dearly,
  It's I loved her more than life,
  But she was nothing but a young flirt
  So she never could be my wife.

3 It's as I was walking one evening,
  It's I walked around the park,
  It's I found her in the arms of another boy,
  God knows it broke my heart.

4 I went to her and asked her
  As plain as words could be,
  "Have you fell in love with another boy
  And turned your back on me?"

[267]

5 She threw her arms around me
  And in these words she said,
  "I love you, dear, with all of my heart,
  God knows, I'd rather be dead.

6 "But your parents, they're against me;
  They talk of me all the time,
  And you are nothing but a hobo,
  God knows you'll never be mine."

7 It's I turned away and left her,
  It's I went on down the track;
  And every step that I would take,
  She seemed to say, "Come back."

8 Next morning I caught a freight train,
  It's I went way down the line,
  It's I said, "I'll go and ask her
  If she'll try me one more time."

9 Now, boys, all take warning
  From a friend that's tried and true.
  Don't fall in love with such a young girl,
  Her love will prove untrue.

10 God knows I've been a rambler,
  It's I rambled all around;
  But if she ever proves true to me
  I'll marry and settle down.

WAY OUT IN IDAHO

B. No. 1634. Blaine Stubblefield, Washington, D.C., 1938.

It is fitting that the man who made this song and the man who composed "Sam Bass" should have used the same tune. For another similar ballad, see "The State of Arkansas," *Cowboy Songs and Other Frontier Ballads*, pp. 283–285 (1938 revised and enlarged edition).

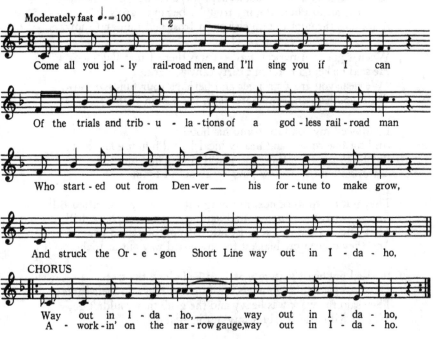

Come all you jol - ly rail-road men, and I'll sing you if I can
Of the trials and trib - u - la - tions of a god - less rail - road man
Who start - ed out from Den-ver___ his for - tune to make grow,
And struck the Or - e - gon Short Line way out in I - da - ho,

CHORUS

Way out in I - da - ho,___ way out in I - da - ho,
A - work-in' on the nar - row gauge, way out in I - da - ho.

1 Come all you jolly railroad men, and I'll sing you if I can
Of the trials and tribulations of a godless railroad man
Who started out from Denver his fortune to make grow,
And struck the Oregon Short Line way out in Idaho.

Chorus:
Way out in Idaho, way out in Idaho,
A-workin' on the narrow-gauge, way out in Idaho.

[269]

2 I was roaming around in Denver one luckless rainy day
   When Kilpatrick's man, Catcher, stepped up to me and did say,
   "I'll lay you down five dollars as quickly as I can
   And you'll hurry up and catch the train, she's starting for Cheyenne."

3 He laid me down five dollars, like many another man,
   And I started for the depot as happy as a clam;
   When I got to Pocatello, my troubles began to grow,
   A-wading through the sagebrush in frost and rain and snow.

4 When I got to American Falls, it was there I met Fat Jack,
   He said he kept a hotel in a dirty canvas shack.
   "We hear you are a stranger and perhaps your funds are low,
   Well, yonder stands my hotel tent, the best in Idaho."

5 I followed my conductor into his hotel tent,
   And for one square and hearty meal I paid him my last cent;
   But Jack's a jolly fellow, and you'll always find him so,
   A-workin' on the narrow-gauge way out in Idaho.

6 They put me to work next morning with a cranky cuss called Bill,
   And they gave me a ten-pound hammer to strike upon a drill;
   They said if I didn't like it I could take my shirt and go,
   And they'd keep my blanket for my board way out in Idaho.

7 It filled my heart with pity as I walked along the track
   To see so many old bummers with their turkeys on their backs;
   They said the work was heavy and the grub they couldn't go,
   Around Kilpatrick's tables way out in Idaho.

8 But now I'm well and happy, down in the harvest camps,
   And there I will continue till I make a few more stamps;
   I'll go down to New Mexico and I'll marry the girl I know,
   And I'll buy me a horse and buggy and go back to Idaho.

III. 5. MINERS' SONGS

"I'm sleepy," he said. "I've been walking all night. Can't sleep when the pain hits me. Have to keep going to keep up the circulation."

The fingers of both of his hands were curled and yellow like the feet of a chicken and the flesh of his arms was pulpy like dry, rotten wood.

"Got this way in the mines," he said. "We was cleaning out an old hole, getting it pumped dry, and pulling out the old machinery. I was foreman and we did a record job. Nobody has equaled our record since, but they wouldn't give us no stove to dry our clothes at. I asked the boss for one, but he said, 'No, I guess you'll get along.'

"We'd take our clothes off wet at night, and when we'd come to put 'em on in the morning they would be frozen. Well, a little while of that and I couldn't turn my head. Three of the other men later died of consumption, and if I didn't die right away, I been dying by inches ever since. Look at those hands."

They were gnarled like chickens' feet.

"The doctor said I ought to sue the company, but I said, 'Aw, hell, no, I'll be all right.' I just had a stiff neck, then, but later on, when it hit my arms, I went to a lawyer. What do you suppose? The man that owned the company had moved to Minnesota and died. And that boss had told lies about us, said that we were lazy. How could he say that when we'd made a record for them? And before he died, a feller told me, that boss confessed to what he had done.

"So nowadays I have to walk. It keeps up the circulation."

OH, MY LIVER AND MY LUNGS

c. No. 597. Mrs. Frost Woodhull, San Antonio, Texas,
1936.

*"I learned this song from my father who used to hear the miners sing it
in Pennsylvania."* —Mrs. Frost Woodhull, *San Antonio, Texas.*

Slow ♩=54

Oh, my liv-er and my lungs, my lights and my legs, They're pain-ing
me, they're pain-ing me; My heart is sad, my head is bad,
And I think I'm go-ing cra - zy. Crushed by__ the
days of__ end-less toil And sleep-less nights of__ woe,__ There is
nought but an-guish__ ev-'ry-where As on through life we go.

1 Oh, my liver and my lungs, my lights and my legs,
   They're paining me, they're paining me;
   My heart is sad, my head is bad,
   And I think I'm going crazy.

2 Crushed by the days of endless toil
   And sleepless nights of woe,
   There is naught but anguish ev'rywhere
   As on through life we go.

[272]

DOWN, DOWN, DOWN

P. 6, *Pennsylvania Folk Songs and Ballads*, George G. Korson, Bucknell University, Lewisburg, Pa. Improvised by William Keating, transcribed and arranged by Melvin LeMon.

"An anthracite mine worker's first day on a new job."

Moderately fast

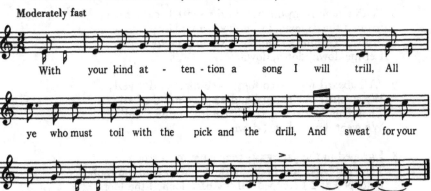

With your kind at-ten-tion a song I will trill, All ye who must toil with the pick and the drill, And sweat for your bread in that hole at Oak Hill, That goes down, down,— down.

1 With your kind attention a song I will trill,
   All ye who must toil with the pick and the drill,
   And sweat for your bread in that hole at Oak Hill,
   That goes down, down, down.

2 "When I was a boy," said my daddy to me,
   "Stay out of Oak Hill, take my warnin'," said he,
   "Or with dust you'll be choked and a pauper you'll be,
   Broken down, down, down."

3 But I went to Oak Hill and I asked for a job,
   A mule for to drive or a gangway to rob;
   The boss said, "Come out, Bill, and follow the mob
   That goes down, down, down."

4 The lampman he squints through the windie at me,
   "What's your name? What's your age? What's your number?" says he.
   "Bill Keating; I'm thirty; my check's twenty-three;
   Mark that down, down, down."

[273]

5 I asked them what tools would I need in the place.
  "Very few," said the boss with a grin on his face;
  "One number six shovel and darn little space,
  While you're down, down, down."

6 With a note from the boss to the shaft I made haste,
  Saluted the topman, in line took my place;
  Sayin', "Gimme a cage, for I've no time to waste,
  Let me down, down, down."

7 "All aboard for the bottom!" the topman did yell;
  We stepped on the cage, and he gave her the bell;
  Then from under our feet like a bat out of—well,
  We went down, down, down.

8 I groped in the gangway; they gave me a scoop.
  The "out" was just fired, muck was heaped to the roof.
  I stooped and I scooped till my back looped the loop,
  Stoopin' down, down, down.

9 You could look at the rib or the face or the top,
  Ne'er a sign of a laggin' or slab or of prop;
  Some day I expect that old mountain to drop
  And come down, down, down.

10 Last pay day my buddy he cussed and he swore,
  In fact it's enough to make any man sore,
  When your wife drags your wages all out in the store,
  While you're down, down, down.

PAY DAY AT COAL CREEK

b. No. 1702. Acc. on 5 string banjo and sung by Pete Steele, Hamilton, Ohio, 1938.

"Pay Day at Coal Creek" was composed at Coal Creek, Tennessee, when the mine exploded and killed nine hundred miners.

"They brought them out and laid the men out on the ground at the drift mouth. Called their wives to come and see if they could know their husbands. They was burned so bad they couldn't tell one from the other. The

company didn't pay no money, not at that time. It broke the company.
Wives never got anything."

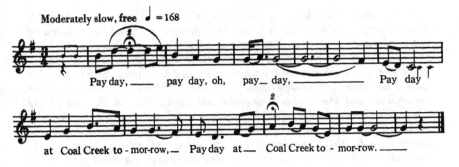

Moderately slow, free ♩ = 168

Pay day, ___ pay day, oh, pay ___ day, _____ Pay day
at Coal Creek to - mor-row, ___ Pay day at ___ Coal Creek to - mor-row. ___

1 Pay day, pay day, oh, pay day,
  Pay day at Coal Creek tomorrow,
  Pay day at Coal Creek tomorrow.

2 Pay day, pay day, oh, pay day,
  Pay day don't come at Coal Creek no more,
  Pay day don't come no more.

3 Bye-bye, bye-bye, oh, bye-bye,
  Bye-bye, my woman, I'm gone,
  Bye-bye, my woman, I'm gone.

4 You'll miss me, you'll miss me, you'll miss me,
  You'll miss me when I'm gone,
  You'll miss me when I'm gone.

5 I'm a poor boy, I'm a poor boy, I'm a poor boy,
  I'm a poor boy and a long ways from home.
  I'm a poor boy and a long ways from home.

6 He's a rider, he's a rider, he's a rider,
  Oh, he's a rider, but he'll leave that rail some time,
  He's a rider, but he'll leave that rail some time.

[275]

THE COAL MINER'S CHILD

ᵃᵇ. No. 2557. Aunt Molly Jackson, New York City,
1939. See Cox, p. 446; Ja.2, p. 48; Sc.2, p. 364.

"This song is a true story concerning a Harlan County miner's child. The miner was killed in the fall-like, and the mother of the child then died in the winter-like in 1928. The same day that the mother was buried, why, this child went to a rich coal operator's house and asked him to give her a home or prepare a home for her where she could have something to eat. He turned her away and thought that she'd went back in the mining camp or somewhere, and the next morning she was found dead in the hall of the house. When the handy man of the place come and reported it, why, this man told him to go and pick up her body and get it out of the way. He didn't see why that the miners' children, them coal miners' trash, should come and die on his hands. Says it looked like they could find some other place to die. And that is the story that I composed this song from."

—AUNT MOLLY JACKSON.

This is a version of the old sentimental ballad, "The Orphan Girl."

Moderately slow, free ♩ = 96

This is the sto-ry of a coal min-er's child,

A lit-tle girl on-ly nine years old,
She died from hun-ger and cold,

She was found dead in a rich man's home,
She was found dead in a rich man's home,

She died from hun-ger and cold.
Yes, she died of hun-ger and cold.

1 This is the story of a coal miner's child,
  A little girl only nine years old,
  She was found dead in a rich man's home,
  She died from hunger and cold,
  She died from hunger and cold,
  She was found dead in a rich man's home,
  Yes, she died of hunger and cold.

2 "I have no home," said the coal miner's child
  At the door of a rich man's hall,
  As she trembling stood on the marble steps
  And leaned against a polished wall.

3 "My father was killed in the coal mines," she said—
  Tears dimmed her eyes so bright,
  "And, last of all, my mother is dead,
  I'm a orphan alone tonight,
  I'm a orphan alone tonight;
  And, last of all, my mother is dead,
  I'm a orphan alone tonight."

4 The night was cold and the snow fell fast,
  But the rich man closed his door,
  And his proud lips spurned with scorn when he said,
  "I've no room, no bread for the poor,
  No room, no bread for the poor";
  His proud lips spurned with scorn when he said,
  "I've no room, no bread for the poor."

5 "I must freeze," she said, as she sank on the steps
  And tried to cover her feet.
  Her ragged dress was covered with snow,
  Yes, covered with snow and sleet.

6 The rich man slep' on a velvet couch,
  And dreamed of his silver and gold,
  While the orphan laid on a bed of snow,
  A-dying from hunger and cold.

7 The morning dawned and the coal miner's child
  Was found lying in his hallway there.
  "Go take up her body and get it out of my way,"
  Was the words the rich man said.

III. 6. FARMERS OF THE SOUTH

The South is singing country, dancing country, fiddling, guitar and banjo-picking country. The spirituals, the blues, ragtime, jazz, and "hill-billy" music came out of the South. It is the country of John Henry, Casey Jones, John Hardy, Stackerlee, Po' Laz'us, Pretty Polly, Wild Bill Jones, and the Boll Weevil. The land is wild and brooding and fertile and gay. Its singing reflects the feeling of the people about their land and its dark and splendid history.

Elsewhere in this volume we print the noble religious songs of the South, its love songs with their tricks and fancies, its tales of fierce brooding passion that brought lovers to their graves, its blues, its work songs, its dance tunes—all made, decorated, or saved up with love by the farm people of the South. Half of the songs in the book, therefore, might well be included in this section, but we have chosen only those songs which have to do with the economic problems of the sharecropper, the farm laborer, the migratory worker, or the small farmer, those which we could feel fairly sure were of folk origin. Here again the South shows itself a singing country, for it has produced songs of lasting strength and merit to tell some of the problems of its rural population.

* * *

Make your cotton and make your corn,
And keep it all in the white folk's barn,
But never you mind about the settlin' time,
The white will bring you out behin'.

* * *

When white man git to worryin',
He ride in de air,
When nigger git to worryin',
Can't go nowhere.

* * *

A man heard a racket in his field. It was old man Boll Weevil whipping Willie Boll Weevil 'cause he couldn't carry two rows of cotton at a time.

[279]

PO' FARMER

No record. Negro share-cropper on the Smithers Plantation, Huntsville, Texas, 1934. Given by A. Lomax.

Moderately slow

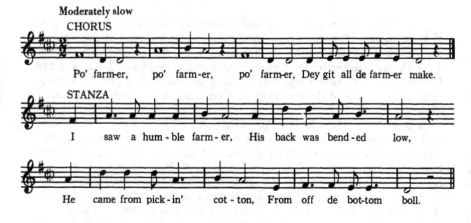

CHORUS

Po' farm-er, po' farm-er, po' farm-er, Dey git all de farm-er make.

STANZA

I saw a hum-ble farm-er, His back was bend-ed low,

He came from pick-in' cot-ton, From off de bot-tom boll.

Chorus:
       Po' farmer, po' farmer, po' farmer,
       Dey git all de farmer make.

1 I saw a humble farmer,
    His back was bended low,
    He came from pickin' cotton,
    From off de bottom boll.

2 Up steps de merchant
    Wid a high-top derby on:
    "Pay me, pay me, Mister Farmer,
    For you to me belong."

3 Up sailed another merchant
    With horses an' buggies fine:
    "Pay me, pay me, Mister Farmer,
    For your corn is shorely mine."

[280]

4 His clo'es is full of patches,
   His hat is full of holes,
   Stoopin' down pickin' cotton,
   From off de bottom boll.

5 At de commissary dere
   His money's in deir bags,
   While his po' little wife an' chillun
   Sit at home in rags.

IT'S HARD ON WE PO' FARMERS

f♯. No. 729. Lemuel Jones, Richmond, Va., 1936.

Moderately fast ♩ = 92

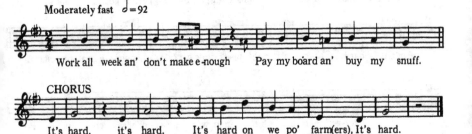

Work all week an' don't make e-nough Pay my board an' buy my snuff.

CHORUS

It's hard, it's hard, It's hard on we po' farm(ers), It's hard.

1 Work all week an' don' make enough
   Pay my board an' buy my snuff.

   Chorus:
       It's hard, it's hard,
       It's hard on we po' farm(ers),
       It's hard.

2 Work all week, in the noonday sun;
   Fifteen cents when Sat'day come.

3 Every morning when I wake up,
   Got to feed my horse and all day cut.

4 Every night when I get home,
   Peas in the pot and a old jawbone.

[281]

AIN'T IT HARD TO BE A RIGHT BLACK NIGGER?

A♭. No. 721. James Baker (Iron Head), Sugar Land,
Texas, 1936. Text composite. See Od.1, pp. 254 ff.; Whi,
385.

*"Dat white man cussed me from de birth o' Saul an' Silas to de death o'
de devil an' called me everything 'cept a chil' o' God."*

Moderately fast, somewhat free ♩ = 104

CHORUS

Ain't it hard to be a right black nig-ger? Po' nig-ger ain' got no___ show.

Ain't it hard__ to be a right black_ nig-ger? Po' nig-ger ain' got no show.

STANZA

Nig-ger and a white man was play-in' sev-en-up, Po' nig-ger ain' got no___ show,___ Nig-ger won the mon-ey, was a-fraid to pick it up, Po' nig-ger ain' got no show.

Chorus:

  Ain't it hard to be a right black nigger?
  Po' nigger ain' got no show.
  Ain't it hard to be a right black nigger?
  Po' nigger ain' got no show.

1 Nigger and a white man was playin' seven-up,
  Po' nigger ain' got no show,
  Nigger won the money, was afraid to pick it up,
  Po' nigger ain' got no show.

2 If you don't go to stealing the white man's money,
  Take away yo' horse and mule;
  If you don't go to stealing the white man's money,
  Take away yo' horse and mule.

3 I told the master my wife was sick,
  Po' nigger ain' got no show,
  "You're tellin' me a lie, you son-of-a-bitch,"
  Po' nigger ain' got no show.

4 I asked my master, "How do you know?"
  Po' nigger ain' got no show,
  "I gave her two dollars an hour ago."
  Po' nigger ain' got no show.

5 I know an old man named Uncle Ned,
  Po' nigger ain' got no show,
  Just about three strands of hair on his head,
  Po' nigger ain' got no show.

6 He had no money, had no home,
  Po' nigger ain' got no show,
  Poor old man always liked to roam,
  Po' nigger ain' got no show.

7 Fer a nickel's worth of crackers and a dime worth of cheese,
  Po' nigger ain' got no show,
  Dey treat him like a dog and do him like dey please,
  Po' nigger ain' got no show.

GEORGIA LAND

d. No. 729. Jim Owens, State Penitentiary, Richmond, Va., 1936. See *PTFLS*, No. 5, p. 178; "Old Joe Clark," Lo.2, p. 277; Bot, pp. 269 ff.; also "Liza Jane," and related songs.

This song is what is known as a sinful reel. In the cool of the evening when a man has nearly finished his plowing, or late Saturday night rattling home from town with a jug under the wagon seat and the lines tied to the handbrake—these are occasions for "Georgia Land." We have heard it all over the South on the lips of rural Negroes, but the stanza which we still like best is the following:

Last year was a very fine year,
For termaters and pertaters.
Papa didn' raise no beans an' greens,
But, Lawd God, the 'taters!

Moderate ♩=84

Stanza 1 only

1. My gal don' wear but-ton-up shoes, Her feet too big for gait-ers, ___

Stanzas 2,3,4

2. My dog died of whoop-ing ___ cough, My mule ___ died'v dis-temp-er, ___

Stanzas 1,2,3,4

1. All she's fit fur a dip of snuff And a yal-low yam ___ po-
2. Me 'n' my gal can't git a - long, *etc.*

ta - to. ___ Jint a ___ head, ___ cen-ter back, ___ Did you

ev - er work on ___ the ___ rail - road track? ___

[284]

1 My gal don' wear button-up shoes,
  Her feet too big for gaiters,
  All she's fit fur—a dip of snuff
  And a yallow yam potato.
      Jint ahead, center back,
      Did you ever work on the railroad track?

2 My dog died of whooping cough,
  My mule died of distemper,
  Me 'n' my gal can't git along,
  She's got a pretty bad temper.
      Tighten on the backband, loosen on the bow,
      And-a whoa! quit pickin' that banjo so!

3 You go saddle the old gray mare,
  And I will plow old muley.
  I'll make a turn 'fore the sun goes down,
  And I'll go back home to Julie.
      Rowdy-o! Rowdy-o!
      If you got the wagon loaded, let me see you go!

4 Takes four wheels to hold a load,
  Takes two mules to pull double,
  Take me back to Georgia Land
  And I won't be no trouble.
      Whoa!

GEORGIA BOY

c'. No. 1029. Mrs. Ruth Clark Cullipher and Angie
Clark, Mullins, S.C., 1937. See Sh, 2:258; Ed, p. 243.

Moderately fast ♩ = 104

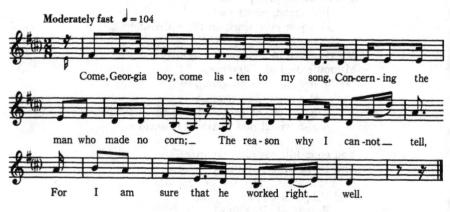

Come, Geor-gia boy, come lis-ten to my song, Con-cern-ing the
man who made no corn;__ The rea-son why I can-not__ tell,
For I am sure that he worked right__ well.

1 Come, Georgia boy, come listen to my song,
  Concerning the man who made no corn;
  The reason why I cannot tell,
  For I am sure that he worked right well.

2 In September his corn was knee-high,
  In October he laid it by,
  In November there came a great frost,
  And you can't tell how much he lost.

3 He went to the field and there he looked in,
  The jimpson weeds were up to his chin,
  The bushes and the grass had grown so high,
  Enough to make this young man cry.

4 In the winter, I was told,
  He went courting, very bold.
  When his courtship first began—
  "My kind sir, did you make any corn?"

[286]

5 "No, kind miss," was his reply.
  "Long ago I laid it by,
  It wasn't worth while to strive in vain,
  For I didn't expect to make one grain."

6 "My kind sir, you ask me to wed.
  If that is your way, we'll have no bread;
  Single I am, and single I'll remain,
  For a lazy man I won't maintain."

HARD TIMES IN THE COUNTRY

g. Columbia Master No. 15565-D (out of print). Acc. on guitar.

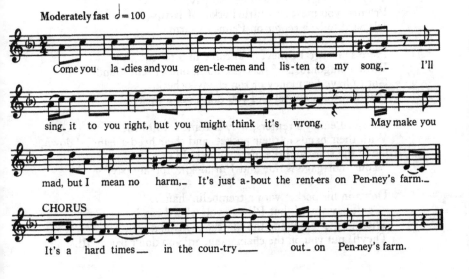

Moderately fast ♩ = 100

Come you la-dies and you gen-tle-men and lis-ten to my song,_ I'll
sing_ it to you right, but you might think it's wrong, May make you
mad, but I mean no harm,_ It's just a-bout the rent-ers on Pen-ney's farm._

CHORUS

It's a hard times_ in the coun-try_ out_ on Pen-ney's farm.

1 Come you ladies and you gentlemen and listen to my song,
  I'll sing it to you right, but you might think it's wrong,
  May make you mad but I mean no harm,
  It's just about the renters on Penney's farm.

Chorus:
>   It's a hard times in the country,
>   Out on Penney's farm.

2   You move out on Penney's farm,
    Plant a little crop of 'bacco, and a little crop of corn,
    Come around to see you, gonna plit and plot
    Till you get yourself a mortgage on everything you've got.

3   Haven't old George Penney got a flatterin' mouth?
    Move you to the country in a little log house,
    Got no windows but the cracks in the wall,
    He will work you summer and he'll rob you in the fall.

4   You'll go in the fields and you'll work all day,
    Way after night, but you get no pay,
    Promise you meat or a little bucket of lard,
    It's hard to be a renter on Penney's farm.

5   Here's George Penney, he'll come into town,
    With a wagonload of peaches, not a one of 'em sound,
    Got to have his money or somebody's check,
    Pay him for a bushel and you don't get a peck.

6   George Penney's renters, they'll come into town,
    With their hands in their pockets and their head a-hangin' down,
    Go in the store and the merchant would say,
    "Your mortgage is due and I'm lookin' for my pay."

7   Down in his pocket with a tremblelin' hand,
    "Can't pay you all but I'll pay you what I can."
    Then to the telephone the merchant made a call,
    They'll put you on the chain gang, an' you don't pay at all.

THE DODGER

d'♭. No. 3230. Emma Dusenberry, Mena, Ark., 1936.
By courtesy of Sidney Robertson, Lawrence Powell and
Charles Seeger. Said to have been used as an anti-Blaine
song in the Cleveland-Blaine campaign.

Mrs. Emma Dusenberry of Mena, Arkansas, sings "The Dodger." She
learned it in the 1880's, when a farmer could still make a living, "just as
sure as he was born."

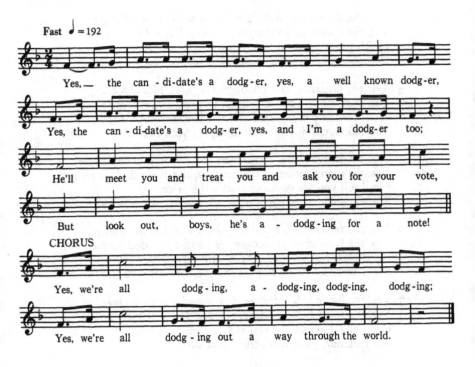

Fast ♩ = 192

Yes,— the can-di-date's a dodg-er, yes, a well known dodg-er,

Yes, the can-di-date's a dodg-er, yes, and I'm a dodg-er too;

He'll meet you and treat you and ask you for your vote,

But look out, boys, he's a-dodg-ing for a note!

CHORUS

Yes, we're all dodg-ing, a-dodg-ing, dodg-ing, dodg-ing;

Yes, we're all dodg-ing out a way through the world.

1 Yes, the candidate's a dodger, yes, a well known dodger,
   Yes, the candidate's a dodger, yes, and I'm a dodger too;
   He'll meet you and treat you and ask you for your vote,
   But look out, boys, he's a-dodging for a note!

[289]

Chorus:
>   Yes, we're all dodging, a-dodging, dodging, dodging;
>   Yes, we're all dodging out a way through the world.

2 Yes, the lawyer he's a dodger, a well known dodger,
  Yes, the lawyer he's a dodger, yes, and I'm a dodger too;
  He'll plead you a case and claim you as a friend,
  But look out, boys, he's easy for to bend!

3 Yes, the doctor he's a dodger, yes, a well known dodger,
  Yes, the doctor he's a dodger, yes, and I'm a dodger too;
  He'll doctor you and cure you for half you possess,
  But look out, boys, he's a-dodging for the rest!

4 Yes, the preacher he's a dodger, yes, a well known dodger,
  Yes, the preacher he's a dodger, yes, and I'm a dodger too;
  He'll preach you a gospel and tell you of your crimes,
  But look out, boys, he's a-dodging for your dimes!

5 Yes, the merchant he's a dodger, yes, a well known dodger,
  Yes, the merchant he's a dodger, yes, and I'm a dodger too;
  He'll sell you the goods at double the price,
  But when you go to pay him, you'll have to pay him twice.

6 Yes, the farmer he's a dodger, yes, a well known dodger,
  Yes, the farmer he's a dodger, yes, and I'm a dodger too;
  He'll plow his cotton, he'll plow his corn,
  He'll make a living just as sure as you're born!

7 Yes, the lover he's a dodger, yes, a well known dodger,
  Yes, the lover he's a dodger, yes, and I'm a dodger too;
  He'll hug you and kiss you and call you his bride,
  But look out, girls, he's telling you a lie!

COTTON–MILL COLIC

d. No. 1629. Acc. on guitar and sung by Joe Sharp of Skyline Farms, Scottsboro, Ala., in Washington, D.C., 1939. By courtesy of Nicholas Ray. See also "Cotton Mill Blues." Decca 5559.

The story of what happens to the cotton farmer when he becomes a cotton-mill worker, with the "collection man" as the villain of the piece.

When you buy clothes on eas-y terms, The col-lect-or treats you like meas-ly worms;

One dol-lar down and then, Lord knows, If you don't make a
No use to col-lect, they're all that way, Peck-in' at your

pay-ment they'll take your clothes. When you go to bed,— you can't
door— till they get your pay. I'm a-gon-na starve, ev'ry-bod-y

sleep,— You owe so much _____ at the end of the week.
will,— You can't make a liv-in' at a cot-ton _____ mill.

1 When you buy clothes on easy terms,
   The collector treats you like measly worms;
   One dollar down and then, Lord knows,
   If you don't make a payment they'll take your clothes.
   When you go to bed, you can't sleep,
   You owe so much at the end of the week.
   No use to collect, they're all that way,
   Peckin' at your door till they get your pay.

[291]

Chorus:
>   I'm a-gonna starve, ev'rybody will,
>   You can't make a livin' at a cotton mill.

2 When you go to work, you work like the devil,
   At the end of the week you're not on the level.
   Pay day comes, you pay your rent,
   When you get through, you've not got a cent
   To buy fat-back meat, pinto beans;
   Now and then you get a turnip green.
   No use to collect, they're all that way,
   You can't get the money to move away.

3 Twelve dollars a week is all I get—
   How in the heck can I live on that?
   I got a wife and fourteen kids,
   We all have to sleep on two bedsteads.
   Patches on my breeches, holes in my hat,
   Ain't had a shave since my wife got fat.
   No use to collect, ever' day at noon—
   Kids get to cryin' in a different tune.

4 They run a few days, and then they stand,
   Just to keep down the workin'man.
   We'll never make it, we never will,
   As long as we stay in a roundin' mill.
   The poor are gettin' poorer, the rich are gettin' rich,
   If I don't starve, I'm a son of a gun.
   No use to collect, no use to rave,
   We'll never rest till we're in our grave.

Chorus:
>   If I don't starve, nobody will,
>   You can't make a livin' at a cotton mill.

Men at Work

CHILLY WINDS

a. No. 1368. Acc. by Bogtrotters Band and sung by Fields Ward, Galax, Va., 1937. Another version of the text appears in John Steinbeck's "Grapes of Wrath." We are assured that this was the song par excellence of the homeless wanderers of the 1930's, especially the "Okies." The tune appears to be related to "I Ain't a-Gonna Study War No Mo'," "Careless Love," "C. C. Rider," "New River Train," and other songs. See Hu, 313.

Based on the Negro song, "I Ain't a-Gonna Be Treated This-a-Way," "Chilly Winds" can be heard wherever there are migratory workers, from the Florida Everglades to the beet fields of Michigan and the orange groves of the Imperial Valley.

Moderately fast ♩ = 112

I'm go-in' where them chil-ly winds — won't blow, darlin' ba - by,

I'm go- in' where them chil -ly winds don't — blow,

When I'm go - in' to my long lone - some — home.

1 I'm goin' where them chilly winds won't blow, darlin' baby,
 I'm goin' where them chilly winds don't blow,
 When I'm goin' to my long lonesome home.

2 Oh, make me a pallet on the floor, darlin' baby, etc.
 For I'm goin' to my long lonesome home.

3 Now who'll be your partner when I'm gone?
 When I'm gone to my long lonesome home?

4 Oh, who'll hoe your corn when I'm gone?

5 Who'll stir the gravy when I'm gone?

6 Oh, it's way down in jail on my knees.

7 Oh, they feed me on corn bread and peas.

8 I ain't got but one old rusty dime.

9 Oh, I'll have a new dollar some old day, darlin' baby,
   Oh, I'll have a new dollar some old day,
   And I'll throw this old rusty dime away.

10 Back, back, old freight train, get your load.

11 Oh, I'm going where the climate suits my clothes.

*   *   *   *   *

Dat road got littler and littler till it jes' run up a tree.

IV

OUTLAWS

OUTLAWS

"I used to think that it was just simply the Devil in people, and that the Devil ruled the people, and that they was corrupt-minded, and that they never did have anything in their minds that was pure and right. But now I have been forced, through misery and depression and through seein' so much misery among the people, that through experience I've learnt that it's just simply that they go beyond control, that they're aggravated so much from their horrible misery and sufferin' that they have to do, they have such a hard life that the people are just simply not theirselves."

—Aunt Molly Jackson.

PASS AROUND YOUR BOTTLE

ab. No. 1601. Acc. on banjo and sung by Walter Williams, Salyersville, Ky., 1937.

"The four of us was rambling through the mountains, a-drinking, and we had a quart of whisky apiece. John would drink like pouring it down a crawfish hole or somepen, and the rest of us would take little light drinks. Well, me an' John, we got away ahead of Earl Lee an' Peanut. So, me an' Earl Lee separated up, an' Earl Lee an' Peanut got together, an' me an' John got together. Me an' John had come to the country there together, and Earl Lee an' Peanut had come together. Well, we got away off down there, an' John he git his little pocketknife out, a Barlow, an' open it up. He'd say this an' that to me an' first one damn thing an' another, an' we'd climb over logs and through damn brushes and everything else until toreckly Earl Lee an' Peanut got up to us pretty close, you know; and Earl Lee had a damn big stick fit fer a fiddle and another big stick fer a bow and they'd plumb stopped there. Earl Lee was playin' the fiddle and Peanut had another big stick, just pickin' it, like it was a banjer or a guitar. Jest a-pickin' away an' a-singin' away. 'Tum, tum, tum, tum, tum.'

"Well, we started off down the hollers, and we ain't went fer till they both had a fiddle and a guitar and a banjer again, jest plinkin' away, a-playin' a fiddle an' singin' 'Little Darlin' ' an' 'Pal o' Mine,' an' 'When the Roses Bloom Agin', and ever damn thing on earth."

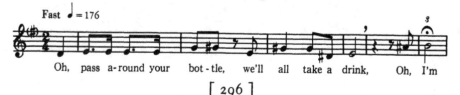

Fast ♩ = 176

Oh, pass a-round your bot - tle, we'll all take a drink, Oh, I'm

bound for an - o - ther spring.— Oh, them— don't like— me can

let— me a - lone, For my darl-ing's gone back on— me.

1 Oh, pass around your bottle, we'll all take a drink,
Oh, I'm bound for another spring.
Oh, them don't like me can let me alone,
For my darling's gone back on me.

2 Well, my old clothes are dirty and torn,
My shoes are full of holes,
Oh, my old hat is hanging all around,
And it's almost touching my nose.

3 Oh, pass around your bottle and we'll all take a drink,
It's been all around this room;
Oh, pass it to the boys that fears no noise,
Although we're far from home.

4 I remember what my old mamma said,
She gave me good advice;
She told me to quit my rambling ways,
And marry me a loving little wife.

5 You can shoot, you can cut, you can rip, you can tear,
You can do whatever you will;
For I ramble around from town to town,
And I drink corn whisky still.

6 When I were young and a-running around,
I had a little money to spend,
I spent it for drink, but I never did think
That my fun would ever end.

[297]

SWEET THING

ab. No. 246. Acc. on guitar and sung by Leroy Allen on
the Cummins State Farm, Ark., 1935. See Sh, 2:357, Lo.2,
153. Version 2, from Knott County, Ky. In the past ten
years this tune has been popular over the radio and on the
phonograph, often as "The Crawdad Song."

1 What you gonna do when the liquor gives out, sweet thing? (2)
 What you gonna do when the liquor gives out?
 A-standing on the corner with your mouth poked out,
 Sweet thing, sweet thing, sweet thing?

2 Danced all night with the bottle in my hand,
 A-looking for the woman ain't got no man.

3 Well, the boiler busted and the smokestack fell,
 Killed my darling dead as hell.

[298]

4 Goin' get me a bucket, gwine to the wood;
   The berries give out, makes rollin' good.

5 I stuck my hook in the crawfish hole,
   I couldn't get it out to save my soul.

6 Wake up, old man, you slept too late,
   The crawfish wagon done passed your gate.

7 What did the old hen say to the rooster?
   "If you gonna catch me, gotta run me down."

8 Oh, what the old hen, he say to the drake?
   "It ain't no fish in this old lake."

9 You get the hook and I got the pole,
   Let's go down to the crawfish hole.

Version 2—The Crawdad Song

1 A-settin' on the ice till my feet got cold,
   A-watchin' that crawdad dig his hole.

2 Crawdad, crawdad, you'd better dig deep,
   For I'm a-goin' to ramble in my sleep.

3 A-settin' on the ice till my feet got hot,
   A-watchin' that crawdad rack and trot.

4 Crawdad, crawdad, you'd better go to hole,
   If I don't catch you, damn my soul.

5 A-settin' on the ice till my feet got numb,
   A-watchin' that crawdad back and come.

6 Shoot your dice and roll 'em in the sand,
   I ain't a-gonna work for no damned man.

7 Apple cider and cinnamon beer,
   Cold hog's head and a nigger's ear.

[299]

THREE NIGHTS DRUNK

bb. No. 1351. Acc. on guitar and mandolin and sung by Mr. and Mrs. E. C. Ball, Rugby, Va., 1937. See "Our Goodman," Child, No. 274; Sh, 1 :267; Sc.2, 2, pp. 231 ff; Be, p. 89.

Moderately fast ♩ = 104

MAN

First night when I came home, as drunk as I could be,—
"Now come, lit-tle wife, my dear lit-tle wife, will you splain this to me?

Found a horse in the sta-ble, where my——horse ought to be.
Here's a horse in the sta-ble, where my—— horse ought to be."

WOMAN

"You blind fool, you sil - ly fool, cain't you nev - er see?—

It's noth-in' but a milk cow your moth-er give— to me."

MAN

"I've trav-elled this wide world o - ver, ten thousand miles or more,—

Sad - dle on a— milk cow's back I nev - er did see— be-fore."

1. MAN

First night when I come home, as drunk as I could be,
Found a horse in the stable, where my horse ought to be.

"Now come, little wife, my dear little wife, will you splain this to me?
Here's a horse in the stable, where my horse ought to be."

[300]

WOMAN

"You blind fool, you silly fool, cain't you never see?
It's nothin' but a milk cow your mother give to me."

MAN

"I've traveled this wide world over, ten thousand miles or more,
Saddle on a milk cow's back I never did see before."

2. MAN

Second night when I come home, drunk as I could be,
Found an overcoat on the rack where my overcoat ought to be.

"Now come, little wife, my dear little wife, will you splain this to me?
Here's an overcoat on the rack, where my overcoat ought to be."

WOMAN

"You blind fool, you silly fool, cain't you never see?
It's nothin' but a bedquilt your granny give to me."

MAN

"I've traveled this wide world over, ten thousand miles or more;
Pockets in a bedquilt I never did see before."

3. MAN

Third night when I come home, drunk as I could be,
Head on the pillow where my head ought to be.

"Now come, little wife, my dear little wife, will you splain this to me?
Here's a head on the pillow where my head ought to be."

WOMAN

"You blind fool, you silly fool, cain't you never see?
It's nothin' but a cabbage head your mother give to me."

MAN

"I've traveled this wide world over, ten thousand miles or more;
Eyes and nose on a cabbage head I never did see before."

[301]

DARLING COREY

bb. No. 828. Aunt Molly Jackson, New York City. See Victor record No. 35838, for banjo accompaniment. Ca, p. 23.

Toast:

Here's to those that wears no clothes and has no wife to mend them,
Here's to a boy that has few dimes but a damn free heart to spend them.

"*There was a woman who used to say a lot of these here rough toasts; her name was Suze Carroll an' her generation was knowed to be brave and tough. She could outcuss, outdrink any man in Clay County, an' she would pass all sorts of rough remarks and jokes, but she couldn't be bought or persuaded to make a dishonest move against her husband.*"

—AUNT MOLLY JACKSON.

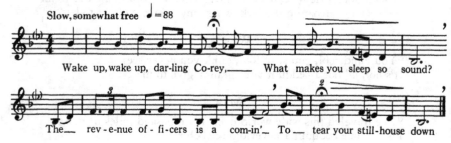

Wake up, wake up, dar-ling Co-rey,— What makes you sleep so sound?
The— rev-e-nue of-fi-cers is a com-in'— To— tear your still-house down

1   Wake up, wake up, darling Corey,
    What makes you sleep so sound?
    The revenue officers is a-comin'
    To tear your stillhouse down.

2   Go away from me, darling Corey,
    Quit hanging around my bed,
    Pretty women run me distracted,
    Corn liquor's killed me stone-dead.

3   The last time I saw darling Corey,
    She had a dram glass in her hand;
    She was drinkin' down her troubles
    With that low-down, dirty man.

4 Last night as I lay on my pillow,
Last night as I lay on my bed,
Last night as I lay on my pillow,
I dreamed darling Corey was dead.

5 I'm going across deep waters,
I'm going across the sea,
I'm going across deep waters,
Going to bring darling Corey to me.

6 Go and dig me a hole in the meadow,
Go and dig me a hole in the ground,
Go and dig me a hole in the meadow,
Just to lay darling Corey down.

7 Don't you hear them bluebirds singing,
Don't you hear that mournful sound,
They're preaching darling Corey's funeral
In the lonesome graveyard ground.

8 The last time I saw darling Corey,
She had a wineglass in her hand,
She was drinking down her troubles
With a low-down, sorry man.

JACK O' DIAMONDS

d♭. No. 89. Acc. with knife guitar and sung by Pete Harris, Richmond, Texas, 1934. Probably derived from Blind Lemon Jefferson's record, "Jack of Diamonds," Paramount 12373.

> *What kinda pants does the gambler wear?*
> *Great big stripes, cost nine dollars a pair.*

This version was recorded from the singing of Pete Harris, a Negro living in Richmond, Texas. Blind Lemon Jefferson of Dallas, the first Negro folk singer to make commercial records, popularized this old Texas gambling song—one of the blues' first cousins. Paramount 12373-A, if you can find this rare record, contains Blind Lemon's version, and furnished us with all but our first and last stanzas.

[303]

Chorus:
 Jack o' Diamonds, Jack o' Diamonds,
 Jack o' Diamonds is a hard card to play.

1 Well, I bet my money in the spring,
 And it set me all in a strain,
 Jack o' Diamonds is a hard card to play.

2 Jack o' Diamonds won this time,
 He did rob a friend of mine,
 Jack o' Diamonds is a hard card to play.

3 Bet the Jack against the Queen,
 It gonna turn yo' money green!
 Jack o' Diamonds is a hard card to play.

4 Bet the Jack against the fo',
 You gonna win right in the do',
 Jack o' Diamonds is a hard card to play.

5 Jack o' Diamonds made me cry,
 Say, I'm gonna gamble till I die,
 Jack o' Diamonds is a hard card to play.

6 Well, I begin to play in the fall,
 Kep' me wearin' my blue overalls,
 Jack o' Diamonds is a hard card to play.

Chorus:
 Oh, li'l' Alice, oh, li'l' Alice,
 Oh, li'l' Alice, keep yo' hole in the wall.

STAVIN' CHAIN

e'. No. 210. Acc. on guitar and sung by Tricky Sam, Huntsville. Texas, 1934. See PTFLS, No. 5, p. 179.

Purported to be a Virginia rounder, Stavin' Chain has been heard from all over the South—a sort of sexy Paul Bunyan. It is worth noting in this connection that we have encountered a number of guitar players nicknamed Stavin' Chain—Little Stavin' Chain, Big Stavin' Chain, etc.—none of whom could or would tell us what his nickname meant. Guitar players, however, have the reputation of being midnight creepers.

This version, sung and censored for us by Tricky Sam of Huntsville, Texas, has been approved by various old-time barroom musicians as an authentic piece of early ragtime of the sort that some might call "a blackguard song."

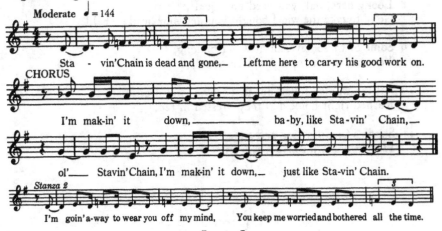

1 Stavin' Chain is dead and gone,
   Left me here to carry his good work on.

Chorus:
   I'm makin' it down, baby, like Stavin' Chain, ol' Stavin' Chain.
   I'm makin' it down, just like Stavin' Chain.

2 I'm goin' away to wear you off my mind,
   You keep me worried and bothered all the time.

3 Stavin' Chain was a man like dis,
   Stood on the corner an' wind his fist.

4 Long and tall, just about my height,
   Won't mistreat you to save yo' life.

5 I tell you, baby, like the Dago tol' the Jew,
   "If you don' likee me, I don' likee you."

6 It ain't but one thing worried my mind,
   Brown-skin gal quit me in the wintertime.

7 I got ten little puppies, one little shaggy houn',
   Take all them puppies to run my brown-skin down.

8 Looky here, gal, you need not squall,
   Goin' to take the wig I bought you, let your head go bald.

9 Some of these days, an' it won't be long,
   You call my name an' I'll be gone.

10 All the women found out that Stavin' was dead,
   Rushed right home and they dressed in red.

11 Stavin's Chain is dead and gone,
   He's in hell with his Stetson on.

MY FATHER GAVE ME A LUMP OF GOLD

d'. No. 863. Mrs. Emma Dusenberry, Mena, Ark.,
1936. Through the courtesy of Lawrence Powell. See
Sh, 2:79; Ja.2, p. 68; Be, p. 259.

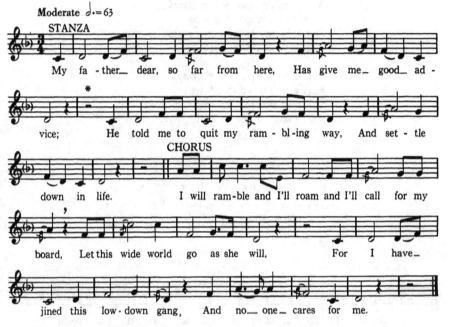

Moderate ♩.=63

STANZA

My fa-ther_ dear, so far from here, Has give me_ good_ ad-

vice; He told me to quit my ram-bl-ing way, And set-tle

CHORUS

down in life. I will ram-ble and I'll roam and I'll call for my

board, Let this wide world go as she will, For I have_

jined this low-down gang, And no_ one_ cares for me.

* With one exception, all half rests in all stanzas and choruses are shortened by one beat.

1 My father dear, so far from here,
Has give me good advice;
He told me to quit my rambling way,
And settle down in life.

Chorus:

I will ramble and I'll roam and I'll call for my board,
Let this wide world go as she will,
For I have jined this low-down gang,
And no one cares for me.

[307]

2 My father gave me a lump of gold,
It pleased me mighty well;
It neither bought me a house nor lot,
Nor saved my soul from hell.

3 My mother dear, so far away,
Has give me good advice;
She told me to quit my rambling way,
And stay at home with her.

4 My sister dear, so far away,
Has give me good advice;
She told me to quit my rambling way,
And marry a pretty little wife.

AS I SET DOWN TO PLAY TIN-CAN

bb. No. 1542. Howard Horne, Hazard, Ky., 1937. See
Sc.2, p. 87; Ga.2, 335; Victor record No. 20534B; Fl.2,
p. 153. Usually titled "The Boston Burglar" or "Po'
Boy."

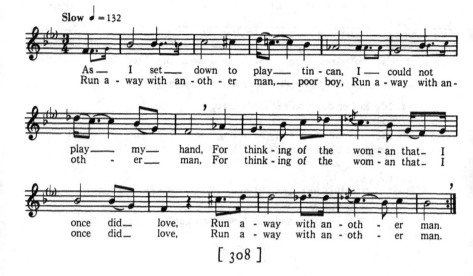

Slow ♩ = 132

As — I set — down to play — tin - can, I — could not
Run a - way with an - oth - er man, — poor boy, Run a - way with an -

play — my — hand, For think - ing of the wom - an that — I
oth - er — man, For think - ing of the wom - an that — I

once did — love, Run a - way with an - oth - er man.
once did — love, Run a - way with an - oth - er man.

1 As I set down to play tin-can,*
   I could not play my hand,
   For thinking of the woman that I once did love,
   Run away with another man.
   Run away with another man, poor boy,
   Run away with another man,
   For thinking of the woman that I once did love,
   Run away with another man.

2 I went down to the big depot,
   The train came rolling by;
   I looked into the window, seen the woman that I loved,
   Bowed down my head and cried,
   Bowed down my head and cried, poor boy,
   Bowed my head and cried,
   I looked into the window, seen the woman that I loved,
   Bowed down my head and cried.

3 I caught the back end of the train,
   I walked right down the aisle,
   I pulled out my big 40-some-odd,
   And I shot that brown-skin child.

4 "Oh, Judge, oh, Judge, kind-hearted Judge,
   Oh, what are you going to do with me?"
   "If I find you guilty, poor boy,
   Going to sentence you to the penitentiaree."

5 The Judge he found me guilty, boys,
   And the clerk he wrote it down;
   He turned me over to the contractor,
   And now I'm penitentiaree-bound.

6 The night was dark and stormy, boys,
   It sure did look like rain;
   Not a friend in all this wide, wide world,
   Nobody knowed my name.

* Usually sung "coon-can."

7 My mother's in her cold, cold grave,
My father's gone away,
My sister married a gambling man,
And I have gone astray,
And I have gone astray, poor boy,
And I have gone astray,
My sister married a gambling man,
And I have gone astray.

LITTLE WILLIE'S MY DARLIN'

c'. No. 98. Acc. on guitar and sung by George W.
Smith, Raleigh, N.C., 1934. See Lo.2, p. 147; also numerous recordings, "Twenty-one Years," "An Answer to
Twenty-one Years," etc.

With "Home on the Range," "Frankie and Albert," "The Red River
Valley," "St. Louis Blues," and a few others, this is among the best known
American folk tunes. Popularized over the air and on commercial records,
it has grown from its humble "Down in the Valley" theme to be best known
of all jailhouse songs. "Twenty-one Years," "An Answer to Twenty-one
Years" are two of the prodigious family of parodies it has fathered. "Little
Willie," sung by a Negro convict in North Carolina, has more charm than
any other version we have heard.

Chorus:

Little Willie's my darlin',
Little Willie's my dear,
If you think I don't love her,
Got a foolish idea.

1 She wrote me one letter,
She sent it by mail,
She sent it in care
Of the Washington jail.

2 Gonna build me one steeple
On the mountain so high,
So I can see Willie
Passin' on by.

3 She said that she loved me
Just to give my heart ease;
Just as soon as my back was turned,
She loved who she pleased.
* Only.

4 I rapped on her window,
I knocked on her do',
She gave me short answer,
"Don't knock there no mo'."

5 Sittin' in the prison
With my back to the wall,
Old corn whisky
Was the cause of it all.

6 The judge said, "Stand up, George,
And dry up your tears;
You're sentenced to Raleigh
For twenty-two years."

7 If I had on' * listened,
To what mother said,
I'd 'a' been there today
In her feather bed.

ADIEU TO THE STONE WALLS

f♯. No. 647. Gant family, Austin, Texas, 1936.

A noticeably modern story of a convict's escape into the "free world"—to the freedom for which every prisoner longs, and about which some of the best prison ballads are made.

Moderately slow ♩ = 120

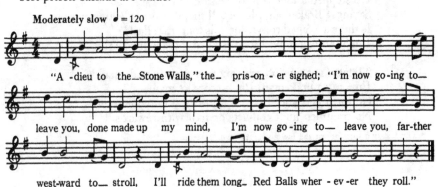

"A-dieu to the Stone Walls," the pris-on-er sighed; "I'm now go-ing to leave you, done made up my mind, I'm now go-ing to leave you, far-ther west-ward to stroll, I'll ride them long Red Balls wher-ev-er they roll."

[311]

1 "Adieu to the Stone Walls," the prisoner sighed;
  "I'm now going to leave you, done made up my mind,
  I'm now going to leave you, farther westward to stroll,
  I'll ride them long Red Balls wherever they roll."

2 I mounted that Red Ball, just about ten o'clock;
  The whistle blowed loudly, the drive-wheels did knock;
  The whistle blowed loudly o'er a lost boy's trail,
  The echoes did mingle far over the hills.

3 The drive wheels were knocking at a forty-mile rate,
  And, boys, I was riding that long Red Ball freight;
  I clumb to the caboose, to all trainmen's place,
  Starvation and death, boys, were both in my face.

4 Then we rolled to a city where they bought me some clothes,
  They dressed me so neatly from my head to my toes;
  They bought me a brake cap, also a white light,
  Saying, "If you're skillful, you'll make it all right,"

5 They tried me awhile, boys, said: "Now you're all right.
  Climb out on the top now, take with you this light."
  I clumb out on top, boys, and I waved them to go,
  A-watchin' my signal conductor below.

6 Then we rolled to the next city where they're searching for me;
  I paid them no mind, boys, you can plainly see.
  Up stepped a lone cop to the side of my car,
  Saying, "Brakeman, please tell me, if it lies in your power,
  Is there a 'scaped convict on this long Red Ball?
  I'm hunting a convict who escaped those Stone Walls." *

7 "That is not my job, sir, you may plainly understand;
  I'm only a brakeman, I'm no convict man.
  Go forth and you'll find him, place it on your records:
  No trainmen hunt convicts or fool with rewards."

* The last two lines repeat the melody of the two preceding.

8 I clumb back on top, boys, and I waved them to go,
A-watchin' my signal conductor below,
A-wavin' so skillful, the brakeman's high ball,
And I left the lone cop on the streets of Stone Walls.

9 My song is now ended, I'll bid you adieu,
My song is now ended, I'll bid you farewell;
My song is now ended, I'll bid you farewell,
To enjoy a heaven instead of a cell.

WE DON'T GET NO JUSTICE HERE IN ATLANTA

e. No. 263. Negro man, State Penitentiary, Milledgeville, Ga., 1934.

"My cell is mighty cold, suh,
And the rain passes through,
My chains are a-clankin'
And I'm feeling mighty blue."

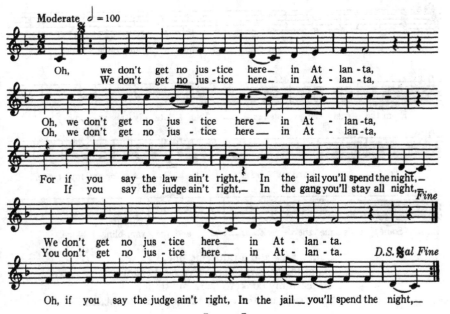

Oh, we don't get no jus-tice here— in At - lan -ta,
We don't get no jus-tice here— in At - lan -ta,

Oh, we don't get no jus - tice here — in At - lan-ta,
Oh, we don't get no jus - tice here — in At - lan-ta,

For if you say the law ain't right,— In the jail you'll spend the night,—
If you say the judge ain't right,— In the gang you'll stay all night,— *Fine*

We don't get no jus - tice here— in At - lan - ta.
You don't get no jus - tice here— in At - lan - ta. *D.S. al Fine*

Oh, if you say the judge ain't right, In the jail— you'll spend the night,—

[313]

Oh, we don't get no justice here in Atlanta,
Oh, we don't get no justice here in Atlanta,
For if you say the law ain't right,
In the jail you'll spend the night,
We don't get no justice here in Atlanta.
Oh, if you say the judge ain't right,
In the jail you'll spend the night,
We don't get no justice here in Atlanta,
Oh, we don't get no justice here in Atlanta,
If you say the judge ain't right,
In the gang you'll stay all night,
You don't get no justice here in Atlanta.

THE REEK AND THE RAMBLING BLADE

e'b. No. 872. Mrs. Emma Dusenberry, Mena, Ark., 1936. By courtesy of Lawrence Powell and Sidney Robertson. See Co, p. 215; Be, p. 136.

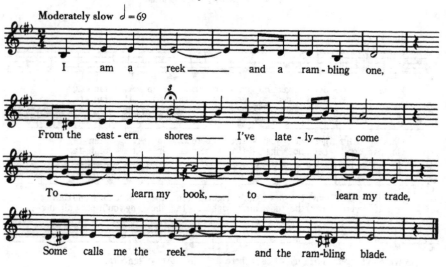

I am a reek and a ram-bling one,
From the east-ern shores I've late-ly come
To learn my book, to learn my trade,
Some calls me the reek and the ram-bling blade.

1 I am a reek and a rambling one,
From the eastern shores I've lately come
To learn my book, to learn my trade,
Some calls me the reek and the rambling blade.

[314]

2 I come here spending money free,
　A-spending money at balls and plays,
　At last my money grew very low
　And then to roving I did go.

3 I married me a handsome wife,
　A girl I loved dear as my life;
　To keep her dressed so neat and gay,
　It caused me to rob on this highway.

4 I robbed old Nelson, I do declare,
　I robbed him on St. James' Square,
　I robbed him of five thousand pounds,
　Dividing with the comrades round.

5 But now I am condemned to die,
　A-many a lady for me cry;
　Pretty Molly weeps, tears down her hair,
　A lady alone left in despair.

6 My father weeps, he maketh moan,
　My mother cries her darling son,
　But all the weeping won't help me
　Or save me from the gallows tree.

7 Now I am dead, laid in my grave,
　The final joy creeps over my head.
　All around my grave play tunes of joy—
　Away goes a reek and the rambling boy.

WHEN FIRST TO THIS COUNTRY A STRANGER I CAME

d♭. No. 65 Acc. on guitar and sung by Foy Gant and Mrs. Gant, Austin, Texas, 1935.

Moderate ♩ = 88 *increasing to* 100 *at end of recording*

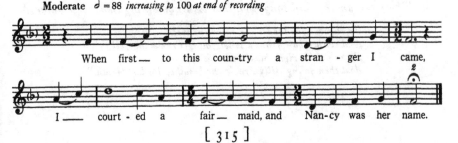

When first— to this coun-try a stran - ger I came,
I — court - ed a fair— maid, and Nan-cy was her name.

[315]

1 When first to this country a stranger I came,
   I courted a fair maid, and Nancy was her name.

2 I courted her for love, her love I didn't obtain;
   Do you think I've any reason or right to complain?

3 I rode to see my Nancy, the pride of my life,
   I courted dearest Nancy, my own heart's true delight.

4 I rode to see my Nancy, I rode both day and night,
   Till I saw a fine gray horse, both plump-looking and white.

5 The sheriff's men, they followed and overtaken me,
   They carted me away to the penitentiary.

6 They opened the door and then they shoved me in,
   They shaved my head and cleared off my chin.

7 They beat me and they banged me, they fed me on dry beans,
   Till I wished to my own soul I'd never been a thief.

8 With my hands in my pockets, my cap put on so bold,
   With my coat of many colors, like Jacob's of old.

*   *   *

"*Jesse James was shot while he was wiping the dust off the picture of his faithful horse. It was the first time he had ever taken his pistols off in his life, and when Ford shot him he fell with his hand on his gun. I had his life in a book once but a couple of summers ago I lent it to a moonshiner from the South—a hell of a nice feller. Well, he had to fly, and he never has returned it. There was another old song, too, that went something like 'Jesse James,'*

"He climbed the ladder, he faced the wall,
   And with a ball from a senet young Frazier he fell,
   He raised his right hand upon his left breast
   And then young Billy Frazier he breathed his last breath."

BRENNAN ON THE MOOR
(An Irish Ballad)

G. No. 1636. Acc. on guitar and sung by Blaine Stubblefield, Washington, D.C. (version from Oregon), 1938.
See Sh, 2:170; Ma, p. 309.

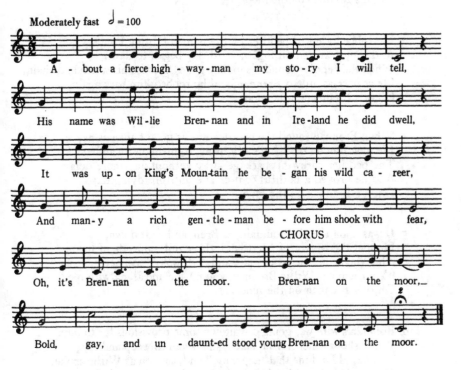

1 About a fierce highwayman my story I will tell,
  His name was Willie Brennan and in Ireland he did dwell,
  It was upon King's Mountain he began his wild career,
  And many a rich gentleman before him shook with fear,
  Oh, it's Brennan on the moor.

Chorus:
      Brennan on the moor,
      Bold, gay, and undaunted, stood young Brennan on the moor.

[317]

2 A brace of loaded pistols he carried night and day,
But he never robbed a poor man all on the King's Highway;
He robbed from the rich like Dick Turpin and Sam Bass,
And he always divided with the widows in distress,
Oh, it's Brennan on the moor.

3 He robbed a noted peddler by the name of Juley Ponds,
And they traveled on together till day began to dawn,
When the peddler found his money gone, likewise his watch and chain,
He at once assaulted Brennan, and he robbed him back again,
Oh, it's Brennan on the moor.

4 When Brennan found the peddler was as good a man as he,
He took him on the King's Highway, companion for to be;
The peddler threw his package away without any more delay,
And he proved a faithful com-er-ade until his dying day,
Oh, it's Brennan on the moor.

5 It was upon King's Mountain, as Brennan he sat down,
He met the Mayor of Moorland, three miles outside of town,
The Mayor he knew Brennan, and, "I think," says he,
"Your name is Willie Brennan, you must come along with me,"
Oh, it's Brennan on the moor.

6 Brennan's wife was going downtown some provisions for to buy,
When she saw her Willie taken, she began to weep and cry;
Said he, "Hand me that tenpenny," and, as soon as Willie spoke,
She handed him a blunderbuss from underneath her cloak,
Oh, it's Brennan on the moor.

7 Now Brennan got his blunderbuss, my story I'll unfold,
He caused the Mayor to tremble and deliver up his gold;
Five thousand pounds were offered for his apprehension there,
But Brennan and the peddler to the mountains did repair,
Oh, it's Brennan on the moor.

8 Now Brennan he is an outlaw all on some mountain high,
 With infantry and cavalry to take him they did try;
 He laughed at them and scorned them until, it was said,
 By a false-hearted woman he was cruelly betrayed,
 Oh, it's Brennan on the moor.

9 In the county of Tipperary in a place called High Moor,
 Where Brennan and his comrades, it's they had suffered sore;
 They lay upon the green grass that grew upon the field,
 And nine wounds they did receive before they would yield,
 Oh, it's Brennan on the moor.

10 Now, Brennan, he is taken, in strong irons he is bound,
 Straightaway they marched him, high walls him did surround;
 When the jury found him guilty the Judge made this reply,
 "For robbing on the King's Highway you are both condemned to die,"
 Oh, it's Brennan on the moor.

11 "Farewell, my dear wife, and likewise my children three,
 And my poor old father who may shed tears for me,
 And my poor old mother who will wring her hands and cry,
 Saying, 'I wish, Willie Brennan, in the cradle you had died.' "
 Oh, it's Brennan on the moor.

 Chorus:
  Brennan on the moor,
  Bold, gay, and undaunted, stood young Brennan on the moor.

THE WILD COLONIAL BOY
(A ballad from Australia)

c. No. 2359. John Norman, Munising, Mich., 1938.
See Ma, p. 317; Ga.2, p. 337.

"No, sir, I do not know where I found this song. I heard it years and years ago, way back workin' around the [lumber] camps somewhere, and then a brother of mine used to sing it, and I picked it up from him. I didn't know any Australians to work in the woods myself, just a few women in town, that's all."

Moderate ♩•=80

Stanza 1 only

There was a wild co - lo nial boy, Jack Dol - lin was his name, —

He was borned in Dub - l - in Cit-y, not so far from Cas - tle - magne

He was his fa - ther's on - ly son, — his — mo-ther's pride and joy, —

So — dear-ly did — those pa-rents love — their wild co - lo - nial boy. —

Stanza 2 and remaining stanzas

At the ear - ly age — of six-teen years — he start-ed his wild ca - reer, —

His courage being un - de - want-ed, — no — dan-ger did — he fear. —

[320]

Outlaws

He robbed the rich to help the poor,—— he shot down Mack - le - roy,——

Who trem-bl-ing gave his gold up to this wild co - lo-nial boy.——

1 There was a wild colonial boy, Jack Dollin was his name,
   He was borned in Dublin City, not so far from Castlemagne,
   He was his father's only son, his mother's pride and joy,
   So dearly did those parents love their wild colonial boy.

2 At the early age of sixteen years he started his wild career,
   His courage being undewanted,* no danger did he fear.
   He robbed the rich to help the poor, he shot down Mackleroy,
   Who trembling gave his gold up to this wild colonial boy.

3 At the early age of eighteen years he left his happy home
   And to Australia's happy land he were inclined to roam;
   He robbed the wealthy squires, their farms he did destroy,
   A terrier to Australia was this wild colonial boy.

4 One day across the prairie as Jack he rode along
   A-listening to the mocking birds as they sang their e-ven-ing song,
   He spied three mounted policemen, Kelly, Davis and Fitzroy,
   They were called out to capture him, the wild colonial boy.

5 "Surrender now, Jack Dollin, you see there's three to one,
   We arrest you in the Queen's name, for you're a plundering son."
   He drew a pistol from his side, made to them this reply,
   "I'll fight but never surrender," said this wild colonial boy.

6 He fired a shot at Kelly which fetched him to the ground,
   While with a shot from Davis' pistol he received a fatal wound,
   When a bullet pierced his brave young heart from the pistol of Fitzroy,
   And that's the way they captured him, this wild colonial boy.

* "Undaunted."

THE VANCE SONG

g. No. 1592. Uncle Branch Higgins, 85 years old, Salyersville, Ky., 1937. Note from Cox, p. 207. See Co, p. 189.

"Some hundred years ago, Abner Vance, a Baptist preacher, was hanged at Abingdon, Virginia, for the killing of Lewis Horton, who had abused Vance's family in his absence. Horton tried to escape, jumped on his horse, and attempted to swim across a river near Vance's house. Vance got his gun and shot him while he was fording the river. After conviction, Vance lay in prison for some time, during which he made a ballad about himself. From the prison window he looked out and saw them erect the scaffold and make the coffin upon which he stood on the day of his execution and preached his own funeral sermon. His son-in-law, Frank Browning, was present, and Vance asked him to turn his back when the trap should fall. A reprieve had been granted the doomed man, but the men who had him in charge hanged him a few minutes before it arrived."

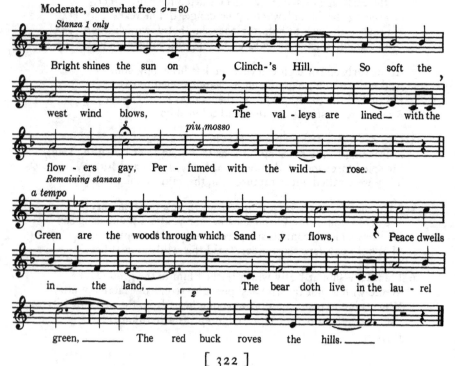

Bright shines the sun on Clinch-'s Hill,___ So soft the west wind blows, The val-leys are lined__ with the flow-ers gay, Per-fumed with the wild__ rose.

Green are the woods through which Sand-y flows, Peace dwells in__ the land,___ The bear doth live in the lau-rel green,___ The red buck roves the hills.___

1 Bright shines the sun on Clinch's Hill,
   So soft the west wind blows,
   The valleys are lined with the flowers gay,
   Perfumed with the wild rose.

2 Green are the woods through which Sandy flows,
   Peace dwells in the land,
   The bear doth * live in the laurel green,
   The red buck roves the hills.

3 But Vance no more on Sandy behold,
   Nor drink its crystal waves,
   The partial judge announced his doom,
   The hunters found his grave.

4 There's Daniel, Bill, and Lewis,
   A lie against me swore,
   In order to take my life away
   That I may be no more.

5 But I and them shall meet again
   When Immanuel's trumpet shall blow,
   Perhaps I'll be wrapped in Abraham's bosom
   When they'll roll in the gulf below.

6 My body it will be laid in the tomb,
   My flesh it will decay,
   But the blood that was shed on Calvary
   Has washed my sins away.

7 Farewell, farewell, my old sweetheart,
   Your face I'll see no more,
   I'll meet you in the world above
   Where parting is no more.

* Pronounced like "both."

THE ROWAN COUNTY CREW

d'ᵇ. No. 932. Mr. and Mrs. George L. White, Grand Saline, Texas, 1937. See Cox, p. 203; Tho.2, p. 5; Co, p. 185. Note from Cox, p. 203.

"A man named Bowling was one of the men who went after Martin, whose wife happened to be visiting him at the time. They brought them back together, but removed her before the killing occurred. Bowling just stepped up to Martin and shot him several times.

"Martin lived a mile east of Morehead, where, some years later, a big lumber company located. Martin had two sons, lads at the time of his murder, and one of them went West. Bowling left the country, too, but after a number of years he came back. He got a job with the lumber company as an inspector of timber, and one day, while he and some others were looking at Martin's grave, which they could see from the camp, Bowling said to them, 'I shot that ———— and I wish he were alive so that I could shoot him again.'

"Martin's younger son overheard the remark, went home, and tried to get his father's pistol; but his mother would not let him have it. Then he sent a telegram to his brother out West, who came home, waited in the wood, shot Bowling, and then went back. The body was rotten before it was found. No one ever knew who shot Bowling, but really everybody knew."

—C. H. Ellis.

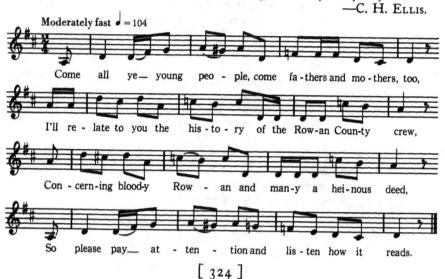

Moderately fast ♩ = 104

Come all ye— young peo - ple, come fa - thers and mo - thers, too,
I'll re - late to you the his - to - ry of the Row-an Coun-ty crew,
Con - cern-ing blood-y Row - an and man-y a hei - nous deed,
So please pay— at - ten - tion and lis - ten how it reads.

1 Come all ye young people, come fathers and mothers, too,
I'll relate to you the history of the Rowan County crew,
Concerning bloody Rowan and many a heinous deed,
So please pay attention and listen how it reads.

2 'Twas in the month of August, 'twas on election day,
Judge Martin shot and wounded, they say by Johnny Clay;
But Martin wouldn't believe it and would not think it so,
He thought it was Clyde Parker that shot the fatal blow.

3 Now Martin had recovered, some months had come and passed,
'Twas in the town of Morehead these fellows met at last,
Parker and a friend or two along the streets did walk;
He seemed to be uneasy with no one for to talk.

4 He walked into Judge Lynn's saloon, he stepped up to the bar,
He little knew that moment he'd met his fatal hour.
He seemed to see death's angels when Martin entered the door;
Some words were passed between them concerning a round before.

5 The people became affrighted and rushed out of the room;
A ball from Martin's pistol put Tolliver in the tomb.
His friends were gathered around him, his wife to weep and wail;
Martin was soon arrested and then confined to jail.

6 Some people thought of lynching him, although the plan would fail;
They put the handcuffs on him until they'd get to jail.
His mind was heavy-laden, he seemed to be in distress;
They put the shackles on him, put him on the night express.

7 Along the road she rumbled all at her usual speed.
There were but two in number to commit this horrible deed;
One were young and handsome and just starting to roam,
He placed the fireman near and bid him not to move.

8 John Martin was in the smoking car accompanied by his wife;
They did not wish her present when they took her husband's life.
They walked up to John Martin with pistols in their hands;
In death he soon was sinking, he died in iron bands.

9 His wife had gone to another car, she heard the horrible sound;
  She cried aloud, "They've killed him! I heard the pistol fire!"
  The death of these two men had caused trouble in our land,
  Caused men to leave their families and take the parting hand.

10 They shot and killed the deputy sheriff, Bumgartner was his name,
  They shot him from the bushes with cool deliberate aim.
  The death of him was horrible, 'twill never be forgot;
  His body was torn and bleeding with forty-four buckshot.

11 I composed this as a warning, so now beware, young men,
  Your pistols will bring you trouble, on this you may depend,
  For in the bottom of a whisky glass a lurking demon dwells,
  'Twill burn the breath of those who drink and send their souls to hell.

HARVEY LOGAN

d. No. 1548. Jimmie Morris, Hazard, Ky., 1937.

"Billy the Kid was to have had his neck stretched today. But since he has taken French leave from the Lincoln County jail, the matter has been indefinitely postponed."

—Las Cruces, New Mexico, *Gazette*, May 13, 1881.

On one Sat-ur-day eve-nin', Just a - round the hour of two,

Har - vey Lo - gan and his part-ner Was play-in' a game of pool,

O my babe, my hon - ey babe.

[326]

1 On one Saturday evenin',
Just around the hour of two,
Harvey Logan and his partner
Was playin' a game of pool,
O my babe, my honey babe.

2 They was playin' for the money,
And the money wouldn't go right,
And that's when old Harvey Logan
Got into a fight,
O my babe, my honey babe.

3 The police heard the racket
And the billets they did break;
Harvey Logan gave 'em a contest
With a smokin' .38,
O my babe, my honey babe.

4 They took him down to Knoxville
And they locked him in the jail;
Because he was a stranger
No one would go his bail,
O my babe, my honey babe.

5 Put the guards before him,
And marched him down the stairs;
Said, "All I want in this wide world
Is the jailer's big fine mare,"
O my babe, my honey babe.

6 "Harvey, now, Harvey,
You know you're doin' me wrong."
Says, "Hush up your cryin', boy,
An' put that saddle on,"
O my babe, my honey babe.

7 He rode across the bridge,
   An' he rode down through the gate;
   He said, "I'd better be makin' time,
   The night is growin' late,"
   O my babe, my honey babe.

8 He rode across the bridge,
   And he looked up at the sky;
   He said, "I'd better be makin' time,
   The night is drawin' nigh,"
   O my babe, my honey babe.

9 He rode down the lane,
   And he rode right through the gate,
   He said, "Goodbye, old Tennessee,
   I'm headin' for another state,"
   O my babe, my honey babe.

DUPREE

d. No. 713. Tune from Walter Roberts, Raiford, Fla.,
1936. Text from Langston Hughes, who heard it in Cleveland in 1936. See Od.2, pp. 56 ff. and p. 123.

1 Betty told Dupree, "Daddy, I want a diamond ring,"
O my Lawd,
Betty told Dupree, "Daddy, I want a diamond ring,"
O my Lawd,
Dupree told Betty, "You can have most anything."

2 He said, "Lay down, little bitty Betty, see what tomorrow bring,
Lord, it may bring sunshine and it may bring a diamond ring."

3 Dupree was a bandit, he was so brave and bold,
He stoled a diamond ring, for some of Betty's jelly roll.

4 So Dupree went to town with a .45 in his hand;
He went after jewelry, but he got the jewelry man.

5 He said, "Look here, Mr. Jewelry Man, won't you show me a diamond,
please,
Because my little bitty Betty want to give her poor heart ease."

6 Dupree hired a taxi, went to Memphis, Tennessee,
Dupree axed the taxi driver, "Wonder will they hang poor me?"

7 Then he went to Chicago, and he was no scary man;
He had a forty-five in his bosom and a Colt kickin' in his hand.

8 Then he shot one big cop, Lawd, and wounded several more.
One fell to his knees cryin', "Please don't shoot me no more."

9 Then he went to the post office to get his evening mail,
But they caught poor Dupree, Lordy, and put him in Atlanta jail.

10 Dupree said to the judge, Lawd, "I ain't been here before."
Judge said, "I'm gonna break your neck, Dupree, so you can't come here
no more."

11 Dupree tol' the lawyer, "Clear me if you can,
For I have money to back me, sure as I'm a man!"

12 The lawyer tol' Dupree, "You are a very brave man,
   But I think that you will go to jail and hang."

13 Dupree's mother said to Betty, "Looky here what you done done—
   Cause my boy to rob and steal and now he's gonna be hung."

14 So Betty weeped and she moaned till she broke out with sweat,
   Said, she moaned and she weeped till her clothes got soppin'-wet.

15 Betty brought him coffee, I swear she brought him tea,
   She brought him all he needed but that big ol' jailhouse key.

16 It was early one mornin' just about the break o' day,
   They had him testifyin', and this is what I heard him say.

17 Dupree tol' the judge, "I'm not so brave and bol',
   But all I wanted was Betty's jelly roll."

18 The judge reared back in his great old cheer,
   Well, the judge told Dupree, "There ain't no mercy here."

19 "Give pappy my clothes, oh, give poor Betty my shoes,
   And if anybody asks you, tell 'em I died with the heartbreakin' blues."

20 So they led him to the scaffold with a black cap over his face.
   Some lonesome graveyard's poor Dupree's restin' place.

21 The choir followed behind him singin' "Nearer My Gawd to Thee."
   Poor Betty she was cryin', "Have mercy on Dupree."

22 Betty said to the hearst driver, "Buddy, drive yo' dead wagon slow,
   You got my man, and he can't come back no mo'."

23 "Sail on, sail on, sail on, Dupree, sail on.
   Don't mind you sailin', but you'll be gone so dog-gone long."

BUGGER BURNS

No record. John T. Vance, Washington, D. C., 1939.

This companion piece for "Brady and Duncan" was furnished us, words, music and note, by John Vance, Chief of the Law Division of the Library of Congress, who has been known to forget his dress suit when he caught a train, but never his guitar. Mr. Vance says:

"*I first heard this song along about 1894 in an alley behind my house on South Upper Street in Lexington, Kentucky. There was a little barrel-house in there where the Negroes congregated on Saturdays, and one of their favorite songs was this 'Bugger Burns' thing. They used to pick it out on the banjo, long before 'Frankie and Johnny' or the blues or any of these cocaine songs ever were heard in that part of the country.*

"*Years later I tried to sing it and could only recall a few stanzas, so I wrote to Lexington to get more stanzas. Sam Johnson, a Negro barber, sent me four or five I didn't have, with the following note: 'Bugger Burns was a policeman in Louisville who had shot and killed several men. Finally a colored man by the name of Danny Major killed him and made his getaway, and the colored folks made up a song about it. There is no words and music to this song.' *"

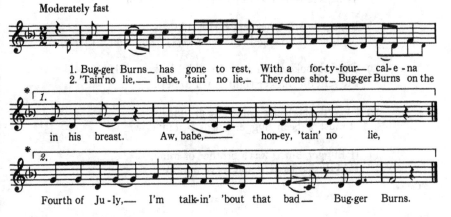

Moderately fast

1. Bug-ger Burns— has gone to rest, With a for-ty-four— cal-e -na
2. 'Tain' no lie,—— babe, 'tain' no lie,— They done shot— Bug-ger Burns on the

* 1.

in his breast.   Aw, babe,——   hon-ey, 'tain' no   lie,

* 2.

Fourth of Ju - ly,—— I'm talk-in' 'bout that bad— Bug-ger Burns.

* The singer of this song states that the two refrains can be alternated at will in succeeding stanzas. Occasionally, stanza 2 is used as a chorus.

1 Bugger Burns has gone to rest,
With a forty-four calena * in his breast.
   Awe, babe, honey, 'tain' no lie.

2 'Tain' no lie, babe, 'tain' no lie,
They done shot Bugger Burns on the Fourth of July,
   I'm talkin' 'bout that bad Bugger Burns.

3 They took ol' Bugger down de dusty road,
His mouth wide open and his eyes was closed.

4 If you don't believe ol' Buggerboo's dead,
Jus' look at that hole in Buggerboo's head.

5 Jus' after Danny'd made his play,
He went to town and made his gitaway.

6 Dan lef' Louisville 'bout half past one,
An' he reached Chattanooga by the settin' of the sun.

7 When Mrs. Burns heard Bugger was dead,
Well, she went right upstairs and dressed in red.

8 Bugger went to heaven, feelin' like a saint,
Said he was an angel, St. Peter says, "You ain't."

9 Gabriel looked him over, he didn' look so well,
He sent ol' Bugger right down to hell.

10 I heard a big noise under the ground,
It must 'a' been Bugger Burns a-goin' down.

11 If Bugger Burns was a brother of mine,
I'd kill that bastard and serve my time.

* Caliber.

DUNCAN AND BRADY

ab. No. 1865. Tune from Camp No. 1, Parchman, Miss., 1933. The air was also whistled "like a mocking bird" by a young negro convict. It seems to be a close relative of "Bad Man Ballad" in *American Ballads and Folksongs*.

Nobody knows where Brady wore his "shinin' star" or in what alley saloon Duncan was bartender. You get the idea, however, that when Duncan cooled Brady's fever down with a forty-four, nobody shed tears at his funeral. In fact, it seems to have been a field day for the ladies, when old King Brady, the bullying peace officer, got "blowed down":

> *When the women in Ioway heard the news,*
> *They wrote it down in old red shoes—*

Miss Scarborough has recorded versions in Texas; Odum and Johnson, fragments in Tennessee; Sandburg's and Gordon's versions mention East St. Louis specifically, and we have others from Texas. A person on a train sang it to me once the way she had heard it in a white caravan show in Kansas. The song comes, probably, from the Mississippi valley. I have made free to combine scattered stanzas so that they tell the story again the way the original may have told it.

Moderately fast ♩= 78

(a) Dun-can, Dun - can was a - tend-in' the bar— When in walked Bra - dy with a shin-in' star, Cried, "Dun-can, Dun - can, you are un-der ar - rest!" And Dun-can shot a hole— in— Bra-dy's breast.

(a) Stanza 5

"Bra-dy, Bra-dy, Bra-dy, don't you know you done wrong?"

1 Duncan, Duncan was a-tendin' the bar
   When in walked Brady with a shinin' star;
   Cried, "Duncan, Duncan, you are under arrest!"
   And Duncan shot a hole in Brady's breast.

2 Brady, Brady cried his level best,
   "Duncan, don't kill me, you've got me best." *
   Duncan says, "Brady, if I got you best,
   You'll hear this forty-four pop in Brady's breast."

3 Brady, Brady had a forty-five,
   Said it would shoot a half a mile.
   Duncan, Duncan had a forty-four,
   And that's what laid poor Brady low.

4 Brady fell down on the barroom floor,
   Cried, "Please, Mr. Duncan, don't you shoot no more!"
   The women cried, "Oh, ain't it a shame,
   He's shot King Brady—gonna shoot him again!"

5 "Brady, Brady, Brady, don't you know you done wrong?
   You broke in my grocery when my game was going on,
   Knockin' down the windows and a-tearin' down doors,
   Now you're layin' dead on my grocery floor."

6 "Mamma, Mamma, Mamma, give me my hat."
   "No, my child, I can't do that,
   Wrap this shawl up around yo' head,
   Go an' see if yo' papa is dead."

7 Mrs. Brady was at home in bed,
   When she got the telegram Brady was dead.
   "Chillun, chillun, put yore hats on yore head,
   An' let's go see if old King Brady is dead."

* You've got the drop on me.

8 "Brady, Brady, why didn't you run,
  When you saw that Duncan had a forty-four gun?
  Oh, Brady, Brady, Brady, you oughter have run;
  You hadn't oughter faced that Gatling gun!"

9 His wife came in in a mighty flirt,
  Wiped up the blood with her underskirt.
  "Hush, my children, and don't you cry,
  We'll all draw a pension when your daddy die."

10 The womens all heard that poor Brady was dead,
  They goes back home and they dresses in red,
  Come a-slippin' an' slidin' up and down the street
  In their big Mother Hubbards and their stockin' feet.

BATSON

c'. No. 95. Acc. on guitar and sung by Stavin' Chain,
Lafayette, La., 1934. Fiddle and guitar accompaniment.

Stavin' Chain said that this long, shuffling, and bloody story—whose
tune and stanza form are evidently derived from "Frankie and Johnny"—
concerns a Lake Charles, Louisiana, murder. Batson, he told us, was a white
day laborer, accused of murdering his employer, Mr. Earle, along with his
whole family. They were found in an open field with only a little red soil
thrown over their bodies. Inquiry fails to confirm Stavin' Chain's story; but
no one who has ever heard him sing this wailing song with his guitar, at
times beating a solemn dirge and then shrieking in hopeless despair can ever
forget it. You've seen and felt a hanging. You notice, too, that the sym-
pathies of the ballad singer rest wholly with the accused, not with his victims.

Moderately fast ♩ = 92 *increasing to 100 at end of recording*

Stanza 1

Bat - son been work - ing for Mis-ter Earle   Six long years to - day,

And ev-er since he been work-ing for Mis-ter Earle,   He nev-er have got a pay.

Cry-in', "Oh, Mam-ma,   I did-n't done— the crime."

Stanza 2

Bat - son asked Mis-ter   Earle,   Can he take a   walk,

Mis-ter Earle   an-swered Bat-son, "You can   go   and come right   back."

Cry-in', "Oh, Mam-ma,   I did-n't done— the crime."

1 Batson been working for Mr. Earle
Six long years today,
And ever since he been working for Mr. Earle,
He never have got a pay.

Cryin', "Oh, Mamma,
I didn't done the crime."

2 Batson asked Mr. Earle,
Can he take a walk,
Mr. Earle answered Batson,
"You can go and come right back."

[336]

3 Batson hitched up Mr. Earle's
   Two bay horse and a wagon,
   Took it back uptown
   To get him a load of feed.

4 When he got back to the house,
   Onhitched those two bay mares,
   And he walked on back uptown,
   See something he really liked.

5 He was walking down Ryan Street
   Looking down in the showcase,
   He thought he had something,
   Something what he really need.

6 'Bout the time he was looking in the showcase
   Here come Mr. Henry Reese,
   Mr. Sheriff, police come a-walking,
   Throwed two forty-fives in his face.

7 Mr. Henry Reese's deputy come a-runnin',
   Slapped him across the face,
   Says, "Stick 'em up, Batson,
   For we constitute you under arrest."

8 Batson asked Mr. Henry Reese,
   "What you arresting me for?"
   Says, "That's all right, Batson,
   You know all about it yourself."

9 'Rested poor little Batson,
   They took him to the county jail,
   And then the people begin to gather
   From miles and miles around.

10 When Batson got in the jailhouse
   Locked up in the place,
   He took a pencil right in his hand
   He marked every day he laid.

[337]

11 Batson told Mr. Sheriff,
   "Don't you know that's wrong?
   You got me charged guilty unfriendly,
   And I know I ain't done the crime."

        Cryin', "Oh, Mamma,
        I never harm no one."

12 Batson begin to cry,
   Tell you what he did do,
   You could hear old Batson crying
   Just like a baby child.

13 The day Batson cried,
   This is the words he said,
   "You're trying me for murder,
   And I know I never harmed no one."

14 Well, the judge found him guilty,
   The clerk he wrote him down,
   The jurymen passed the sentence,
   Poor Batson, he had to be hung.

15 Batson begin to wonder,
   Batson begin to moan,
   Batson told his people,
   "You just have to leave your home.

16 "You may bring me coffee,
   You may bring me tea,
   You got to bring me everything I want
   'Cept that black jailhouse key."

17 "Now you may dress in red,
   You may dress in black,
   You may dress any color you want,
   But you'll never bring Batson back."

[338]

18 Batson's little girl begin to wonder,
   Batson's little girl begin to cry,
   Batson's little child begin to ask him,
   "Daddy, what they going to do with you?"

19 Batson's mother cried,
   Batson's sister cry,
   Batson's sister asked him,
   "When you coming back again?"

20 They brought poor Batson to the gallows,
   They brought him back to the hall,
   Batson asked the judge
   If they going to take his life.

21 Batson asked the judge
   Was they going to take his life;
   Judge asked Mr. Batson,
   "Haven't you done that crime?"

22 Batson begin to moan,
   Batson begin to groan,
   Batson begin to tell those people
   He'd never see home no more.

23 Batson told his brother,
   The day they brought him back at home,
   Says, "If your brother has to lose his life,
   I tell you what I want you to do."

24 Batson asked the sheriff,
   He asked him that two, three times,
   Says, "All I want you to do for me,
   Take care of my two little girls."

25 Batson's mother cried,
   Batson's mother cried,
   Batson's mother had tears a-running
   Clean out of her eyes.

[339]

26 They brought him home to the gallows,
    They brought him back to the jail,
    He started looking around over the people,
    To see 'em for the last, last time.

27 They brought his coffin,
    The day he come to die,
    And he told the sheriff,
    "That's the last thing I'm going to lay down."

28 Then the priest told Batson,
    "Black box takes you down,"
    Says, "Here comes your black box,
    You'll never rise again."

29 They put a black bonnet above his head,
    They put a rope right on his neck,
    They put handcuffs on his hands,
    Balls and chains on his foot.

30 The people begin to cry,
    "Umm-mm-mm,
    Um-mmmm-mmmm,
    Poor Batson he is dead and gone."

31 The clear blood run out of his eyes,
    Nobody they couldn't see his face,
    Had a tongue stuck out out of his mouth
    Six inches long.

32 A rubber-tired buggy,
    Decorated horse,
    You know they brought Batson to the graveyard,
    Says, they brought his family back.

33 His wife walked up to the grave,
    Fell down on her knees,
    Says, "Lord, have mercy,"
    Says, "Batson, are you gone?"

34 Batson's wife began to pray,
    Pray as hard as she could,
    Prayed so much until it looked like
    The Lord done answered her prayer.

35 I thought I heard somebody say
    Awhile before she left,
    Says, "You're goin' leave me,
    But I'll meet you some lonesome day."

36 Batson's little girl cry,
    Batson's little child cry,
    That's all he asked them people,
    "Take keer of them two little girls."

37 Um-mmm,
    Um-mmm-mmm,
    Um-mmm,
    The tears run out of his eyes.

38 Think I heared somebody say,
    "Bye-bye, Batson, bye-bye,
    Bye-bye, Batson, bye-bye"—
    And I believe he's dead and gone.

PO' LAZ'US *

b to bb. No. 246. Tune, Judge Williams, Tucker Farm,
Little Rock, Ark. Composite text from this and a number
of other recorded sources. See Od.2, pp. 50 ff., 90 ff.; Lo.2,
p. 91; also "Take This Hammer," this volume, p. 380.

I am go-ing out West, part-ner, Way out West 'mong the rob-bers;
I am go-ing out West, part-ner, Way out West 'mong the rob-bers,
Be a rob-ber too, Wo Lawd-y, be a rob-ber too.

1 I am going out West, partner,
   Way out West 'mong the robbers;
   I am going out West, partner,
   Way out West 'mong the robbers,
   Be a robber too,
   Wo—Lawdy, be a robber too.

2 Dey was ol' bad Laz'us, partner,
   He was a bully from a baby;
   He got blowed down,
   Wo—Lawdy, he got blowed down.

3 Ol' Laz'us, he walked on, partner,
   Walked on the commissary counter;
   He walked away,
   Wo—Lawdy, he walked away.

4 All de people, people, partner,
   They begin to start to talkin';
   "He done gone home,
   Wo—Lawdy, he done gone home."

* For another tune, see *American Ballads and Folk Songs*. Both versions are sung as work songs,
and their connection with such songs as "Every Mail Day" and "Muley on the Mountain" is
intimate.

5 Lawd, the captain told the sergeant, partner,
"Go out and bring me Laz'us;
Bring him dead or alive,
Wo—Lawdy, bring him dead or alive."

6 Dat ol' sergeant, he rambled, partner,
Rambled dose mountains over;
Couldn't find him dere,
Wo—Lawdy, couldn't find him dere.

7 Says, he spied ol' Laz'us, partner,
Way in between two mountains;
Blowed him down,
Wo—Lawdy, Lawdy, blowed him down.

8 Well, he shot bad Laz'us, partner,
Shot him wid a great big number,
Wid a four-by-five,
Wo—Lawdy, wid a four-by-five.

9 Well, they come a-draggin', partner,
The po' boy back to his shanty,
Right by his heels,
Wo—Lawdy, right by his heels.

10 Lawd, they drug po' Laz'us, partner,
One-half mile to his shanty,
An' dey walked away,
Wo—Lawdy, an' dey walked away.

11 Well-a, Laz'us he spoken, partner,
"Partner, please turn me over
Off my wounded side,
Wo—Lawdy, off my wounded side."

12 Well-a, Laz'us' ol' father, partner,
He come a-cussin' and a-swearin',
"Let the fool go down,
Wo—Lawdy, let the fool go down."

[343]

13 Well-a, Laz'us' ol' father, partner,
   Said, "No better for the rascal,
   He's mean and bad,
   Wo—Lawdy, he's mean and bad."

14 Says-a, Laz'us' ol' mother, partner,
   She never stopped her sewing;
   She began to cry,
   Wo—Lawdy, she began to cry.

15 She was cryin' 'bout dat trouble, partner,
   Trouble she'd had with Laz'us,
   Four years ago,
   Wo—Lawdy, four years ago.

16 Says-a, Laz'us told his sister, partner,
   Tol' his li'l' baby sister,
   "Lawd, I won't live,
   Wo—Lawdy, Lawdy, I won't live."

17 Well, ol' Laz'us he cried out, partner,
   "One more cool drink of water,
   Before I die,
   Wo—Lawdy Lawd, before I die."

18 Says-a, "Go an' tell my, partner,
   Tell my Grandma Julie,
   Oh, I'm goin' die,
   Wo—Lawdy, Lawd, I'm goin' to die.

19 "If I live to ever, partner,
   Ever to make it over,
   Be bad no mo',
   Wo—Lawdy, be bad no mo'."

20 Lawd, the sergeant he spoken, partner,
   Sergeant he spoken to the captain,
   "Gonna lose my job,
   Wo—Lawdy, gonna lose my job.

21 "Well, the reason I shot that, partner,
   Shot that po' boy Laz'us,
   He was too bad,
   Wo—Lawdy, he was too bad."

22 Says, "Cap'n, Cap'n, partner,
   Don't you see I'm dyin'
   An' won't come 'roun',
   Wo—Lawdy, an' won't come 'roun'?"

23 "Well-a, I ain't mad about, partner,
   'Bout you blowin' me down, sir;
   Lawd, that's yo' job,
   Wo—Lawdy, Lawdy, that's yo' job."

24 Lawdy, we gonna bury, partner,
   Po' boy Laz'us Sunday mornin'.
   'Bout nine o'clock,
   Wo—Lawdy, 'bout nine o'clock.

25 Well-a, Laz'us' father, partner,
   He sure was hardhearted;
   Wouldn't say a word,
   Wo—Lawdy, wouldn't say a word.

26 Well-a, Laz'us' brother, partner,
   He wouldn't go to th' buryin',
   Said, "I'm glad he's dead,
   Wo—Lawdy, Lawd, I'm glad he's dead."

27 Now, ol' Laz'us' sister, partner,
   She couldn't go to the buryin';
   Didn't have no shoes,
   Wo—Lawdy, didn't have no shoes.

   (*A pause—then the gang sings:*)

28 Captain, did you hear about, partner,
   All your men gonna leave you?
   Well, next pay day,
   Wo—Lawdy, well, next pay day.

V

HOLLERS AND BLUES

HOLLERS AND BLUES

"Hollering songs" represent a distinct type of Negro folk singing. Usually they consist of a two-line stanza in which the singer repeats the first verse two or three times and the last verse once—the whole introduced and followed by long drawn-out moaning or "yodling" or shouts in the tempo and mood of the tune he has been singing. They are sung with an open throat—shouted, howled, growled, or moaned in such fashion that they will fill a stretch of country and satisfy the wild and lonely and brooding spirit of the worker. The holler is a musical platform from which the singer can freely state his individual woes, satirize his enemies, and talk about his woman.

The country Negro worker lightens the tedium of his labor by these musical cries: a plowman, turning sandy furrows in the long cotton rows of a lonely swamp field; the mule skinner, driving his team, with trace chains clanking, up and down in the dust of a levee bank; a roustabout, shouting the beat for the feet of his companions as, like an endless chain, they stagger under a load up the gangplank or, in double-time, hurry down on the other side—"them niggers keep hollerin' all the time." The melodies are so free that it is impossible to give an adequate picture of them even by transcribing entire songs in musical notation. In mood they run the gamut of the worker's emotional life: his loves and sorrows, his hope and despair, his weariness, his resentment.

> "*Oo—oo—oo—oo—uh!*
> *If I feels tomorrow like I feels today*
> *Take a long freight train wid a red caboose to carry my blues away.*"

"That's Enoch hollerin'," said Mrs. Tartt one night, as we sat on her porch near Livingston, Alabama.

Although the singer was some distance away, the cry seemed to fill completely the void of dark silence about us. The pitch started high but grew to a climax unbelievably high for a deep voice like his, and then faded gradually into a mournful wail, ending in a jumble of words. The call was thrice repeated.

[348]

"Hopeless, remote, stark loneliness," I managed to say, for a feeling near to fear had tightened my heart.

"Enoch is like a shy bird of the night," Mrs. Tartt said. "Many people in Livingston have never seen him except perhaps after night when he flits by them in the darkness. Every night he comes out on the wooded end of the long bridge leading into Livingston and cries his woes to heaven. He lives alone in a cabin back in the woods. It will be a hard job to get him to sing into your microphone, but I'll try; Enoch is a little off, you know."

Two or three nights afterwards Enoch's cry rang out startlingly near. I ran out and found him standing like a piece of darkness itself near the trunk of a great oak tree. When I asked him to come nearer the microphone, he answered me with a burst of nervous, explosive laughter. I was a long time getting him near the machine where I could secure a recording. Between the hollers I could only catch the words,

"Just a few more weeks and I won't be here long."

He laughed again and seemed mightily pleased at the sound of his own voice when I played back the record. Neither then nor afterwards did he utter a spoken word.

The next December I sent Enoch a Christmas card in care of Mrs. Tartt. Probably he had never before received a letter. She delivered the card to Enoch on Christmas Day along with a big Christmas dinner. Enoch appeared the following day. No card but another dinner. For two weeks Enoch came back at dinnertime inquiring for another card.

"He thought your Christmas card was a meal ticket," commented Mrs. Tartt.   —Adventures of a Ballad Hunter.

ROUSTABOUT HOLLER

c. No. 2658. Henry Truvillion, Newton, Texas, 1939.

Chanting:

Now boys, we're on the steamer Natchez,
And we got to load this here cotton and cottonseed here
Before anybody can shut his eyes like he's asleep;
So we might just as well tear around
Get us a gobo apiece.
Let's go on and load this stuff, what do you say?
We're up here and got it to do.
Where you at there, you old nub-fingered nappy?
Let's hear from you, blow your horn, let's load some cotton.

Moderate, free ♩ = 96

Oh, _____ Po' roust-a-bout

don't have no home, _____ Makes his liv-in' on his shoul-der bone. _____

* This is the tune of stanza 1. Most of the remaining stanzas can be fitted to it with slight altera-tions; several must be sung as free variants on the basic pattern.

1 Oh-h-h-h,
   Po' roustabout don't have no home,
   Makes his livin' on his shoulder bone.

2 Oh-h-h-h,
   Wake up, sleepy, and tell your dream,
   I want to make you acquainted with the two blue seams.*

3 Oh-h-h-h,
   Midnight was my cry, 'fo' day was my creep,
   I got a pretty little girl in big New Orleans, lives on Perdida Street.

* Sacks of cottonseed had two blue stripes running from bottom to top.

4 Oh-h-h-h,
    If yo' shoulder bone gets so' this time,
    Git you a little sody an' turpentine.

5 Oh-h-h-h,
    I left my home in '84,
    And I ain't never been dere no more.

6 Oh-h-h-h,
    I know my sweetie goin' open the do',
    As soon as she hear the *Natchez* blow.

7 Oh-h-h-h,
    The *Natchez* up the bayou an' she done broke down,
    She got her head toward Memphis, but she's New-Orleans-boun'.

8 Oh-h-h-h,
    Did you hear Daniel in the lion den?
    Lord, have mercy, hear me now.

9 Oh-h-h-h,
    Po' roustabout don't have no home,
    Here today and tomorrow gone.

10 Oh-h-h-h,
    'Fo' day was my cry, midnight was my creep,
    I got a sweet little gal in big New Orleans, I does all I can to please.

11 Oh-h-h-h,
    Catch this here sack, boys, and leave it go,
    Take her down the river further, 'cause they ain't no mo'.

TROUBLE, TROUBLE

f♯. No. 948. James Hale, Atmore, Ala., 1937. See Od.2, p. 40.

1. Trouble, trouble, I had them all my day, Trouble, trouble, trouble, had them all my day, Well, it seem like trouble go'n' let me to my grave. *Gid-dap o-ver dere Spot; come here, Hat-tie! Whoa dere! Gid-dap dere! Pow!*

2. Well, I'm gwine back South, Mamma, where de weather suit my clo(thes), Well, I'm go'n' back South, babe, where de weather suit my clo(thes), Well, I'm gonna lay out on dat green grass an' look up at de sky. *Gee o-ver dere, Pok-ey. Come 'ere now, Spot. Jes' look at you!*

3. Well,— so man-y a— day,— Mam-ma,— laid in

my —— cell an' moan, —— So man-y day,—Lawd, laid in my

cell an'—— moan,—Well,I'm think-in'a-bout my— ba-by, —— Lawd, an'—

yo'—— hap-py home. *What I told you o - ver dere, ol' mule?*

Git up o - ver dere, An' give me a pull now, Spot-light, you an' ol' Hat-tie!

4. Well, —— Mam - ma, Mam-ma, —— hear an' lis-ten to my— sec-ond

mind, —— Hey, —— hey,Mam - ma, lis-ten to my sec-ond —— mind,—Well, I

don't b'lieve I'd'a'been here,—wring-in' my— hand — an' cry'n. *Whoa dere!*

1 Trouble, trouble, I had them all my day,
  Trouble, trouble, trouble, had them all my day,
  Well, it seem like trouble go'n' let me to my grave.

  Giddap over dere, Spot; come here, Hattie!
  Whoa dere! Giddap dere! Pow! *

2 Well, I'm gwine back South, Mamma, where de weather suit my clothes,
  Well, I'm go'n back South, babe, where de weather suit my clothes,
  Well, I'm gonna lay out on dat green grass—an' look up at de sky.

  Gee over dere, Pokey. Come 'ere now, Spot,
  Jes' look at you!

3 Well, so many a day, Mamma, laid in my cell an' moan,
  Well, so many a day, Lawd, laid in my cell an' moan,
  Well, I'm thinkin' about my baby, Lawd, an' yo' happy home.

  What I told you over dere, ol' mule? Git up over dere,
  An' give me a pull now, Spotlight, you an' ol' Hattie!

4 Well, Mamma, Mamma, here an' listen to my second mind,
  Hey, hey, Mamma, listen to my second mind,
  Well, I don't b'lieve I'd 'a' been here, wringin' my hand an' cryin'.

  Whoa dere!

* Imitation of the sound of a popping whip lash.

MAMMA, MAMMA

c′. No. 210. A. Haggerty (Track Horse), Huntsville,
Texas, 1934. See "Go Down, Ol' Hannah."

1 Well, it's Mamma, Mamma, O Lawd, you don't know;
And it's Mamma, Mamma, Mamma, you don't know.

2 Well, it's trouble I've been havin', Mamma, ain't gonna have no mo',
Mamma, this trouble I've been havin', ain't gonna have no mo'!

3 Little boy, if you see my Mamma, will you please tell her for me,
Lawd, to see that governor, tell him to set me free?

4 Mamma, some goes this summer, O Lawd, some goes this fall;
Mamma, but it's so many bullies don't go at all.

GO DOWN, OL' HANNAH

b♭. No. 199. Ernest Williams and a group, Sugar Land, Texas, 1933. See Lo.2, p. 58.

Little boy, little boy, who fooled you here?
Little boy, little boy, who fooled you here?
Did they tell you it was a heaven?
You found a burning hell.

Little boy, you oughta knowed you couldn't hold 'em,
Little boy, you oughta stayed at home,
Picked up chips for yo' mammy
And blowed yo' daddy's ho'n.

The slow-drag work songs that grew up in what the old prisoners call the "red heifer" days in the Texas penitentiary stand, along with the Negro spirituals, as the greatest American folk songs. As the hoes and cane knives flash in the sun, the plaintive melodies speak of tired bodies, aching limbs, stifling heat. The "red heifer" was somebody's jocular nickname for the cowhide lash used on the leased convicts as they rolled in the burning hell of the Brazos bottom cane fields. They were leased out by the state to individual plantation owners, and these men, according to the prisoners, weren't particular about whom they hit or who fell out with sunstroke. A "Mister Cunningham" * gets honorable mention by the convicts, and in 1904, the songs say, you ought to have been down on his place; they were finding a dead man at every turnrow. Ol' Hannah was beaming, and the bullies were screaming. It was an act of heroism, as the stanzas quoted above make tenderly clear, to be able to "hold 'em"—to survive.

"Ol' Hannah was shinin' way up there, an' we was tryin' to pull her down."

* At that time under Texas law (long since repealed), convicts were rented out as laborers to owners of large plantations.

[356]

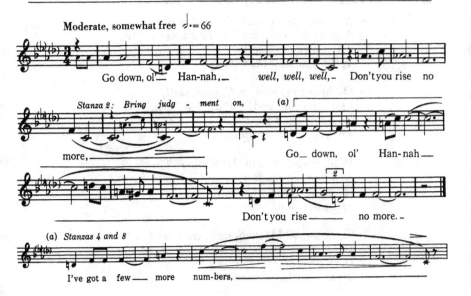

Moderate, somewhat free ♩. = 66

Go down, ol' Han-nah,— well, well, well, - Don't you rise no more,

Stanza 2: Bring judg - ment on, (a)

Go— down, ol' Han-nah—

Don't you rise——— no more. -

(a) Stanzas 4 and 8

I've got a few— more num-bers, —

1 Go down, ol' Hannah, *well, well, well,*
  Don't you rise no more, *don't you rise no more;*
  Go down, ol' Hannah,
  Don't you rise no more.

2 If you rise in the mornin', *well, well, well,*
  Bring judgment on, *bring judgment on.*
  I ain't tired of livin',
  But I got so long.

3 My mamma called me, *well, well, well,*
  An' I answered, "Ma'am," *and I answered, "Ma'am";*
  "Ain't you tired of rollin'
  For Cunnin'ham?"

4 "I'm tired of rollin', *well, well, well,*
  But I ain't got long, *but I ain't got long,*
  I've got a few more numbers,
  And then I'll be gone."

[357]

5 My papa called me, *well, well, well,*
  And I answered, "Sir," *and I answered "Sir,"*
  "If you tired of rollin',
  What you stay there for?"

6 Ol' long-time man, *well, well, well,*
  Hol' up your head, *hol' up your head;*
  You may get a pardon,
  An' you may drop dead.

7 Well, it's some on the buildin', *well, well, well,*
  And some on the farm, *and some on the farm,*
  It's some in the graveyard
  And some gone home.

8 Go down, ol' Hannah, *well, well, well,*
  Don't you rise no more, *don't you rise no more;*
  If you rise in the mornin',
  Set the world on fire.

MAKE ME A GARMENT

g. No. 682. Roscoe McLean, State Penitentiary, Raiford, Fla., 1936. Contains lines from "Barbara Allen."

Roscoe McLean, who hollered this holler and contributed other lovely folk songs to the Folk Song Archive, for more than a year has been in the tuberculosis ward of the Florida Penitentiary. Recently I talked with Roscoe —he could only whisper as he peered through the woven wire netting, sobbing his despair. He will never sing again.

Slow, somewhat free, on the basis of a steady beat of ♩ = 120

Mam-ma, Mam-ma___ (ng _____), make me_ a ___ gar-ment,_

And_ make it long,_____ white and _ nar-row.

Get a-long, boys, and _ gath-er 'round me,___

Come pay my_ fine,_____ come and get me.___

1 Mamma, Mamma, make me a garment,
   And make it long, white, and narrow.

2 Mamma, Mamma, look on my pillow
   And you will find some money.

3 Get along, boys, and gather 'round me,
   Come pay my fine, come and get me.

4 My true love died the other day
   I believe I'll die tomorrow.

GO DOWN, YOU LITTLE RED RISING SUN

g to a♭. No. 682. Roscoe McLean, State Penitentiary, Raiford, Fla., 1936. See Od.2, p. 82, last stanza; Sh, 2:278.

1 Uh—go down, go down, you little red,
  Redder than rouge rising sun,
  And don't you never—uh—bring day,
  Great Godamighty, no more.

2 To the pine, to the pine, where the sun,
  Great Godamighty, don't shine,
  You got to shiver when the cold,
  Great Godamighty, wind blows.

3 Lord, I wish to my soul that old bald—
  Bald-head Judge was dead,
  And green grass growing round,
  Great Godamighty, his head.

4 Lord, I left my home in nine—
  Nineteen hundred and ten,
  And I ain't never, oh, been back,
  Great Godamighty, again.

5 "Oh, Mamma, Mamma, why'n't you pray,
   Great Godamighty, for yo' child?
   For the grand jury tryin' to have,
   Great Godamighty, him hung."

6 "Oh, son, oh, son, what in the world,
   Great Godamighty, you done,
   For the grand jury tryin' to have,
   Great Godamighty, you hung?"

7 "Mamma, Mamma, you just pray,
   Great Godamighty, for me,
   And I never will do wrong,
   Great Godamighty, no more.

8 "I ain't killed no man and I ain't robbed,
   Great Godamighty, no train,
   And I ain't did no man,
   Great Godamighty, no crime."

PRISON MOAN *

bb. No. 270. Robert Higgins, State Prison, Raleigh, N.C., 1934.

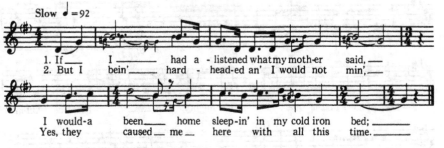

1 If I had a-listened what my mother said,
   I would 'a' been home sleepin' in my cold iron bed;

2 But I bein' hardheaded an' I would not min',
   Yes, they caused me here with all this time.

* A hymnlike tune used as a prison holler.

[361]

3 But if I overcome this trouble I'm in,
   Lawd, I never no mo' will live in sin.

4 When I was a free man I had plenty friends;
   Now I'm in trouble, an' they won' come in.

5 Lawd, in struggle I'll stretch my hands to Thee,
   Lawd, in trouble, no other help I know.

6 But if Thou withdrew Thyself from me;
   I would wonder where then shall I go.

7 Lawd, if I could hear my dear old mother
   When she pray for me once again!

8 Trouble have caused me to weep, an' it's caused me to moan,
   An' it caused me to leave my happy home.

LIGHTS IN THE QUARTERS BURNIN' MIGHTY DIM

f♯. No. 693. Johnny Maxwell, State Penitentiary, Raiford, Fla., 1936.

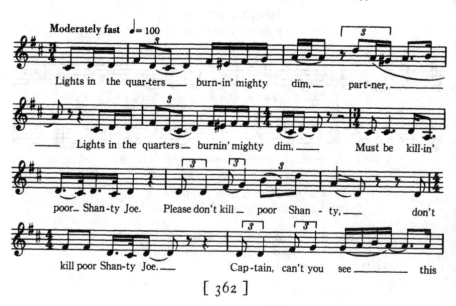

Moderately fast ♩ = 100

Lights in the quar-ters___ burn-in' mighty dim, ___ part-ner, _____

Lights in the quarters __ burnin' mighty dim, ___ Must be kill-in'

poor __ Shan-ty Joe. Please don't kill __ poor Shan - ty, ___ don't

kill poor Shan-ty Joe. __ Cap-tain, can't you see _____ this

[362]

four o' clock ris - in's — 'bout to kill — poor me? — Cap -

tain, — can't you see — this four o'clock trouble 'bout to kill poor me? —

Lights in the quarters burnin' mighty dim, partner,
Lights in the quarters burnin' mighty dim,
Must be killin' poor Shanty Joe.
Please don't kill poor Shanty, don't kill poor Shanty Joe.
Captain, can't you see this four o'clock risin's 'bout to kill poor me?
Captain, can't you see this four o'clock trouble 'bout to kill poor me?

EADIE

g. No. 190. Lightning and Dave Tippen, Darrington
State Farm, Texas, 1934.

Slow, very free ♩ = 112

Go way, — Ea - die, you dir - ty dog, — Wo, —

Ea - die, — go — way; — Go — way, — Ea - die, — you

dir - ty dog, — Wo, Ea - die, — go — way. —

1 Go way, Eadie, you dirty dog,
Wo, Eadie, go way;
Go way, Eadie, you dirty dog,
Wo, Eadie, go way.

[363]

2 Go way, Eadie, quit worryin' me,
  Wo, Eadie, go way.

3 Told you once and I told you twice,
  Wo, Eadie, go way.

4 Next time I tell you goin' take your life,
  Wo, Eadie, go way.

"*Now this here is a blues. You never heard a white man could sing the blues in your life, have you? You know the reason why? They don't have them. Blues was composed up by the Negro people when they was under slavery. They was worried.*

"*When you lie down at night sometime, it ain't too hot and it ain't too cold, but you turning from side to side. What's the matter? Blues got you. When you get up in the morning, the blues is walkin' 'round your bed. You may have a mother and a father and a sister and a brother and maybe a girl friend, and none of them ain't done you nothin'. Anyhow you don't want no talk out of 'em. What's the matter with you? The blues got you.*"

—LEAD BELLY.

"*The blues are made by working people, both Negroes and whites, when they have a lot of problems to solve about their work, when their wages are low and they don't have no way to exist hardly and they don't know which way to turn and what to do, whenever they're low in spirit and actually feeling blue.*

"*I used to hear a bunch of colored boys that belonged to an old colored preacher by the name of Steve Crews that lived right over from us. They was next-door neighbors but they lived just across the track—the mining track, that is. I'd rather hear them sing that 'Lordy, Lordy Blues' than eat.*"

—AUNT MOLLY JACKSON.

I BEEN A BAD, BAD GIRL

d'. No. 692. Ozella Jones, State Penitentiary, Raiford, Fla., 1936.

If the Bessie Smith enthusiasts could hear Ozella Jones or some other clear-voiced Southern Negro girl sing the blues, they might, we feel, soon forget their idol with her brassbound, music-hall throat. The blues, sung

[364]

by an unspoiled singer in the South, sung without the binding restrictions of conventional piano accompaniment or orchestral arrangement, grow up like a wild flowering vine in the woods. Their unpredictable, incalculably tender melody bends and then swings and shivers with the lines like a reed moving in the wind. The blues then show clearly their country origin, their family connection with the "holler."

Moderate, somewhat free ♩.=63

Stanzas 1, 2 and 4

I been a bad,— bad girl,———— would-n' treat no bod — — y right, ———— I been a bad,— bad girl,———— ——— would-n' treat no - bod — — y right, They want to give me thir(ty)-five years, some one want-ed to take my life.—

Stanzas 3 and 5

Now'm so— sor-ry, e - ven the day I ——— was born, — Now'm so— sor-ry, e - ven the day I — was born, I want to say to all you bad— fell-as that— you— are in— the wrong.

* When "Judge" and "I'm" are sung to this measure, the singer makes a slow slide from the *g* to the *b*♭.

1 I been a bad, bad girl, wouldn' treat nobody right,
   I been a bad, bad girl, wouldn' treat nobody right,
   They want to give me thirty-five years, some one wanted to take my life.

2 Judge, please don't kill me, I won't be bad no mo',
   Judge, please don't kill me, I won't be bad no mo',
   I'll listen to ev'ybody, something I never done befo'.

3 Now I'm so sorry, even the day I was born,
   Now I'm so sorry, even the day I was born,
   I want to say to all you bad fellas that you are in the wrong.

4 I'm sittin' here in prison with my black cap on,
   I'm sittin' here in prison with my black cap on,
   Boys, remember this even when I am gone.

5 Now I'm so sorry, even the day I was born,
   Now I'm so sorry, even the day I was born,
   I want to say to all you bad fellas that you are in the wrong.

SUN GONNA SHINE IN MY DOOR SOME DAY

a^b. No. 1331. Acc. on accordion and sung by Jesse
Harris (blind), Livingston, Ala., 1937.

We once asked Jelly Roll Morton, hot composer and pianist, what instruments the boys were playing in country towns in Mississippi and Alabama in 1901 and 1902. "They didn't have nothing," he said, "only a bunch of guys on the street corners and in those little low-life honky-tonks that would sing the blues all day, the same thing over and over and in between times, beat on some old guitar, or blow a harmonica or pull on a windjammer until they could think of the next verse."

Blind Jesse Harris, now dead, was pulling on his old accordion even longer ago in the country around Livingston, Alabama. In those days it might have had two lungs, but when we recorded him it only had one. With that one lung, nevertheless, Jesse could play more blues than most two-handed piano combinations—in between times while he was thinking of the next verse.

[366]

1 Been in dat jailhouse, expectin' a fine,
Looked through the door, no friend could I find.

Chorus:

It's no matter, Lord, I know,
Sun gonna shine in my door some day.

2 Standin' 'round here hungry, ain't got a dime,
Look like my friends ought to come see me some time.

3 Me and my buddy, got thick and thin,
My buddy got away, but I got in.

4 Lordy, Lordy, Lordy, Lord,
Used to be your reg'lar, now I've got to be your dog.

THE RISING SUN BLUES

e. No. 1404. Georgia Turner, Middlesboro, Ky., 1937.
Other stanzas, Bert Morton, Manchester, Ky., No. 1496.

The fact that a few of the hot jazzmen who were in the business before the war have a distant singing acquaintance with this song, indicates that it is fairly old as blues tunes go. None of them, however, has information at his fingertips about the mother who ran a "blue-jean" shop, about the "house they call the Rising Sun," or about the young lady it proved the ruin of. We have heard it sung only by Southern whites. "Rising Sun," as a name for a bawdy house, occurs in a number of unprintable songs of English origin.

Moderately slow ♩.= 54

1. There is a house in New Or-leans, they call the
2. If I had lis-tened what Mam-ma said, I'd'a' been at
5. The on-ly thing a drunk-ard needs is a suit-case
6. Fills his glass-es to the brim, pass-es

1. Ris-ing Sun, It's been the ru-in of
2. home to-day, Being so young and
5. and a trunk, The on-ly time he's
6. them a-round, On-ly pleas-ure he

1. man-y poor girl, and me O God, for one.
2. fool-ish, poor boy, let a ram-bler lead me a-stray.
5. sat is-fied is when he's on a drunk.
6. gets out of life is ho-bo-in' from town to town.

3. Go tell my ba-by sis-ter nev-er do like I have done,
4. My moth-er she's a tai-lor, she sold those new blue jeans,

3. To shun that house in New Or-leans they call the Ris-ing Sun.
4. My sweet-heart, he's a drunkard, Lord, Lord, drinks down in New Or-leans.

Hollers and Blues

7. One foot is on the plat-form and the o-ther one on the train,
8. Going back to New Or-leans,— My race is al-most run,

7. I'm go-ing back to— New— Or-leans, to— wear that ball and chain.
8. Going back to spend the rest of my— life be-neath that Ris-ing Sun.

1 There is a house in New Orleans, they call the Rising Sun,
  It's been the ruin of many poor girl, and me, O God, for one.

2 If I had listened what Mamma said, I'd 'a' been at home today,
  Being so young and foolish, poor boy, let a rambler lead me astray.

3 Go tell my baby sister never do like I have done,
  To shun that house in New Orleans they call the Rising Sun.

4 My mother she's a tailor, she sold those new blue jeans,
  My sweetheart, he's a drunkard, Lord, Lord, drinks down in New
    Orleans.

5 The only thing a drunkard needs is a suitcase and a trunk,
  The only time he's satisfied is when he's on a drunk.

6 Fills his glasses to the brim, passes them around,
  Only pleasure he gets out of life is hoboin' from town to town.

7 One foot is on the platform and the other one on the train,
  I'm going back to New Orleans, to wear that ball and chain.

8 Going back to New Orleans, my race is almost run,
  Going back to spend the rest of my life beneath that Rising Sun.

BIG FAT WOMAN

a^b. No. 255. Negro quartet, Bellewood Farms, Atlanta, Ga., 1936.

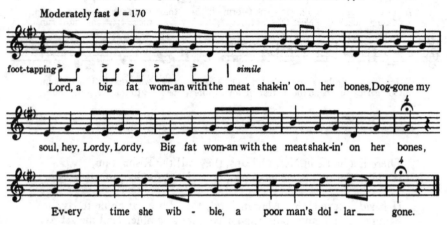

1 Lord, a big fat woman with the meat shakin' on her bones,
Doggone my soul, hey, Lordy, Lordy,
Big fat woman with the meat shakin' on her bones,
Every time she wibble, a poor man's dollar gone.

2 I don't want no sugar sprinkled in my tea,
Doggone my soul, hey, Lordy, Lordy,
Don't want sugar sprinkled in my tea,
Lord, the gal I got is sweet enough for me.

3 I don't want no black woman to fry no meat for me,
Doggone my soul, hey, Lordy, Lordy,
No black woman to fry no meat for me,
'Cause she's so black and evil I'm scared might pizen me.

4 Lord, a brown-skinned woman make a preacher lay his Bible down,
Doggone my soul, hey, Lordy, Lordy,
Brown-skinned woman make a preacher lay his Bible down,
But a jet-black woman make a jack rabbit hug a hound.

5 The blues jumped a rabbit and run him for a solid mile,
Doggone my soul, hey, Lordy, Lordy,

[370]

Blues jumped a rabbit and run him for a solid mile,
When the blues overtook him, he cried like a baby child.

6 When a woman gets the blues, she hang her head and cry,
Doggone my soul, hey, Lordy, Lordy,
Woman get the blues, she hang her head and cry,
When a man gets the blues he catch that train and rides.

I'M A STRANGER HERE

f. No. 541. Acc. on guitar and sung by Mrs. Louise Henson, San Antonio, Texas, 1937.

They say Bix Beiderbecke has been the only white man who could sing the blues. We submit that this is a limited view, for the blues have been for some time common property of Negro and white singers, although the creative source has been with the Negroes until recently. The two following tunes of Mrs. Henson's, a San Antonio "hill-billy" singer, are of Negro derivation; yet despite their texts they show a developing quality quite their own.

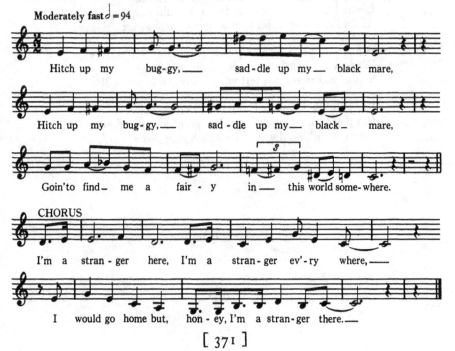

Moderately fast ♩=94

Hitch up my bug-gy,___ sad-dle up my___ black mare,

Hitch up my bug-gy,___ sad-dle up my___ black___ mare,

Goin'to find___ me a fair-y in___ this world some-where.

CHORUS

I'm a stran-ger here, I'm a stran-ger ev'-ry where,___

I would go home but, hon-ey, I'm a stran-ger there.___

[371]

1 Hitch up my buggy, saddle up my black mare,
  Hitch up my buggy, saddle up my black mare,
  Goin' to find me a fairy in this world somewhere.

  Chorus:
      I'm a stranger here, I'm a stranger ev'rywhere,
      I would go home but, honey, I'm a stranger there.

2 I'm worried now, but I won't be worried long,
  I'm worried now, but I won't be worried long,
  It takes a worried man to sing a worried song.

3 Baby caught that Katy, she left me a mule to ride,
  Baby caught that Katy, she left me a mule to ride,
  When the train pulled out that mule laid down and died.

4 Looked down that road as far as I could see,
  Looked down that road as far as I could see,
  And a little bitty hand kept a-wavin' back at me.

5 When you get a woman, man, you better get you two,
  When you get a woman, boy, you better get you two,
  'Cause you never can tell what a woman goin' to do.

6 I'm goin' back home, I'm goin' to settle down,
  I'm goin' back home, Lord, I'm goin' to settle down,
  'Cause I ain't no dog and I won't be dogged around.

I'M WORRIED NOW BUT I WON'T BE WORRIED LONG

f. No. 541. Acc. on guitar and sung by Mrs. Louise Henson, San Antonio, Texas, 1937.

Moderate ♩ = 80

Went to sleep, babe, last night in a snow-white feather bed,—

I woke up this mornin' with the blues all a-round my head,

I'm worried now but I won't be wor-ried long.

1 Went to sleep, babe, last night in a snow-white feather bed,
  I woke up this mornin' with the blues all around my head,
  I'm worried now but I won't be worried long.

2 See the sun rose this mornin', I was sleepin' on the floor,
  I had no one to love me and I had no place to go,
  I'm worried now but I won't be worried long.

3 This world is so crooked until you don't know what to do,
  Each time you try to hold your head up, some one's downing you,
  I'm worried now but I won't be worried long.

4 'Druther be down on a river sitting out on a holler log
  Than to have my sweet baby treat me like a dog,
  I'm worried now but I won't be worried long.

5 Going to Waco next summer, ain't comin' back till fall,
  If I don't get the one I want, ain't comin' back at all,
  I'm worried now but I won't be worried long.

[373]

LINES FROM THE BLUES

Woman Blues

It's so cold and shiny till the birds can't hardly sing,
I wouldn't hate it so much, but she soak my diamond ring.

Then I asked the doctor to give me some strychnine,
To stop that brown-skinned woman from rollin' 'cross my mind.

The doctor told me to lay my head on Jay Gould's railroad iron,
And 1009 would ease my trouble' mind.

I been drinkin' plenty sody water to keep my nature down,
And you know when I get started I'm hell, hell all over town.

I ain't no monkey and you never seen me climb no tree,
I can't see why you want to make a monkey outa me.

It was late last night when I fell across my bed,
I didn't have no pretty baby to hold my achin' head.

"Don't you mistreat her because she's young and wild,
I want you to remember that you've once been a child."

Goin' to snatch me a palin' off my back-yard fence,
Goin' whale my baby till she learn some sense.

I went down to the depot and looked upon the board,
Asked the operator which way my brown-skin woman go.

He says, "If you'll 'scribe yo' woman, I'll tell you which way she's gone."
I says, "She's a seal-skinned brown, chocolate to the bone."

My woman got a tooth and it glisten in the sun,
Soon as she git able, gonna give me one.

Don' write no letter, telegram may get lef',
I want to see you, baby, talk with you myself.

[374]

"Gimme a few risings, settings of that lonesome sun
I'll be back, baby, don't you break and run."

"Baby, baby, would you cry about a lonesome dime,
You got a home as long as I got mine."

What makes your rooster crow about the dawn of day?
To let the kid man know the workingman's on his way.

The stars is fallin', it ain't long time till day,
That's to notify Teddie that the Big Bear's on his way.

I'm goin' where the water tastes like sherry wine,
 Cause the water roun' here taste like turpentine.

Ain't it hard to stumble when you ain't got no place to fall?
In this wide world I ain't got no place at all.

Levee Camp Blues

Oh, the long line skinner gets a dollar a day,
But the short line skinner gets hell to pay.

Captain, captain, don't you think it's mighty hard
Work me all day on 'lasses and lard?

Oh, the nigger lick 'lasses, white folks lick 'em, too,
I wonder what in the world a po' Mexican's gonna do.

You know, captain, I ain't to blame,
You can't get the harness on Stavin' Chain.

He shake his head and he jump so high,
I'm 'fraid he might kick me an' I might die.

[375]

Chain Gang Blues

Some on the right of way, some on the farm,
Some in the chain gang, buddy, and some gone home.

I used to be a bully jest like you,
And now you see what bull'in' has brought me to.

Wake up, lifetime man, hold up your head,
Well, you may get a pardon and you may drop dead.

Mamma have told me, have come to pass,
Says, "Drinkin' an' gamblin' be your ruin at las'."

I'm lyin' in jail with my back turned to the wall,
Thinkin' 'bout my baby, I done lost it all.

If I leave here walking, captain, you'll know I'm free,
If I leave here runnin', captain, don't follow me.

If you beat me to the Brazis, to the Brazis line,
Captain, I'll be sillum seen, captain, and hard to find.

You boys listen what the captain said,
"If you work well, give you cold corn bread,
If you won't work, I'll kill you dead."

VI

NEGRO GANG SONGS

NEGRO GANG SONGS

As he made his work songs, the Negro cleared the land of the South, worked its plantations, built its railroads, raised its levees, and cut its roads. When he worked with a group of his fellows in a situation where a regular work rhythm was possible, he sang simple, highly rhythmic songs; and every ax, pick, or hoe fell on the same beat. When he picked cotton or did some other form of work in which it was not possible to adhere to a regular rhythm, his songs rose and fell with the free and swinging movement of his breathing. The words of these songs were not designed for the ear of the Lord, nor for the ear of the white boss. In them the Negro was likely to speak his free and open mind.

The songs in this section, or songs like them, were formerly sung all over the South, wherever a gang of Negroes was at work. With the coming of machines, however, the work gangs were broken up. The songs then followed group labor into its last retreat, the road gang and the penitentiary. For the state, the most profitable way of handling convicts in the South is to use them for road repair and construction, or to have them pay for their own keep by farming large plantations. These men come together from every section of the state, bringing songs—both the "sinful songs" and the spirituals—current in their communities. Some of them have been singers, migratory workers, wandering guitar pickers in the free world. These make ready recruits for the men who work in groups, and make the work go more easily by adapting its rhythm to the rhythm of a song.

In the penitentiary, therefore, Negro "sinful" music (the term often applied to any secular song) has been concentrated and preserved as nowhere else. The men are lonely and dependent on themselves for amusement and consolation. These conditions in themselves are enough to produce and nurture songs. In our visits to all the large prison camps in the South we have found songs in abundance—blues, ballads, gang songs, hollers—colored by the melancholy solitude of prison life.

The movement of these songs varies in accord with the fast or slow rhythm of the work and with the moods of the singers. In driving a lazy mule team the song is likely to be mournful, while wood-cutting evokes spirited and gay tunes. The Negro sings, even under the hard regime of penitentiary life. In fact some of the most notable of his folk songs seem to have grown there.

"If you don' sing, you sho' git worried."

* * *

I's worked all summer an' I's worked all fall,
Den I hatter to take Christmas in my overalls.

* * *

TAKE THIS HAMMER

a to b♭. No. 726. Clifton Wright and gang, Richmond, Va., 1936. Other stanzas from Ga., Ala., N.C., and Fla. See Od.2, pp. 105, 112, 120; Lo.2, p. 84, p. 91; Whi, p. 259; Hu, p. 327.

1 *I went to the captain with my hat in my hand,—*
"Woncha please have mercy on a long-time man?"
"Cain' pick no cotton, cain' pull no corn,
Ain' got no business on this man's farm."

2 Take this hammer, (*huh!*) carry it to the captain, (*huh!*)
  Take this hammer, (*huh!*) carry it to the captain, (*huh!*)
  Take this hammer, (*huh!*) carry it to the captain, (*huh!*)
  Tell him I'm gone, tell him I'm gone. (*huh!*)

3 If he ask you (*huh!*) was I runnin', (*huh!*)
  Tell him I's flyin', tell him I's flyin'. (*huh!*)

4 If he ask you (*huh!*) was I laughin', (*huh!*)
  Tell him I's cryin', tell him I's cryin'. (*huh!*)

5 Cap'n called me, (*huh!*) called me "a nappy-headed devil," (*huh!*)
  That ain't my name, that ain't my name. (*huh!*)

6 I don't want no (*huh!*) peas, cornbread, neither molasses, (*huh!*)
  They hurt my pride, they hurt my pride. (*huh!*)

7 I don't want no (*huh!*) cold iron shackles (*huh!*)
  Around my leg, around my leg. (*huh!*)

8 Cap'n got a big gun, (*huh!*) an' he try to play bad. (*huh!*)
  Go'n' take it in the mornin' if he make me mad. (*huh!*)

9 I'm go'n' make these (*huh!*) few days I started, (*huh!*)
  Then I'm goin' home, then I'm goin' home. (*huh!*)

DON'T TALK ABOUT IT

a. No. 268. Negro convicts, State Penitentiary, Raleigh, N.C., 1934. Final two stanzas from Texas, 1935. See Od.2, pp. 76, 106.

It was so hot dat a grindstone melted and runned into the shade to cool off.

Moderately fast ♩=92 *increasing to 104 at end of recording*

LEADER
Ju - ly the red bird (*hanh!*), red bird, Au-gus' the fly._____ (*hanh!*)

GROUP
If Ju-ly ain't a hot__ month (*hanh!*), hot month, I hope I may die. (*hanh!*)

CHORUS
Now__ don't__ talk a - bout it,__(*hanh!*)'Bout it, if you do I'll cry.____ (*hanh!*)

Don't__ talk a - bout it,__ (*hanh!*) 'Bout it, if you do I'll__ die.(*hanh!*)

* The above notation is a transcription of the principal (continuous) voice parts heard on the record.

1 July the redbird, (*hanh!*) redbird, Augus' the fly. (*hanh!*) *
  If July ain't a hot month, (*hanh!*) hot month, I hope I may die. (*hanh!*)

> *Chorus 1:*
>   Now don't talk about it, (*hanh!*)
>   'Bout it, if you do I'll cry. (*hanh!*)
>   Don't talk about it, (*hanh!*)
>   'Bout it, if you do I'll die. (*hanh!*)

2 Wake up in the mornin', Lawd, between four an' five,
  Lawd, pick an' shovel, hammer right by my side.

3 Little bit o' cabbage, yellow-belly beans,
  Little more corn bread, buddy, than I ever seen.

4 Some on the right o' way, buddy, some on the farm,
  Some in the buildin', Lawdy, an' some gone home.

5 I used to be a bully, bully, jes' like you,
  But you see what bull'in', Lawdy, has brought me to.

> *Chorus 2:*
>   Now don't talk about it, (*hanh!*)
>   'Bout it, if you do I'll cry. (*hanh!*)
>   Don't crowd aroun' me, (*hanh!*)
>   'Roun me, if you do I'll die. (*hanh!*)

* A tree-chopping song. The explosive "*hanh!*" comes with the ax-strokes.

DIDN' OL' JOHN CROSS THE WATER ON HIS KNEES?

bb. No. 265. Negro convicts, Reed Camp, S.C., 1934.
See Od.2, p. 193; Me, p. 154; Jo.2, 63; also "Pauline,"
this volume, p. 402.

Responding to the prejudice against singing secular songs ("reels" or "sinful songs"), Negro convicts sometimes sing spirituals to the rhythm of their work. This nobly simple and restrained verse contains the text for a chapter of Negro history.

1 Didn' ol' John (*huh!*) cross the water, water on his knees? (*huh!*)
Didn' ol' John (*huh!*) cross the water (*huh!*) on his knees? (*huh!*)
Let us all (*huh!*) bow down, (*huh!*) good Lawd, an' face, face de risin'
sun. (*huh!*)
Didn' ol' John (*huh!*) cross the water, water on his knees? (*huh!*)

2 Let us all sing together, 'gether on our knees,
  Let us all sing together on our knees,
  Let us all bow down, good Lawd, an' face, face de risin' sun,
  Let us all sing together, 'gether on our knees.

4 Didn' ol' John wade the water, water on his knees?
  Didn' ol' John wade the water on his knees?
  Let us all bow down, good Lawd, an' face, face de risin' sun,
  Didn' ol' John wade the water, water on his knees?

MARTHY HAD A BABY

f to *f*♯. No. 693. Roscoe McLean, Florida State Penitentiary, Raiford, Fla., 1936.

Marthy had a baby and she said ____ 'twas mine,

Marthy had a ____ baby ____ and she said ____ 'twas mine,

Marthy ____ had a ____ ba - by, ____

Oo - hoo, Lordy Lord, ____ she ____ said 'twas mine. ____

1 Marthy had a baby and she said 'twas mine,
  Marthy had a baby and she said 'twas mine,
  Marthy had a baby,
  Oo-hoo, Lordy Lord, she said 'twas mine.

2 It must have been the walker's,* 'cause it had blue eyes, (2)
  It must have been the walker's,
  Oo-hoo, Lordy Lord, she said 'twas mine.

* The "walking" boss, usually a white man.

[385]

3 The walker couldn't stand to hear the baby cry, (2)
The walker couldn't stand to,
Oo-hoo, Lordy Lord, to hear him cry.

4 Oh, me an' my buddy started lopin' on down the road, (2)
Oh, me an' my buddy started lopin',
Oo-hoo, Lordy Lord, on down the road.

5 Bulldog bit the devil and the devil died, (2)
Bulldog bit the devil,
Oo-hoo, Lordy Lord, the devil died.

LORD, IT'S ALL, ALMOST DONE

d. No. 225. Negro convict, Wetumka, Ala., 1934. See Od.1, p. 258; BB, p. 26.

Did you boys hear
What the captain said?
"If the boys work,
Gonna treat you pretty well,
But if you don't work,
Gonna give you plenty hell."

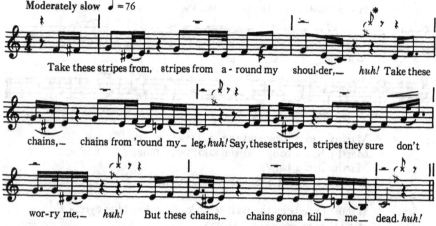

* In most work songs the "*huh*'s" are more or less within the normal range of the voices. In this
song they are pitched at an exceptional height, on and around a twelfth above the highest sung tone
of the song.

[386]

CHORUS

Lord, it's all, al - most ___ done, *huh!* Lord, it's all, al - most ___

done, *huh!* Lord, it's all, al - most ___ done, Noth-in' but to

bring them ___ yal -low wom - ens o - ver here. *huh!*

1 Take these stripes from, stripes from around my shoulder, *huh!*
Take these chains, chains from 'round my leg, *huh!*
Say, these stripes, stripes they sure don't worry me, *huh!*
But these chains, chains gonna kill me dead. *huh!*

Chorus:
    Lord, it's all, almost done, *huh!*
    Lord, it's all, almost done, *huh!*
    Lord, it's all, almost done,
    Nothin' but to bring them yallow womens over here. *huh!*

2 An' if it wasn't for, wasn't for my good captain,
Lord, I would of, would of been gone down,
By he liked, liked my hard rollin',
Then he gave me little narrow round.

3 Says, she whispered, whispered to her mother,
"Mother, I can't, can't see how he stand,"
Says, "He ain't, ain't but sweet sixteen,
An' they drivin' him like a man."

4 Says, she carried me, carried me to her parlor,
Lord, she cooled me, cooled me with her fan,
Says, she swore by, swore by the man who made her,
"Mother, I do, do love a railroad man."

Variant Chorus:
Railroad man ain't got no home,
Railroad man ain't got no home,
Railroad man ain't got no home,
Here today, Lord, tomorrow he'll be gone.

5 Well, she told me, told me that she loved me,
Jus' to give my, give my po' heart ease,
Just as soon as, soon as I got in trouble,
Well, she turned her, turned her back on me.

6 On Monday, Monday, I was arrested,
On Tuesday locked up in jail,
On Wednesday my trial was attested,
On Thursday nobody wouldn't go my bail.

7 On Friday me an' my baby was a-walkin',
On Saturday she throwed me out of doors,
On Sunday me an' my baby was a-talkin',
On Monday she pawned all my clothes.

8 Needn't to come here, come here buckin' an' jumpin' *
Lawd, you sho, sho can't stand,
Lawd, it's ol', ol' buckin' an' jumpin'
Have been the death of, death of many a good man.

* " 'Buckin' an' jumpin' ' or 'buck-jumpin' ' means to do field work the easy, shoddy way and to conceal this fact from your boss or your driver."

AIN'T WORKIN' SONG

d^b. No. 1336. Charley Campbell, Alabama State Docks,
Mobile, Ala., 1937.

On the docks, at Mobile, Alabama, a collector of folk songs has just recorded a song by a Negro longshoreman, Charley Campbell.

COLLECTOR: Was that a work song that you've just sung?

CHARLEY: Boss, this here ain't no workin' song; it's a ain't workin' song!

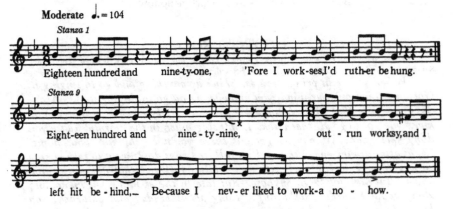

Moderate ♩. = 104

Stanza 1

Eighteen hundred and nine-ty-one, 'Fore I work-ses, I'd ruth-er be hung.

Stanza 9

Eight-een hundred and nine-ty-nine, I out-run worksy, and I

left hit be-hind,— Be-cause I nev-er liked to work-a no-how.

1 Eighteen hundred and ninety-one,
  'Fore I workses, I'd ruther be hung.

2 Eighteen hundred and ninety-two,
  Me an' old worksy, we done been through.

3 Eighteen hundred and ninety-three,
  Me and old worksy, we can't agree.

4 Eighteen hundred and ninety-four,
  I lef' old worksy standin' at de workhouse door.

5 Eighteen hundred and ninety-five,
  'Fore I workses, I be bad lie.

6 Eighteen hundred and ninety-six,
  Me an' old worksies, we business out of fix.

[389]

7 Eighteen hundred and ninety-seven,
  Work killed my brother and sont him to heaven.

8 Eighteen hundred and ninety-eight,
  I lef' old worksy standin' at de workhouse gate.

9 Eighteen hundred and ninety-nine,
  I outrun worksy, and I left hit behind,
  Because I never liked to work-a nohow.

I GOT TO ROLL

No record. From the singing of Bess Brown Lomax and Alan Lomax, learned from Black Sampson in the Nashville Penitentiary, 1937. See Od.2, p. 101.

"When you're in prison, you can think up anything and go to singing it. Got something on your mind, you know, and you go to singing it. On Mondays—we call that 'Blue Monday'—you ain't studyin' 'bout singing. You know you got to go all that week. Don't sing much in the mornin' 'cause you don't feel good. When you get out there you'd be thinkin' 'bout home. Right after dinner, when they bellies full, the boys don't want to talk or sing either; they're feelin' lazy with their bellies full and that hot sun comin' down. But you got to go anyhow. But late in the evenin', you know, and along about Saturday, we'd sing. 'Long about Friday and Saturday, you know the week is all about done, and, man, you go to singing then. Down there, we call Saturday 'Christmas Eve' and Sunday 'Christmas' 'cause we know when Sunday comes we ain't gonna work. —Louisiana Negro.

Slow

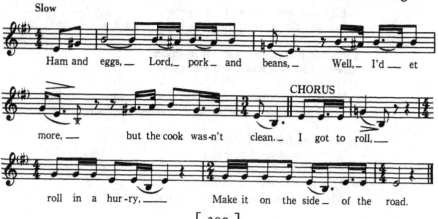

Ham and eggs, __ Lord, __ pork __ and beans, __ Well, __ I'd __ et

CHORUS

more, __ but the cook was-n't clean. __ I got to roll, __

roll in a hur-ry, ____ Make it on the side __ of the road.

1 Ham and eggs, Lord, pork and beans,
  Well, I'd et more, but the cook wasn't clean.

Chorus:
    I got to roll, roll in a hurry,
    Make it on the side of the road.

2 If I'd 'a' knowed my cap'n was mean,
  I never would 'a' left St. Augustine. (*Chorus.*)

3 If I'd 'a' knowed my cap'n was blind,
  I wouldn't 'a' went to work till half past nine. (*Chorus.*)

4 If I'd 'a' knowed my cap'n was bad,
  I wouldn't 'a' sold that special that I once did had. (*Chorus.*)

YOU KICKED AND STOMPED AND BEAT ME

f. No. 1857. Bowlegs, State Penitentiary, Parchman, Miss., 1933.

Cap'n, if I get a letter an' Mamma says, "Come home."
Cap'n, yo' flat-back shotgun ain' gonna hold me long.

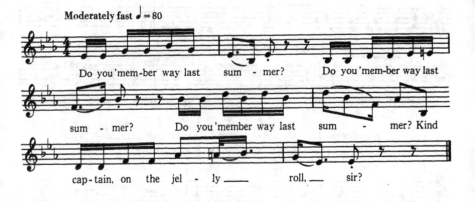

1 Do you 'member way last summer? (3)
  Kind captain, on the jelly roll, sir?

[391]

2 Well, you kicked and stomped and beat me; (3)
Kind cap'n, and you call that fun, sir.

3 If I catch you in my home town, (3)
Goin' to make you run, sir.

DRIVE IT ON

a^b. No. 245. Group of convicts, Cummins State Farm, Ark., 1934.

A gay, rollicking gang work song with a spirited tempo, interspersed with shouts of physical enjoyment, used for ax work.

I'm gonna preach to my diamond,* hammer ring,
Listen what I'm gonna preach, suh, hammer ring.
If you walk, I'll drive you, hammer ring,
If you drive, I'll ride you, hammer ring,
If you lead, I'll follow you, hammer ring,
I'm heavy lo——oaded, hammer ring,
Loaded with my diamond, hammer ring.

* Axe blade.

* These or other shouts accompany each stanza at this point.

[392]

1 Well-a, jumpin', Jumpin' Judy, (2)
   Oh, Captain, was a mighty fine girl, oh, Lawd,
   Oh, drive it on.

2 Well-a, Judy brought de jumpin',
   Oh, Captain, to this whole round world, oh, Lawd,

3 Well, did you hear 'bout Berta Robbins,
   Oh, Captain, and a little Berta Lee, oh, Lawd?

4 Lawd, and both of them got 'rested,
   Oh, Captain, in the down-town jail, oh, Lawd,

5 Oh, Lawd, it's one of them got six months,
   Oh, Captain, and the other got a year, oh, Lawd,

6 Oh, well, you remember last winter,
   Oh, Captain, when the weather was cold, oh, Lawd,

7 Oh, well, you had me way out yonder,
   Oh, Captain, on that long ferry road, oh, Lawd,

8 Oh, well, you kicked and stomped and beat me,
   Oh, Captain, and you called it fun, oh, Lawd,

9 Well, I may meet you over in Memphis,
   Oh, Captain, we're going t' have a little run, oh, Lawd,

10 Well, yonder come Elnora,
   Oh, Captain, how in the world do you know? Oh, Lawd,

11 Umberella on her shoulder,
   Oh, Captain, piece of paper in her hand, oh, Lawd,

12 Well, I heard her tell the sergeant,
   Oh, Captain, "God, I love my man," oh, Lawd,

13 Well, did you ever been dishonored?
   Oh, Cap'n, and taken to the pen, oh, Lawd,
   Oh, Lawdy, Lawd.

[393]

14 Well, if you don't stop stealin',
　　Oh, Captain, then you're gwine again, oh, Lawd,
　　Oh, drive it on.

15 Well, it's every Monday mornin',
　　Oh, Captain, when the iron gong ring, oh, Lawd,

16 Well, we go marchin' to the table,
　　Oh, Captain, find the same old thing, oh, Lawd,
　　Oh, Lawdy, Lawd.

17 Well, if anybody asks you,
　　Oh, Captain, who sung this song, oh, Lawd,
　　Oh, Lawdy, Lawd.

18 Just tell him it's three parts of devil,
　　Oh, Captain, that's been here and gone, oh, Lawd,
　　Oh, Lawdy, Lawd.

O LAWD I WENT UP ON THE MOUNTAIN

a. No. 248. Group led by Kelly Page, Cummins State
Farm, Ark., 1934.

What men think about in prison is "women." On Sundays they stand
in the dormitories clinging to the big iron bars, they stand there looking at
nothing, saying nothing, with their arms wrapped around the bars. The
name of the girl they sing about in Mississippi and Arkansas nowadays is
Rosie, sometimes Roxie. From Arkansas comes this tender advice to Roxie.

> *Roxie, Roxie, if you were mine,*
> *You wouldn' do nothin' but starch an' i'on.*
>
> *Roxie gal, you promised me,*
> *You'd never marry till I went free.*
>
> *Roxie, Roxie, doncha wait on me,*
> *So long rollin' I may never go free.*
>
> *Every evenin' when the sun goes down,*
> *Big leg Roxie restin' on my mind.*
>
> *I was rollin' when you come along,*
> *And I'll be rollin' when you started home.*

[394]

The prisoner lets out a long moan like a lonely steamboat whistle and hollers,

I fills her pocket full of silver and her mouth full of gold,
Every time I kiss her, my blood runs chilly co-o-old.

Then he remembers how lonely he is,

She said that she loved me, but she told me a lie,
She hasn't been to see me, Lawd, since last July.

He remembers where he is and puts the bitterness of the prisoner into these two lines,

Ain' but the one thing worries my mind:
World full of women, an' ain' nary one mine.

"O Lawd, I Went Up on the Mountain" is a compost of old blues verses and a blues tune set to the rhythm of the woodyard axes.

O Lawd, I went up on the moun-tain, looked at the ris-in' sun,—
Hey, hey, hey, hey;—— O Lawd, I went up on the moun - tain,
looked at the ris-in' sun,—— Hey, hey,— hey. I says-uh, "You-uh can't
do me,— oh, like Lo - re - na done."— Hey, — hey, hey, hey.

* In the middle of the second stanza the men begin to double-cut, i.e., to alternate their axe strokes, which from then on occur regularly on the first beat of each measure.

1 O Lawd, I went up on the mountain, looked at the risin' sun,
   Hey, hey, hey, hey;
   O Lawd, I went up on the mountain, looked at the risin' sun,
   Hey, hey, hey.
   I says-uh, "You can't do me, oh, like Lorena done."
   Hey, hey, hey, hey.

2 Oh, well, she picks yo' pockets and rush you through the do',
   An' she say, "Hurry, big man, over yonder in West Arco."

3 "Oh, did you get that letter, I throwed in your back yard?
   I would 'a' done been to see you, yo' white folks got me barred."

4 Oh, well, just look over yonder, oh, where the sun done gone,
   I says, "She's makin' her way back to where Saint Mary has gone."

5 I says, "She goes to bed with her, her head rag on her head,"
   I says, "You ask her how about it, she'll swear she's almost dead."

6 Oh, well, it's T for Texas, it's T for Tennessee,
   I says, "It's T for the woman that thinks a world of me."

7 O Lawd, I went to the graveyard, looked in my rider's face,
   I says, "I wished to good Lawd she's in another place."

8 O Lawd, my feets all muddy, and it's pourin' down rain,
   O Lawd, my woman's down in Cummins, I love her just the same.

LONG SUMMER DAY

a to *bb*. No. 196. Clear Rock, Sugar Land and Taylor, Texas, 1933.

Me an' my pardner an' my pardner's frien'
Can pick mo' cotton than a gin can gin.

Me an' my pardner can pick a bale,
Can pick mo' cotton than de scales can weigh.

Me an' my pardner an' two or three mo'
Can pick mo' cotton than a boat can hold.

* * *

Moderate ♩ = 132

Stanza 1*

Long sum-mer day makes a white man— la - zy,— Long sum-mer day,

Well, a long sum-mer day makes a white man la - zy, Long sum-mer day.

Stanza 2

Well, a long— sum-mer day make a nig-ger run a-way, sir,—

Long sum-mer day, Well, a long sum-mer day make a

nig - ger run a - way, sir, Long sum - mer day.

* Remaining stanzas may be sung to the tune either of stanza 1 or of stanza 2.

1 Long summer day makes a white man lazy,
  Long summer day,
  Well, a long summer day makes a white man lazy,
  Long summer day.

2 Well, a long summer day make a nigger run away, sir,
  Long summer day,
  Well, a long summer day make a nigger run away, sir,
  Long summer day.

3 Well, a-pickin' that cotton in the bottom field, sir,
  Long summer day,
  Well, it's gatherin' up the cotton in the bottom field, sir,
  Long summer day.

4 Well, he run away to see Miss Mary,
   Long summer day,
   Well, he run right away to see his baby,
   Long summer day.

5 Well, the white man sont and got him a doctor, etc.

6 Well, "Go back to the field, you got no fever," etc.

7 Well, the summer day makes a nigger feel lazy, etc.

GODAMIGHTY DRAG

From the singing of Alan Lomax, learned from Augustus Haggerty and group of Negroes. Huntsville Penitentiary, Texas, 1934.

His nickname was Track Horse, and he's dead now. His body was a thick wedge of strength that could tie a rainbow round his shoulder * all day under the hot broiling sun, and he had the voice of a lead man for both work songs and spirituals. The lead man has to have a strong carrying voice, but most of all he has to dare to thrust out ahead of the rhythm with his verse lines so that the refrain bursts out of the gang like beer out of a bunghole.

In his "Godamighty Drag"—"drag" here meaning a hot, syncopated tempo—each prisoner tells his own story. When one leader slacks his singing, another prisoner speaks his individual mind, and the group roars assent —"Wo, Lawdy!"—as if to say, "That's true for you and the same damn thing happened to me."

"I" and "me" in the Negro work songs, blues, and hollers are always thus expressions of the feeling of the Negro community as well as of the individual who is singing. The first person singular means, "I, the Negro woman or man"—not self-consciously so, but because, as the song passes from one singer to another with its burden of common experience, it can invisibly and immediately belong to the individual singer. The melodic and literary forms involved are so universally familiar that the material can be remolded with facility by each victim of "the blues." The root of this communal quality is the community tragedy in the life of the Southern Negro.

*   *   *

Look over yonder where the sun done gone,
It may be a cemetery, but it's my home.

*   *   *

* The shimmering arc of the whirling axe.

Slow

Mam-ma and Pa-pa, Wo-ho, Lawd-y, Mam-ma and

Pa-pa, God-a-might-y God knows, Done tol' me a lie, suh, Wo,

Lawd-y, Done tol' me a lie, suh,— Wo-ho, my Lawd.

1 Mamma and Papa,
Wo-ho, Lawdy,
Mamma and Papa,
Godamighty God knows,
Done tol' me a lie, suh,
Wo, Lawdy,
Done tol' me a lie, suh,
Wo-ho, my Lawd.

2 Done told me they'd pardon
me,*
Well, next July, suh.

3 June, July, and August,
Done come an' gone, suh.

4 Left me here rollin',
On this ol' farm, suh.

5 When Hannah † go to beamin',
Make you think about your
mamma.

6 When the boys go to steamin',
Make a nigger run away, suh.

7 Oh, me an' my pardner,
We went to the Brazis.

8 And he could not swim, suh,
And he could not swim.

9 I crossed him over,
On a live-oak limb.

10 Ride, old dog-man,
You better ride, old dog-man.

11 When the Brazis was risin',
Riley walked the water.

* Each couplet to be expanded as in the first stanza.
† The sun.

JOHNNY, WON'T YOU RAMBLE?

G, g. No. 190. Lightning and a group of convicts,
Darrington State Farm, Texas, 1934.

Said by Texas convicts to be one of the oldest songs on the Colorado
River, this song seems to have had its origin in the days of slavery. It shows
that the Negroes looked neither at slavery nor at their masters through
rose-colored glasses.

Moderately fast ♩ = 63

FIRST SINGER

Well, I went down in Hell-town To see the Dev-il chain down,

FIRST SINGER

John-ny, won't you ram - ble?__ Hoe, hoe, hoe.

SECOND SINGER

Well, I went down__ in Hell-town To see the Dev-il chain down,

John-ny, won't you ram - ble?__ Hoe, hoe,__ hoe.

* The above notation is a transcription of the two parts heard on the record.

1 Well, I went down in Hell-town
  To see the Devil chain down,
  Johnny, won't you ramble?
  Hoe, hoe, hoe.
               } *bis*

[400]

2 Ol' Massa an' ol' missis
   Settin' in the parlor,
   Johnny, won't you ramble?
   Hoe, hoe, hoe.
   Jus' fig'in, an' a plannin'
   How to work a nigger harder,
   Johnny, won't you ramble?
   Hoe, hoe, hoe.

3 Ol' Massa's gonna kill a little
   Bitty ol' fattenin' calf,
   Johnny, won't you ramble?
   Hoe, hoe, hoe.
   When the bullies heard they gonna kill him,
   You oughta seen them try to laugh,
   Johnny, won't you ramble?
   Hoe, hoe, hoe.

4 Ol' Mistis gonna kill the bully's
   Little bitty red Jersey bull,
   Johnny, won't you ramble?
   Hoe, hoe, hoe.
   Ol' Mistis told old Massa
   That "it'll give the bullies a bellyful,"
   Johnny, won't you ramble?
   Hoe, hoe, hoe.

5 I looked up on the hill
   And spied old Massa ridin',
   Johnny, won't you ramble?
   Hoe, hoe, hoe.
   Had a bull whip in one hand,
   A cowhide in the other,
   Johnny, won't you ramble,
   Hoe, hoe, hoe.

6 Pocketful of leather strings
   To tie your hands together,
   Johnny, won't you ramble,
   Hoe, hoe, hoe.

"Ol' Massa, don't you whip me,
I'll give you half a dollar,"
Johnny, won't you ramble?
Hoe, hoe, hoe.

7 "No, no, bully boy,
I'd rather hear you holler."
Johnny, won't you ramble? } *bis*
Hoe, hoe, hoe.

PAULINE

𝅗𝅥. No. 176. Allen Prothero, Tennessee Penitentiary,
Nashville, Tenn., 1933. See "Didn' Ol' John Cross the
Water on His Knees?", p. 384.

In the Nashville penitentiary Allen Prothero, a Negro convict from
Chattanooga, sang "Pauline" in tones as clear as a silver trumpet. White
friends interested themselves in his case, but the Governor's parole found
Allen Prothero dead from tuberculosis—"galloping consumption." This
song will stand as a monument to him. It shows its kinship with a whole
school of work songs,* but it is his own highly individual rearrangement and,
we think, one of the tenderest, most delicate love songs that ever came out
of a human throat.

What's in a name? These names—Frankie, Rosie, Roxie, Jumpin' Judy,
Hattie Bell, Eadie, Marthy, Julie Ann, and Pauline—these women, the
heroines of Negro work songs, will live as long as there are lovers of folk
melodies.

* Cf. "Didn' Ol' John Cross the Water," etc.

Slow ♩ = 66

Paul - ine,_____ Paul -ine, ___ I don' love ___ no-body but you.

Lawd, I'm go-in'_____ to my shan-ty, ___ I'm gonna lie ___ down,

[402]

Lawd, I'm go-in'——— to my shan-ty,—— I'm go'n' lie down,—

Well, it's oh, —— Lawd-y—— me, well, it's trou-ble —— I do see, ——

Lawd, I'm go-in'——— to my shan-ty, — I'm gon-na lie —— down.

see,—— You been a long, —— long time 'bout makin' up, — Lawd, in yo' min'.

Introductory:
> Pauline, Pauline,
> I don' love nobody but you.

Stanzas:

1 Lawd, I'm goin' to my shanty, I'm gonna lie down,
   Lawd, I'm goin' to my shanty, I'm go'n' lie down,
   Well, it's oh, Lawdy me, well, it's trouble I do see,
   Lawd, I'm goin' to my shanty, I'm gonna lie down.

2 Lawd, I'm goin' back home to Pauline, (2)
   Well, I'm goin' back home, well, I'm goin' to lie down,
   You been a long, long time 'bout makin' it up, Lawd, in yo' min'.

3 Lawd, I walked and I cried all night long, (2)
   Lawd, it's oh, Lawdy me, Lawd, it's trouble I do see,
   You been a long, long time 'bout makin' it up, Lawd, in yo' min'.

[403]

4 I'm gonna write one mo' letter, gonna write no mo', (2)
   Well, it's oh, Lawdy me, well, it's trouble I do see,
   You been a long, long time 'bout makin' it up, Lawd, in yo' min'.

LOOK DOWN THAT LONESOME ROAD

d'. No. 267. Group of convicts, Reed Prison Camp,
Boykin, S.C., 1934. See Sc.1, p. 73; Od.2, p. 46. The
popular version is copyrighted by Nathaniel Shilkret, N. Y.,
1928.

Slow ♩ = 76

Look— down, look— down— That— long, lone-some road,—

Where you— and I,— I must— go.

1 Look down, look down
  That long, lonesome road,
  Where you and I,
  I must go.

2 Stand back, stand back,
  All you five-and-ten-cent men,
  Got a man knockin' on,
  On yo' door.

3 Hattie Bell, Hattie Bell,
  Oh, she my own, own true love,
  Darlin', what have,
  Have I done?

* * *

*I been up and down this river from end to end,
Ain't found no heaven nowhere I been.*

[404]

BIBLIOGRAPHY

This is a supplement to the bibliography published in *American Ballads and Folk Songs* (1934). The intention is to list the most important books and pamphlets of American folk songs which have been published since that date, together with a few of the most valuable articles which have appeared in the *Journal of American Folk-Lore* (*JAFL*) and the *Southern Folklore Quarterly* (*SFQ*). If space permitted, the list might be extended greatly by adding titles of choral and solo arrangements. The bibliographer is Harold W. Thompson of Cornell University, who has found these works useful in his courses in American folk literature, conducted at Cornell University and at the New York College for Teachers at Albany.

ANDERSON, A. O., "Geography and Rhythm," *University of Arizona Bulletin*, Vol. 4, No. 8. Tucson: University of Arizona, 1935.

ANDREWS, A. O., *The Gift to Be Simple: Songs, Dances and Rituals of the American Shakers*. New York: J. J. Augustin, 1940.

BARBEAU, MARIUS, *Folk-Songs of Old Quebec*. National Museum of Canada, Bulletin 75, Ottawa, 1936.
   Fifteen songs.

BARNES, R. A., *I Hear America Singing*. Philadelphia: J. C. Winston Co., 1937.
   Introduction by Carl Van Doren. Illustrations by Robert Lawson. No tunes, not all folk songs, but an attractive book for young people.

BARRY, PHILLIPS, *Folk Music in America*. Introduction by George Herzog. W.P.A., Federal Theatre Project, Publication No. 80-S, June 1939. New York: National Service Bureau.
   The most important essays by a great scholar, dating from 1909 to 1937, with a bibliography of Barry's writings.

BELDEN, H. M., *Ballads and Songs Collected by the Missouri Folk-Lore Society* (*University of Missouri Studies*, Vol. XV, No. 1). Columbia, Mo.: University of Missouri, 1940.
   Wide range of songs, splendidly edited.

BLEGEN, T. C., AND RUUD, M. B., *Norwegian Emigrant Songs and Ballads*. Minneapolis: University of Minnesota Press, 1937.

BOGGS, R. S., Annual bibliographies of American Folklore in the *SFQ*, 2:43–48, 3:45–58, 4:23–50.

BOTKIN, B. A., *The American Play-Party Song, with a Collection of Oklahoma Texts and Tunes*. Lincoln: University of Nebraska, 1937.

[405]

BREWSTER, P. G., *Ballads and Songs of Indiana* (Indiana University Publications, Folklore Series, No. 1). Bloomington: Indiana University, 1940.

BUCHANAN, ANNABEL MORRIS, Choral arrangements of white spirituals and folk-hymns. New York: J. Fischer & Bro., 1935–1936.

BUCHANAN, ANNABEL MORRIS, *Folk Hymns of America.* New York: J. Fischer & Bro., 1938.
> Excellent notes, useful accompaniments.

BUCHANAN, ANNABEL MORRIS, Bibliography of Folk Music of America. For National Federation of Music Clubs. Ithaca, N. Y.: National Federation Publisher, 1939.

Bulletin of the Folksong Society of the Northeast.
> This series ended with No. 12 (1937), upon the death of its lamented editor, Phillips Barry.

CAMBIAIRE, C. P., *East Tennessee and Western Virginia Mountain Ballads.* London: Mitre Press, 1935.

CAMPBELL, MARIE. An important series of ballads from the Kentucky mountains, published in the *SFQ*: "Liquor Ballads," 2:157–164 (1938); "Funeral Ballads," 3:107–116 (1939); "Feuding Ballads," 3:165–172 (1939).

CARY, M. B., JR., "Mademoiselle from Armentières," in *JAFL*, 47:369–376 (1934).

CHAPPELL, L. W., *John Henry: A Folk-Lore Study.* Jena, Germany: W. Biedermann, 1933.

CHAPPELL, L. W., *Folksongs of Roanoke and the Albemarle.* Morgantown, W. Va.: Ballard Press, 1939.

CHASE, RICHARD, *Old Songs and Singing Games.* Chapel Hill: University of North Carolina Press, 1938.

COLCORD, J. C., *Songs of American Sailormen.* New York: W. W. Norton & Co., Inc., 1938.
> The standard American collection, an enlargement of *Roll and Go* (1924), now out of print.

COX, J. H., *Folk-Songs Mainly from West Virginia.* Introduction and supplementary references by H. Halpert. W.P.A., Federal Theatre Project, Publication No. 81–S. New York: National Service Bureau, 1939.

COX, J. H., *Traditional Ballads Mainly from West Virginia.* Edited by H. Halpert. W.P.A., Federal Theatre Project, Publication No. 75-S. New York: National Service Bureau, 1939.
> Has a valuable bibliography.

DENSMORE, FRANCES, *Cheyenne and Arapaho Music* (Southwest Museum Papers, No. 10). Los Angeles: Southwest Museum, 1936.

DENSMORE, FRANCES, *The American Indians and Their Music.* New York: Woman's Press, 1936.
> Revised edition of a book written in popular style by a distinguished scholar.

Bibliography

DOWNES, OLIN, AND SIEGMEISTER, ELIE, *A Treasury of American Song*. New York: Howell, Soskin & Co., 1940.

EDDY, M. O., *Ballads and Songs from Ohio*. Introduction by J. H. Hanford. New York: J. J. Augustin, 1939.

FISH, H. D., *Four and Twenty Blackbirds*. Illustrated by Robert Lawson. New York: Frederick A. Stokes Co., 1937.
    Nursery rhymes in a charming book for children.

FLANDERS, H. H., *A Garland of Green Mountain Song*. Northfield, Vt.: A. W. Peach, 1934.

FLANDERS, H. H., AND NORFLEET, HELEN, *Country Songs of Vermont*. Schirmer's American Folksong Series, Set 19. New York: G. Schirmer, Inc., 1937.

FLANDERS, H. H., AND OTHERS, *The New Green Mountain Songster: Traditional Folk Songs of Vermont*. New Haven: Yale University Press, 1939.

FORD, IRA W., *Traditional Music of America*. New York: E. P. Dutton & Co., 1940.

GARDNER, E. E., *Folklore from the Schoharie Hills, New York*. Ann Arbor: University of Michigan Press, 1937.
    One chapter of "Songs and Ballads," some of them with tunes, and one chapter of "Rhymes and Games."

GARDNER, E. E., AND CHICKERING, G. J., *Ballads and Songs of Southern Michigan*. Ann Arbor: University of Michigan Press, 1939.

GELLERT, LAWRENCE, *Negro Songs of Protest*. New York: American Music League, 1936.

Gold Rush Ballads: The Forty-Niners, ed. Cornel Lengyel. San Francisco: W.P.A. of Northern California, 1940.

GORDON, R. W., *Folk-Songs of America*. W.P.A., Federal Theatre Project, Publication No. 73-S. New York: National Service Bureau, 1938.
    Fifteen articles by one of the leading collectors, reprinted from the New York *Times*, 1927–1928.

HALPERT, HERBERT, "Some Ballads and Folk Songs from New Jersey," in *JAFL*, 52:52–69 (1939).

HAUGEN, EINAR, "Norwegian Emigrant Songs and Ballads," in *JAFL*, 51:69–75 (1938).

HENDREN, J. W., *A Study of Ballad Rhythm, with Special Reference to Ballad Music* (Princeton Studies in English, No. 14). Princeton: Princeton University Press, 1936.

HENRY, M. E., *A Bibliography for the Study of American Folk-Songs*. London: Mitre Press, 1937.

HENRY, M. E., *Folk-Songs from the Southern Highlands*. New York: J. J. Augustin, 1937.

HERZOG, GEORGE, "Musical Typology in Folksong," in *SFQ*, 1:49–55 (June, 1937).

HERZOG, GEORGE, *Research in Primitive and Folk Music in the United States* (Bulletin No. 24). Washington, D. C.: American Council of Learned Societies, 1936.

HORNE, D. D., "An Inquiry into the Musical Backgrounds of Folk Songs of the Southern Mountains," in *Tennessee Folklore Society Bulletin,* 4:70–81 (Maryville, Tenn., 1938).

HUDSON, A. P., *Folksongs of Mississippi and Their Background.* Chapel Hill: University of North Carolina Press, 1936.

HUDSON, A. P., AND HERZOG, G., *Folk Tunes from Mississippi,* ed. G. Herzog. National Play Bureau, W.P.A., Federal Theatre Project, Publication No. 25. New York: National Service Bureau, 1937.

HUDSON, A. P., *Folk Tunes from Mississippi,* 2nd ed., ed. G. Herzog and H. Halpert, with Preface by E. S. Woodward. W.P.A., Federal Theatre Project, Publication No. 25. New York: National Service Bureau, 1937.

HUSTVEDT, S. B., *A Melodic Index of Child's Ballad Tunes* (Publications of the University of California Southern Branch in Languages and Literatures, Vol. I, No. 2). Berkeley: University of California Press, 1936.

JACKSON, G. P., "Did Spirituals First Develop in the Northeast?" in *SFQ,* 3:1–4 (1939).

JACKSON, G. P., *Spiritual Folk-Songs of Early America.* New York: J. J. Augustin, 1937.

JOHNSON, J. R., *Rolling Along in Song.* New York: Viking Press, 1937.
   A chronological survey of Negro music in the United States, with illustrations.

KARPELES, MAUD, *Folk-Songs from Newfoundland.* London: Oxford University Press, 1934.

KIRKLAND, E. C., AND M. M., "Popular Ballads Recorded in Knoxville, Tennessee," in *SFQ,* 2:65–80 (1938).

KORSON, GEORGE, *Minstrels of the Mine Patch.* Philadelphia: University of Pennsylvania Press, 1938.

LINSCOTT, E. H., *Folk-Songs of Old New England.* Introduction by J. M. Carpenter. New York: Macmillan Co., 1939.
   Wide range and charming presentation.

LOMAX, J. A. AND ALAN, *Cowboy Songs and Other Frontier Ballads.* Rev. and enlarged ed. New York: Macmillan Co., 1938.
   The standard collection.

LOMAX, J. A. AND ALAN, *Negro Folk Songs as Sung by Lead Belly.* Musical notation by George Herzog. New York: Macmillan Co., 1936.
   Important. Has fascinating biography of the singer.

LONGINI, M. D., "Folk Songs of Chicago Negroes," in *JAFL,* 52:96–111 (1939).

MATTESON, MAURICE, AND HENRY, M. E., *Beech Mountain Folk-Songs and Ballads.* Schirmer's American Folk-Song Series, Set 15. New York: G. Schirmer, 1936.

McDOWELL, L. L., *Songs of the Old Camp Ground.* Ann Arbor: Edwards Bros., Inc., 1937.
   Religious songs from Tennessee.

McDOWELL, L. L. AND F. L., *Folk Dances of Tennessee: Old Play Party Games of the Caney Fork Valley.* Smithville, Tenn.: L. L. McDowell, 1938.

Bibliography

Nebraska Folklore Pamphlets.
  Valuable material collected and mimeographed by the Federal Theatre Project, at Lincoln, Nebraska. See especially Nos. 1, 3, 11, 15, 16, 18, 20, 22, 24.
NEELY, CHARLES, "Four British Ballads in Southern Illinois," in *JAFL*, 52:75–81 (1939).
NEESER, R. W., *American Naval Songs and Ballads*. New Haven: Yale University Press, 1938.
  Valuable for texts; no tunes.
NILES, J. J., *Ballads, Carols, and Tragic Legends from the Southern Appalachian Mountains*. Schirmer's American Folk-Song Series, Set 20. New York: G. Schirmer, 1938.
NILES, J. J., *More Songs of the Hill-Folk*. Set 17. New York: G. Schirmer, 1936.
NILES, J. J., *Seven Kentucky Mountain Songs*. New York: G. Schirmer, 1929.
NILES, J. J., *Songs of the Hill-Folk*. Set 14. New York: G. Schirmer, 1934.
OWENS, B. A., "Songs of the Cumberlands," in *JAFL*, 49:215–242 (1936).
  From Pike County, Kentucky.
PIKE, R. E., "Folk Songs from Pittsburg, New Hampshire," in *JAFL*, 48:337–351 (1935).
POUND, LOUISE, *Folk-Song of Nebraska and the Central West: A Syllabus* (Nebraska Academy of Science Publications, Vol. IX, No. 3). Lincoln, 1915.
POUND, LOUISE, "Some Texts of Western Songs," in *SFQ*, 3:25–32 (1939).
POWELL, JOHN, "In the Lowlands Low," in *SFQ*, 1:1–12 (1937).
  Story of an exciting discovery of folk-music.
RANDOLPH, V., AND CLEMENS, N., "Ozark Mountain Party Games," in *JAFL*, 49:199–206 (1936).
Report of the Committee on Folksong of the Popular Literature Section of the Modern Language Association of America (published as Vol. I, No. 2, of the *SFQ*, 1937).
  Valuable articles by Barry, Davis, Herzog, J. A. Lomax, and Reed Smith, with a list of collectors and other persons interested in the ballad and folk song in the United States and Canada.
SCARBOROUGH, DOROTHY, *A Song Catcher in Southern Mountains*. New York: Columbia University Press, 1937.
SIEGMEISTER, ELIE. See DOWNES, OLIN.
SMITH, REED, "A Glance at the Ballad and Folksong Field," in *SFQ*, Vol. I, No. 2, 7–18 (1937).
  Includes a list of the Child ballads found in the U. S. and Canada.
SMITH, REED, "The Traditional Ballad in America, 1933," in *JAFL*, 47:64–75 (1934).
SMITH, REED, AND RUFTY, H., *American Anthology of Old-World Ballads*. New York: J. Fischer & Bro., 1937.
  With accompaniments and admirable notes; perhaps the best collection available for professional singers.

Southern Folklore Quarterly. 1937–   . Published by the University of Florida in cooperation with the Southeastern Folklore Society.

SPIVACKE, HAROLD, "The Archive of American Folk-Song in the Library of Congress," in *SFQ*, Vol. II, No. 1, 31–36 (1938).

STOUT, E. J., *Folklore from Iowa*. New York: J. J. Augustin, 1936.

TAYLOR, ARCHER, "A Finding-List of American Song," in *SFQ*, Vol. I, No. 3, 17–24 (1937).

Tennessee Folklore Society Bulletin, 1935–

THOMAS, JEAN, *Ballad Makin' in the Mountains of Kentucky*. New York: Henry Holt & Co., 1939.

    Interesting study of backgrounds.

THOMPSON, H. W., *Body, Boots and Britches*. Philadelphia: J. B. Lippincott Co., 1940.

    Not primarily a collection of folk songs, but contains the texts of more than a hundred ballads and other songs, without music, gathered in New York State.

THOMPSON, STITH, *Motive-Index of Folk-Literature* (*Indiana University Studies*, Nos. 96, 97, 100, 101, 105, 106, 108, 109, 110, 111, 112; also issued as *FF Communications*, Nos. 106–109, 116, 6 vols.). Bloomington, Ind.: Indiana University, 1932–5.

    Monumental work; important in classifying.

TREAT, A. E., "Kentucky Folksong in Northern Wisconsin," in *JAFL*, 52:1–51 (1939).

UMBLE, JOHN, "The Old Order Amish, Their Hymns and Hymn Tunes," in *JAFL*, 52:82–95 (1939).

WHEELER, M., AND BRIDGE, C. G., *Kentucky Mountain Folk-Songs*. Introduction by Edgar Stillman-Kelley. Boston: Boston Music Co., 1937.

    With accompaniments.

INDEX OF SONGS

Index of Songs

INDEX OF FIRST LINES

Index of First Lines

A CATALOG OF SELECTED DOVER BOOKS IN ALL FIELDS OF INTEREST

100 BEST-LOVED POEMS, Edited by Philip Smith. "The Passionate Shepherd to His Love," "Shall I compare thee to a summer's day?" "Death, be not proud," "The Raven," "The Road Not Taken," plus works by Blake, Wordsworth, Byron, Shelley, Keats, many others. 96pp. $5\frac{3}{16}$ x $8\frac{1}{4}$. 0-486-28553-7

100 SMALL HOUSES OF THE THIRTIES, Brown-Blodgett Company. Exterior photographs and floor plans for 100 charming structures. Illustrations of models accompanied by descriptions of interiors, color schemes, closet space, and other amenities. 200 illustrations. 112pp. $8\frac{3}{8}$ x 11. 0-486-44131-8

1000 TURN-OF-THE-CENTURY HOUSES: With Illustrations and Floor Plans, Herbert C. Chivers. Reproduced from a rare edition, this showcase of homes ranges from cottages and bungalows to sprawling mansions. Each house is meticulously illustrated and accompanied by complete floor plans. 256pp. $9\frac{3}{8}$ x $12\frac{1}{4}$. 0-486-45596-3

101 GREAT AMERICAN POEMS, Edited by The American Poetry & Literacy Project. Rich treasury of verse from the 19th and 20th centuries includes works by Edgar Allan Poe, Robert Frost, Walt Whitman, Langston Hughes, Emily Dickinson, T. S. Eliot, other notables. 96pp. $5\frac{3}{16}$ x $8\frac{1}{4}$. 0-486-40158-8

101 GREAT SAMURAI PRINTS, Utagawa Kuniyoshi. Kuniyoshi was a master of the warrior woodblock print — and these 18th-century illustrations represent the pinnacle of his craft. Full-color portraits of renowned Japanese samurais pulse with movement, passion, and remarkably fine detail. 112pp. $8\frac{3}{8}$ x 11. 0-486-46523-3

ABC OF BALLET, Janet Grosser. Clearly worded, abundantly illustrated little guide defines basic ballet-related terms: arabesque, battement, pas de chat, relevé, sissonne, many others. Pronunciation guide included. Excellent primer. 48pp. $4\frac{3}{16}$ x $5\frac{3}{4}$. 0-486-40871-X

ACCESSORIES OF DRESS: An Illustrated Encyclopedia, Katherine Lester and Bess Viola Oerke. Illustrations of hats, veils, wigs, cravats, shawls, shoes, gloves, and other accessories enhance an engaging commentary that reveals the humor and charm of the many-sided story of accessorized apparel. 644 figures and 59 plates. 608pp. $6\frac{1}{8}$ x $9\frac{1}{4}$. 0-486-43378-1

ADVENTURES OF HUCKLEBERRY FINN, Mark Twain. Join Huck and Jim as their boyhood adventures along the Mississippi River lead them into a world of excitement, danger, and self-discovery. Humorous narrative, lyrical descriptions of the Mississippi valley, and memorable characters. 224pp. $5\frac{3}{16}$ x $8\frac{1}{4}$. 0-486-28061-6

ALICE STARMORE'S BOOK OF FAIR ISLE KNITTING, Alice Starmore. A noted designer from the region of Scotland's Fair Isle explores the history and techniques of this distinctive, stranded-color knitting style and provides copious illustrated instructions for 14 original knitwear designs. 208pp. $8\frac{3}{8}$ x $10\frac{7}{8}$. 0-486-47218-3

Browse over 9,000 books at www.doverpublications.com

CATALOG OF DOVER BOOKS

ALICE'S ADVENTURES IN WONDERLAND, Lewis Carroll. Beloved classic about a little girl lost in a topsy-turvy land and her encounters with the White Rabbit, March Hare, Mad Hatter, Cheshire Cat, and other delightfully improbable characters. 42 illustrations by Sir John Tenniel. 96pp. 5$\frac{3}{16}$ x 8$\frac{1}{4}$. 0-486-27543-4

AMERICA'S LIGHTHOUSES: An Illustrated History, Francis Ross Holland. Profusely illustrated fact-filled survey of American lighthouses since 1716. Over 200 stations — East, Gulf, and West coasts, Great Lakes, Hawaii, Alaska, Puerto Rico, the Virgin Islands, and the Mississippi and St. Lawrence Rivers. 240pp. 8 x 10$\frac{3}{4}$. 0-486-25576-X

AN ENCYCLOPEDIA OF THE VIOLIN, Alberto Bachmann. Translated by Frederick H. Martens. Introduction by Eugene Ysaye. First published in 1925, this renowned reference remains unsurpassed as a source of essential information, from construction and evolution to repertoire and technique. Includes a glossary and 73 illustrations. 496pp. 6$\frac{1}{8}$ x 9$\frac{1}{4}$. 0-486-46618-3

ANIMALS: 1,419 Copyright-Free Illustrations of Mammals, Birds, Fish, Insects, etc., Selected by Jim Harter. Selected for its visual impact and ease of use, this outstanding collection of wood engravings presents over 1,000 species of animals in extremely lifelike poses. Includes mammals, birds, reptiles, amphibians, fish, insects, and other invertebrates. 284pp. 9 x 12. 0-486-23766-4

THE ANNALS, Tacitus. Translated by Alfred John Church and William Jackson Brodribb. This vital chronicle of Imperial Rome, written by the era's great historian, spans A.D. 14-68 and paints incisive psychological portraits of major figures, from Tiberius to Nero. 416pp. 5$\frac{3}{16}$ x 8$\frac{1}{4}$. 0-486-45236-0

ANTIGONE, Sophocles. Filled with passionate speeches and sensitive probing of moral and philosophical issues, this powerful and often-performed Greek drama reveals the grim fate that befalls the children of Oedipus. Footnotes. 64pp. 5$\frac{3}{16}$ x 8 $\frac{1}{4}$. 0-486-27804-2

ART DECO DECORATIVE PATTERNS IN FULL COLOR, Christian Stoll. Reprinted from a rare 1910 portfolio, 160 sensuous and exotic images depict a breathtaking array of florals, geometrics, and abstracts — all elegant in their stark simplicity. 64pp. 8$\frac{3}{8}$ x 11. 0-486-44862-2

THE ARTHUR RACKHAM TREASURY: 86 Full-Color Illustrations, Arthur Rackham. Selected and Edited by Jeff A. Menges. A stunning treasury of 86 full-page plates span the famed English artist's career, from *Rip Van Winkle* (1905) to masterworks such as *Undine, A Midsummer Night's Dream,* and *Wind in the Willows* (1939). 96pp. 8$\frac{3}{8}$ x 11. 0-486-44685-9

THE AUTHENTIC GILBERT & SULLIVAN SONGBOOK, W. S. Gilbert and A. S. Sullivan. The most comprehensive collection available, this songbook includes selections from every one of Gilbert and Sullivan's light operas. Ninety-two numbers are presented uncut and unedited, and in their original keys. 410pp. 9 x 12. 0-486-23482-7

THE AWAKENING, Kate Chopin. First published in 1899, this controversial novel of a New Orleans wife's search for love outside a stifling marriage shocked readers. Today, it remains a first-rate narrative with superb characterization. New introductory Note. 128pp. 5$\frac{3}{16}$ x 8$\frac{1}{4}$. 0-486-27786-0

BASIC DRAWING, Louis Priscilla. Beginning with perspective, this commonsense manual progresses to the figure in movement, light and shade, anatomy, drapery, composition, trees and landscape, and outdoor sketching. Black-and-white illustrations throughout. 128pp. 8$\frac{3}{8}$ x 11. 0-486-45815-6

Browse over 9,000 books at www.doverpublications.com

THE BATTLES THAT CHANGED HISTORY, Fletcher Pratt. Historian profiles 16 crucial conflicts, ancient to modern, that changed the course of Western civilization. Gripping accounts of battles led by Alexander the Great, Joan of Arc, Ulysses S. Grant, other commanders. 27 maps. 352pp. 5⅜ x 8½. 0-486-41129-X

BEETHOVEN'S LETTERS, Ludwig van Beethoven. Edited by Dr. A. C. Kalischer. Features 457 letters to fellow musicians, friends, greats, patrons, and literary men. Reveals musical thoughts, quirks of personality, insights, and daily events. Includes 15 plates. 410pp. 5⅜ x 8½. 0-486-22769-3

BERNICE BOBS HER HAIR AND OTHER STORIES, F. Scott Fitzgerald. This brilliant anthology includes 6 of Fitzgerald's most popular stories: "The Diamond as Big as the Ritz," the title tale, "The Offshore Pirate," "The Ice Palace," "The Jelly Bean," and "May Day." 176pp. 5⅜ x 8½. 0-486-47049-0

BESLER'S BOOK OF FLOWERS AND PLANTS: 73 Full-Color Plates from Hortus Eystettensis, 1613, Basilius Besler. Here is a selection of magnificent plates from the *Hortus Eystettensis*, which vividly illustrated and identified the plants, flowers, and trees that thrived in the legendary German garden at Eichstätt. 80pp. 8⅜ x 11. 0-486-46005-3

THE BOOK OF KELLS, Edited by Blanche Cirker. Painstakingly reproduced from a rare facsimile edition, this volume contains full-page decorations, portraits, illustrations, plus a sampling of textual leaves with exquisite calligraphy and ornamentation. 32 full-color illustrations. 32pp. 9⅜ x 12¼. 0-486-24345-1

THE BOOK OF THE CROSSBOW: With an Additional Section on Catapults and Other Siege Engines, Ralph Payne-Gallwey. Fascinating study traces history and use of crossbow as military and sporting weapon, from Middle Ages to modern times. Also covers related weapons: balistas, catapults, Turkish bows, more. Over 240 illustrations. 400pp. 7¼ x 10⅛. 0-486-28720-3

THE BUNGALOW BOOK: Floor Plans and Photos of 112 Houses, 1910, Henry L. Wilson. Here are 112 of the most popular and economic blueprints of the early 20th century — plus an illustration or photograph of each completed house. A wonderful time capsule that still offers a wealth of valuable insights. 160pp. 8⅜ x 11. 0-486-45104-6

THE CALL OF THE WILD, Jack London. A classic novel of adventure, drawn from London's own experiences as a Klondike adventurer, relating the story of a heroic dog caught in the brutal life of the Alaska Gold Rush. Note. 64pp. 5³⁄₁₆ x 8¼. 0-486-26472-6

CANDIDE, Voltaire. Edited by Francois-Marie Arouet. One of the world's great satires since its first publication in 1759. Witty, caustic skewering of romance, science, philosophy, religion, government — nearly all human ideals and institutions. 112pp. 5³⁄₁₆ x 8¼. 0-486-26689-3

CELEBRATED IN THEIR TIME: Photographic Portraits from the George Grantham Bain Collection, Edited by Amy Pastan. With an Introduction by Michael Carlebach. Remarkable portrait gallery features 112 rare images of Albert Einstein, Charlie Chaplin, the Wright Brothers, Henry Ford, and other luminaries from the worlds of politics, art, entertainment, and industry. 128pp. 8⅜ x 11. 0-486-46754-6

CHARIOTS FOR APOLLO: The NASA History of Manned Lunar Spacecraft to 1969, Courtney G. Brooks, James M. Grimwood, and Loyd S. Swenson, Jr. This illustrated history by a trio of experts is the definitive reference on the Apollo spacecraft and lunar modules. It traces the vehicles' design, development, and operation in space. More than 100 photographs and illustrations. 576pp. 6¾ x 9¼. 0-486-46756-2

A CHRISTMAS CAROL, Charles Dickens. This engrossing tale relates Ebenezer Scrooge's ghostly journeys through Christmases past, present, and future and his ultimate transformation from a harsh and grasping old miser to a charitable and compassionate human being. 80pp. 5³⁄₁₆ x 8¼. 0-486-26865-9

COMMON SENSE, Thomas Paine. First published in January of 1776, this highly influential landmark document clearly and persuasively argued for American separation from Great Britain and paved the way for the Declaration of Independence. 64pp. 5³⁄₁₆ x 8¼. 0-486-29602-4

THE COMPLETE SHORT STORIES OF OSCAR WILDE, Oscar Wilde. Complete texts of "The Happy Prince and Other Tales," "A House of Pomegranates," "Lord Arthur Savile's Crime and Other Stories," "Poems in Prose," and "The Portrait of Mr. W. H." 208pp. 5³⁄₁₆ x 8¼. 0-486-45216-6

COMPLETE SONNETS, William Shakespeare. Over 150 exquisite poems deal with love, friendship, the tyranny of time, beauty's evanescence, death, and other themes in language of remarkable power, precision, and beauty. Glossary of archaic terms. 80pp. 5³⁄₁₆ x 8¼. 0-486-26686-9

THE COUNT OF MONTE CRISTO: Abridged Edition, Alexandre Dumas. Falsely accused of treason, Edmond Dantès is imprisoned in the bleak Chateau d'If. After a hair-raising escape, he launches an elaborate plot to extract a bitter revenge against those who betrayed him. 448pp. 5³⁄₁₆ x 8¼. 0-486-45643-9

CRAFTSMAN BUNGALOWS: Designs from the Pacific Northwest, Yoho & Merritt. This reprint of a rare catalog, showcasing the charming simplicity and cozy style of Craftsman bungalows, is filled with photos of completed homes, plus floor plans and estimated costs. An indispensable resource for architects, historians, and illustrators. 112pp. 10 x 7. 0-486-46875-5

CRAFTSMAN BUNGALOWS: 59 Homes from "The Craftsman," Edited by Gustav Stickley. Best and most attractive designs from Arts and Crafts Movement publication — 1903-1916 — includes sketches, photographs of homes, floor plans, descriptive text. 128pp. 8¼ x 11. 0-486-25829-7

CRIME AND PUNISHMENT, Fyodor Dostoyevsky. Translated by Constance Garnett. Supreme masterpiece tells the story of Raskolnikov, a student tormented by his own thoughts after he murders an old woman. Overwhelmed by guilt and terror, he confesses and goes to prison. 480pp. 5³⁄₁₆ x 8¼. 0-486-41587-2

THE DECLARATION OF INDEPENDENCE AND OTHER GREAT DOCUMENTS OF AMERICAN HISTORY: 1775-1865, Edited by John Grafton. Thirteen compelling and influential documents: Henry's "Give Me Liberty or Give Me Death," Declaration of Independence, The Constitution, Washington's First Inaugural Address, The Monroe Doctrine, The Emancipation Proclamation, Gettysburg Address, more. 64pp. 5³⁄₁₆ x 8¼. 0-486-41124-9

THE DESERT AND THE SOWN: Travels in Palestine and Syria, Gertrude Bell. "The female Lawrence of Arabia," Gertrude Bell wrote captivating, perceptive accounts of her travels in the Middle East. This intriguing narrative, accompanied by 160 photos, traces her 1905 sojourn in Lebanon, Syria, and Palestine. 368pp. 5⅜ x 8½. 0-486-46876-3

A DOLL'S HOUSE, Henrik Ibsen. Ibsen's best-known play displays his genius for realistic prose drama. An expression of women's rights, the play climaxes when the central character, Nora, rejects a smothering marriage and life in "a doll's house." 80pp. 5³⁄₁₆ x 8¼. 0-486-27062-9

Browse over 9,000 books at www.doverpublications.com

DOOMED SHIPS: Great Ocean Liner Disasters, William H. Miller, Jr. Nearly 200 photographs, many from private collections, highlight tales of some of the vessels whose pleasure cruises ended in catastrophe: the *Morro Castle, Normandie, Andrea Doria, Europa,* and many others. 128pp. 8⅞ x 11¾. 0-486-45366-9

THE DORÉ BIBLE ILLUSTRATIONS, Gustave Doré. Detailed plates from the Bible: the Creation scenes, Adam and Eve, horrifying visions of the Flood, the battle sequences with their monumental crowds, depictions of the life of Jesus, 241 plates in all. 241pp. 9 x 12. 0-486-23004-X

DRAWING DRAPERY FROM HEAD TO TOE, Cliff Young. Expert guidance on how to draw shirts, pants, skirts, gloves, hats, and coats on the human figure, including folds in relation to the body, pull and crush, action folds, creases, more. Over 200 drawings. 48pp. 8¼ x 11. 0-486-45591-2

DUBLINERS, James Joyce. A fine and accessible introduction to the work of one of the 20th century's most influential writers, this collection features 15 tales, including a masterpiece of the short-story genre, "The Dead." 160pp. 5³⁄₁₆ x 8¼.
0-486-26870-5

EASY-TO-MAKE POP-UPS, Joan Irvine. Illustrated by Barbara Reid. Dozens of wonderful ideas for three-dimensional paper fun — from holiday greeting cards with moving parts to a pop-up menagerie. Easy-to-follow, illustrated instructions for more than 30 projects. 299 black-and-white illustrations. 96pp. 8⅜ x 11.
0-486-44622-0

EASY-TO-MAKE STORYBOOK DOLLS: A "Novel" Approach to Cloth Dollmaking, Sherralyn St. Clair. Favorite fictional characters come alive in this unique beginner's dollmaking guide. Includes patterns for Pollyanna, Dorothy from *The Wonderful Wizard of Oz,* Mary of *The Secret Garden,* plus easy-to-follow instructions, 263 black-and-white illustrations, and an 8-page color insert. 112pp. 8¼ x 11. 0-486-47360-0

EINSTEIN'S ESSAYS IN SCIENCE, Albert Einstein. Speeches and essays in accessible, everyday language profile influential physicists such as Niels Bohr and Isaac Newton. They also explore areas of physics to which the author made major contributions. 128pp. 5 x 8. 0-486-47011-3

EL DORADO: Further Adventures of the Scarlet Pimpernel, Baroness Orczy. A popular sequel to *The Scarlet Pimpernel,* this suspenseful story recounts the Pimpernel's attempts to rescue the Dauphin from imprisonment during the French Revolution. An irresistible blend of intrigue, period detail, and vibrant characterizations. 352pp. 5³⁄₁₆ x 8¼. 0-486-44026-5

ELEGANT SMALL HOMES OF THE TWENTIES: 99 Designs from a Competition, Chicago Tribune. Nearly 100 designs for five- and six-room houses feature New England and Southern colonials, Normandy cottages, stately Italianate dwellings, and other fascinating snapshots of American domestic architecture of the 1920s. 112pp. 9 x 12. 0-486-46910-7

THE ELEMENTS OF STYLE: The Original Edition, William Strunk, Jr. This is the book that generations of writers have relied upon for timeless advice on grammar, diction, syntax, and other essentials. In concise terms, it identifies the principal requirements of proper style and common errors. 64pp. 5⅜ x 8½. 0-486-44798-7

THE ELUSIVE PIMPERNEL, Baroness Orczy. Robespierre's revolutionaries find their wicked schemes thwarted by the heroic Pimpernel — Sir Percival Blakeney. In this thrilling sequel, Chauvelin devises a plot to eliminate the Pimpernel and his wife. 272pp. 5³⁄₁₆ x 8¼. 0-486-45464-9

AN ENCYCLOPEDIA OF BATTLES: Accounts of Over 1,560 Battles from 1479 B.C. to the Present, David Eggenberger. Essential details of every major battle in recorded history from the first battle of Megiddo in 1479 B.C. to Grenada in 1984. List of battle maps. 99 illustrations. 544pp. 6½ x 9¼. 0-486-24913-1

ENCYCLOPEDIA OF EMBROIDERY STITCHES, INCLUDING CREWEL, Marion Nichols. Precise explanations and instructions, clearly illustrated, on how to work chain, back, cross, knotted, woven stitches, and many more — 178 in all, including Cable Outline, Whipped Satin, and Eyelet Buttonhole. Over 1400 illustrations. 219pp. 8⅜ x 11¼. 0-486-22929-7

ENTER JEEVES: 15 Early Stories, P. G. Wodehouse. Splendid collection contains first 8 stories featuring Bertie Wooster, the deliciously dim aristocrat and Jeeves, his brainy, imperturbable manservant. Also, the complete Reggie Pepper (Bertie's prototype) series. 288pp. 5⅜ x 8½. 0-486-29717-9

ERIC SLOANE'S AMERICA: Paintings in Oil, Michael Wigley. With a Foreword by Mimi Sloane. Eric Sloane's evocative oils of America's landscape and material culture shimmer with immense historical and nostalgic appeal. This original hardcover collection gathers nearly a hundred of his finest paintings, with subjects ranging from New England to the American Southwest. 128pp. 10⅝ x 9.

0-486-46525-X

ETHAN FROME, Edith Wharton. Classic story of wasted lives, set against a bleak New England background. Superbly delineated characters in a hauntingly grim tale of thwarted love. Considered by many to be Wharton's masterpiece. 96pp. 5³⁄₁₆ x 8 ¼.

0-486-26690-7

THE EVERLASTING MAN, G. K. Chesterton. Chesterton's view of Christianity — as a blend of philosophy and mythology, satisfying intellect and spirit — applies to his brilliant book, which appeals to readers' heads as well as their hearts. 288pp. 5⅜ x 8½.

0-486-46036-3

THE FIELD AND FOREST HANDY BOOK, Daniel Beard. Written by a co-founder of the Boy Scouts, this appealing guide offers illustrated instructions for building kites, birdhouses, boats, igloos, and other fun projects, plus numerous helpful tips for campers. 448pp. 5³⁄₁₆ x 8¼. 0-486-46191-2

FINDING YOUR WAY WITHOUT MAP OR COMPASS, Harold Gatty. Useful, instructive manual shows would-be explorers, hikers, bikers, scouts, sailors, and survivalists how to find their way outdoors by observing animals, weather patterns, shifting sands, and other elements of nature. 288pp. 5⅜ x 8½. 0-486-40613-X

FIRST FRENCH READER: A Beginner's Dual-Language Book, Edited and Translated by Stanley Appelbaum. This anthology introduces 50 legendary writers — Voltaire, Balzac, Baudelaire, Proust, more — through passages from *The Red and the Black, Les Misérables, Madame Bovary,* and other classics. Original French text plus English translation on facing pages. 240pp. 5⅜ x 8½. 0-486-46178-5

FIRST GERMAN READER: A Beginner's Dual-Language Book, Edited by Harry Steinhauer. Specially chosen for their power to evoke German life and culture, these short, simple readings include poems, stories, essays, and anecdotes by Goethe, Hesse, Heine, Schiller, and others. 224pp. 5⅜ x 8½. 0-486-46179-3

FIRST SPANISH READER: A Beginner's Dual-Language Book, Angel Flores. Delightful stories, other material based on works of Don Juan Manuel, Luis Taboada, Ricardo Palma, other noted writers. Complete faithful English translations on facing pages. Exercises. 176pp. 5⅜ x 8½. 0-486-25810-6

FIVE ACRES AND INDEPENDENCE, Maurice G. Kains. Great back-to-the-land classic explains basics of self-sufficient farming. The one book to get. 95 illustrations. 397pp. 5⅜ x 8½. 0-486-20974-1

FLAGG'S SMALL HOUSES: Their Economic Design and Construction, 1922, Ernest Flagg. Although most famous for his skyscrapers, Flagg was also a proponent of the well-designed single-family dwelling. His classic treatise features innovations that save space, materials, and cost. 526 illustrations. 160pp. 9⅜ x 12¼.
0-486-45197-6

FLATLAND: A Romance of Many Dimensions, Edwin A. Abbott. Classic of science (and mathematical) fiction — charmingly illustrated by the author — describes the adventures of A. Square, a resident of Flatland, in Spaceland (three dimensions), Lineland (one dimension), and Pointland (no dimensions). 96pp. 5³⁄₁₆ x 8¼.
0-486-27263-X

FRANKENSTEIN, Mary Shelley. The story of Victor Frankenstein's monstrous creation and the havoc it caused has enthralled generations of readers and inspired countless writers of horror and suspense. With the author's own 1831 introduction. 176pp. 5³⁄₁₆ x 8¼. 0-486-28211-2

THE GARGOYLE BOOK: 572 Examples from Gothic Architecture, Lester Burbank Bridaham. Dispelling the conventional wisdom that French Gothic architectural flourishes were born of despair or gloom, Bridaham reveals the whimsical nature of these creations and the ingenious artisans who made them. 572 illustrations. 224pp. 8⅜ x 11. 0-486-44754-5

THE GIFT OF THE MAGI AND OTHER SHORT STORIES, O. Henry. Sixteen captivating stories by one of America's most popular storytellers. Included are such classics as "The Gift of the Magi," "The Last Leaf," and "The Ransom of Red Chief." Publisher's Note. 96pp. 5³⁄₁₆ x 8¼. 0-486-27061-0

THE GOETHE TREASURY: Selected Prose and Poetry, Johann Wolfgang von Goethe. Edited, Selected, and with an Introduction by Thomas Mann. In addition to his lyric poetry, Goethe wrote travel sketches, autobiographical studies, essays, letters, and proverbs in rhyme and prose. This collection presents outstanding examples from each genre. 368pp. 5⅜ x 8½. 0-486-44780-4

GREAT EXPECTATIONS, Charles Dickens. Orphaned Pip is apprenticed to the dirty work of the forge but dreams of becoming a gentleman — and one day finds himself in possession of "great expectations." Dickens' finest novel. 400pp. 5³⁄₁₆ x 8¼.
0-486-41586-4

GREAT WRITERS ON THE ART OF FICTION: From Mark Twain to Joyce Carol Oates, Edited by James Daley. An indispensable source of advice and inspiration, this anthology features essays by Henry James, Kate Chopin, Willa Cather, Sinclair Lewis, Jack London, Raymond Chandler, Raymond Carver, Eudora Welty, and Kurt Vonnegut, Jr. 192pp. 5⅜ x 8½. 0-486-45128-3

HAMLET, William Shakespeare. The quintessential Shakespearean tragedy, whose highly charged confrontations and anguished soliloquies probe depths of human feeling rarely sounded in any art. Reprinted from an authoritative British edition complete with illuminating footnotes. 128pp. 5³⁄₁₆ x 8¼. 0-486-27278-8

THE HAUNTED HOUSE, Charles Dickens. A Yuletide gathering in an eerie country retreat provides the backdrop for Dickens and his friends — including Elizabeth Gaskell and Wilkie Collins — who take turns spinning supernatural yarns. 144pp. 5⅜ x 8½. 0-486-46309-5

HEART OF DARKNESS, Joseph Conrad. Dark allegory of a journey up the Congo River and the narrator's encounter with the mysterious Mr. Kurtz. Masterly blend of adventure, character study, psychological penetration. For many, Conrad's finest, most enigmatic story. 80pp. 5³⁄₁₆ x 8¼. 0-486-26464-5

HENSON AT THE NORTH POLE, Matthew A. Henson. This thrilling memoir by the heroic African-American who was Peary's companion through two decades of Arctic exploration recounts a tale of danger, courage, and determination. "Fascinating and exciting." — *Commonweal*. 128pp. 5⅜ x 8½. 0-486-45472-X

HISTORIC COSTUMES AND HOW TO MAKE THEM, Mary Fernald and E. Shenton. Practical, informative guidebook shows how to create everything from short tunics worn by Saxon men in the fifth century to a lady's bustle dress of the late 1800s. 81 illustrations. 176pp. 5⅜ x 8½. 0-486-44906-8

THE HOUND OF THE BASKERVILLES, Arthur Conan Doyle. A deadly curse in the form of a legendary ferocious beast continues to claim its victims from the Baskerville family until Holmes and Watson intervene. Often called the best detective story ever written. 128pp. 5³⁄₁₆ x 8¼. 0-486-28214-7

THE HOUSE BEHIND THE CEDARS, Charles W. Chesnutt. Originally published in 1900, this groundbreaking novel by a distinguished African-American author recounts the drama of a brother and sister who "pass for white" during the dangerous days of Reconstruction. 208pp. 5⅜ x 8½. 0-486-46144-0

THE HUMAN FIGURE IN MOTION, Eadweard Muybridge. The 4,789 photographs in this definitive selection show the human figure — models almost all undraped — engaged in over 160 different types of action: running, climbing stairs, etc. 390pp. 7⅞ x 10⅝. 0-486-20204-6

THE IMPORTANCE OF BEING EARNEST, Oscar Wilde. Wilde's witty and buoyant comedy of manners, filled with some of literature's most famous epigrams, reprinted from an authoritative British edition. Considered Wilde's most perfect work. 64pp. 5³⁄₁₆ x 8¼. 0-486-26478-5

THE INFERNO, Dante Alighieri. Translated and with notes by Henry Wadsworth Longfellow. The first stop on Dante's famous journey from Hell to Purgatory to Paradise, this 14th-century allegorical poem blends vivid and shocking imagery with graceful lyricism. Translated by the beloved 19th-century poet, Henry Wadsworth Longfellow. 256pp. 5³⁄₁₆ x 8¼. 0-486-44288-8

JANE EYRE, Charlotte Brontë. Written in 1847, *Jane Eyre* tells the tale of an orphan girl's progress from the custody of cruel relatives to an oppressive boarding school and its culmination in a troubled career as a governess. 448pp. 5³⁄₁₆ x 8¼. 0-486-42449-9

JAPANESE WOODBLOCK FLOWER PRINTS, Tanigami Kônan. Extraordinary collection of Japanese woodblock prints by a well-known artist features 120 plates in brilliant color. Realistic images from a rare edition include daffodils, tulips, and other familiar and unusual flowers. 128pp. 11 x 8¼. 0-486-46442-3

JEWELRY MAKING AND DESIGN, Augustus F. Rose and Antonio Cirino. Professional secrets of jewelry making are revealed in a thorough, practical guide. Over 200 illustrations. 306pp. 5⅜ x 8½. 0-486-21750-7

JULIUS CAESAR, William Shakespeare. Great tragedy based on Plutarch's account of the lives of Brutus, Julius Caesar and Mark Antony. Evil plotting, ringing oratory, high tragedy with Shakespeare's incomparable insight, dramatic power. Explanatory footnotes. 96pp. 5³⁄₁₆ x 8¼. 0-486-26876-4

Browse over 9,000 books at www.doverpublications.com

THE JUNGLE, Upton Sinclair. 1906 bestseller shockingly reveals intolerable labor practices and working conditions in the Chicago stockyards as it tells the grim story of a Slavic family that emigrates to America full of optimism but soon faces despair. 320pp. 5 3/16 x 8¼. 0-486-41923-1

THE KINGDOM OF GOD IS WITHIN YOU, Leo Tolstoy. The soul-searching book that inspired Gandhi to embrace the concept of passive resistance, Tolstoy's 1894 polemic clearly outlines a radical, well-reasoned revision of traditional Christian thinking. 352pp. 5 3/16 x 8¼. 0-486-45138-0

THE LADY OR THE TIGER?: and Other Logic Puzzles, Raymond M. Smullyan. Created by a renowned puzzle master, these whimsically themed challenges involve paradoxes about probability, time, and change; metapuzzles; and self-referentiality. Nineteen chapters advance in difficulty from relatively simple to highly complex. 1982 edition. 240pp. 5⅜ x 8½. 0-486-47027-X

LEAVES OF GRASS: The Original 1855 Edition, Walt Whitman. Whitman's immortal collection includes some of the greatest poems of modern times, including his masterpiece, "Song of Myself." Shattering standard conventions, it stands as an unabashed celebration of body and nature. 128pp. 5 3/16 x 8¼. 0-486-45676-5

LES MISÉRABLES, Victor Hugo. Translated by Charles E. Wilbour. Abridged by James K. Robinson. A convict's heroic struggle for justice and redemption plays out against a fiery backdrop of the Napoleonic wars. This edition features the excellent original translation and a sensitive abridgment. 304pp. 6⅛ x 9¼. 0-486-45789-3

LILITH: A Romance, George MacDonald. In this novel by the father of fantasy literature, a man travels through time to meet Adam and Eve and to explore humanity's fall from grace and ultimate redemption. 240pp. 5⅜ x 8½. 0-486-46818-6

THE LOST LANGUAGE OF SYMBOLISM, Harold Bayley. This remarkable book reveals the hidden meaning behind familiar images and words, from the origins of Santa Claus to the fleur-de-lys, drawing from mythology, folklore, religious texts, and fairy tales. 1,418 illustrations. 784pp. 5⅜ x 8½. 0-486-44787-1

MACBETH, William Shakespeare. A Scottish nobleman murders the king in order to succeed to the throne. Tortured by his conscience and fearful of discovery, he becomes tangled in a web of treachery and deceit that ultimately spells his doom. 96pp. 5 3/16 x 8¼. 0-486-27802-6

MAKING AUTHENTIC CRAFTSMAN FURNITURE: Instructions and Plans for 62 Projects, Gustav Stickley. Make authentic reproductions of handsome, functional, durable furniture: tables, chairs, wall cabinets, desks, a hall tree, and more. Construction plans with drawings, schematics, dimensions, and lumber specs reprinted from 1900s *The Craftsman* magazine. 128pp. 8⅛ x 11. 0-486-25000-8

MATHEMATICS FOR THE NONMATHEMATICIAN, Morris Kline. Erudite and entertaining overview follows development of mathematics from ancient Greeks to present. Topics include logic and mathematics, the fundamental concept, differential calculus, probability theory, much more. Exercises and problems. 641pp. 5⅜ x 8½. 0-486-24823-2

MEMOIRS OF AN ARABIAN PRINCESS FROM ZANZIBAR, Emily Ruete. This 19th-century autobiography offers a rare inside look at the society surrounding a sultan's palace. A real-life princess in exile recalls her vanished world of harems, slave trading, and court intrigues. 288pp. 5⅜ x 8½. 0-486-47121-7

Browse over 9,000 books at www.doverpublications.com